A Book Of

HUMAN RESOURCE MANAGEMENT

For
MBA Semester - II
As Per Pune University's New Syllabus
Effective from June 2013

Prof. Sharad D. Geet
M.A. (Eco.), M.Com., LL.B., D.C.L.

Mrs. Asmita A. Deshpande
B.Com., M.B.A.

HUMAN RESOURCE MANAGEMENT – MBA : (Sem. - II) ISBN 978-93-83750-65-8

First Edition : December 2013

© : **Authors**

The text of this publication, or any part thereof, should not be reproduced or transmitted in any form or stored in any computer storage system or device for distribution including photocopy, recording, taping or information retrieval system or reproduced on any disc, tape, perforated media or other information storage device etc., without the written permission of Author with whom the rights are reserved. Breach of this condition is liable for legal action.

Every effort has been made to avoid errors or omissions in this publication. In spite of this, errors may have crept in. Any mistake, error or discrepancy so noted and shall be brought to our notice shall be taken care of in the next edition. It is notified that neither the publisher nor the author or seller shall be responsible for any damage or loss of action to any one, of any kind, in any manner, therefrom.

Published By :
NIRALI PRAKASHAN
Abhyudaya Pragati, 1312, Shivaji Nagar,
Off J.M. Road, PUNE – 411005
Tel - (020) 25512336/37/39, Fax - (020) 25511379
Email : niralipune@pragationline.com

Printed By :
Repro Knowledgecast Limited,
Thane

DISTRIBUTION CENTRES

PUNE

Nirali Prakashan
119, Budhwar Peth, Jogeshwari Mandir Lane
Pune 411002, Maharashtra
Tel : (020) 2445 2044, 66022708, Fax : (020) 2445 1538
Email : niralilocal@pragationline.com

Nirali Prakashan
S. No. 28/27, Dhyari,
Near Pari Company, Pune 411041
Tel : (020) 24690204, Fax : (020) 24690316
Email : bookorder@pragationline.com

MUMBAI
Nirali Prakashan
385, S.V.P. Road, Rasdhara Co-op. Hsg. Society Ltd.,
Girgaum, Mumbai 400004, Maharashtra
Tel : (022) 2385 6339 / 2386 9976, Fax : (022) 2386 9976
Email : niralimumbai@pragationline.com

DISTRIBUTION BRANCHES

NAGPUR
Pratibha Book Distributors
Above Maratha Mandir, Shop No. 3, First Floor,
Rani Jhanshi Square, Sitabuldi, Nagpur 440012,
Maharashtra, Tel : (0712) 254 7129

JALGAON
Nirali Prakashan
34, V. V. Golani Market, Navi Peth, Jalgaon 425001,
Maharashtra, Tel : (0257) 222 0395
Mob : 94234 91860

BENGALURU
Pragati Book House
House No. 1, Sanjeevappa Lane, Avenue Road Cross,
Opp. Rice Church, Bengaluru – 560002.
Tel : (080) 64513344, 64513355,
Mob : 9880582331, 9845021552
Email:bharatsavla@yahoo.com

KOLHAPUR
Nirali Prakashan
New Mahadvar Road,
Kedar Plaza, 1st Floor Opp. IDBI Bank
Kolhapur 416 012, Maharashtra. Mob : 9855046155

CHENNAI
Pragati Books
9/1, Montieth Road, Behind Taas Mahal, Egmore,
Chennai 600008 Tamil Nadu, Tel : (044) 6518 3535,
Mob : 94440 01782 / 98450 21552 / 98805 82331, Email : bharatsavla@yahoo.com

RETAIL OUTLETS

PUNE

Pragati Book Centre
157, Budhwar Peth, Opp. Ratan Talkies,
Pune 411002, Maharashtra
Tel : (020) 2445 8887 / 6602 2707, Fax : (020) 2445 8887

Pragati Book Centre
Amber Chamber, 28/A, Budhwar Peth,
Appa Balwant Chowk, Pune - 411002, Maharashtra,
Tel : (020) 20240335 / 66281669
Email : pbcpune@pragationline.com

Pragati Book Centre
676/B, Budhwar Peth, Opp. Jogeshwari Mandir,
Pune 411002, Maharashtra
Tel : (020) 6601 7784 / 6602 0855

PBC Book Sellers and Stationers
152, Budhwar Peth, Pune 411002, Maharashtra
Tel : (020) 2445 2254 / 6609 2463

MUMBAI
Pragati Book Corner
Indira Niwas, 111 - A, Bhavani Shankar Road, Dadar (W), Mumbai 400028, Maharashtra
Tel : (022) 2422 3526 / 6662 5254, Email : pbcmumbai@pragationline.com

www.pragationline.com info@pragationline.com

Preface ...

Human Resource Management deals with a wide variety of topics such as Human Resource Planning, Training and Development, Human Resource Procurement, Performance Management, Employee Appraisal and Compensation, Employee Relations and so on.

These topics are important from the view point of development and growth of organisations and employees. There is an urgent need for effective utilisation of human resources to attain individual, organisational and national goals in this era of keen competition, privatisation, globalisation and liberalisation.

Human Resource Management has assumed great importance at the corporate level and HRM has become a driving force in success of an organisation. Considering these aspects, various topics have been explained in this text book as per the new revised syllabus of Pune University.

We therefore have great pleasure in bringing out this book of Human Resource Management incorporating chapters on SHRM, HR Procurement, Training and Development, Employee Appraisal, Managing Employee Relations to meet the requirements of various topics prescribed for the examination.

We sincerely hope that the students and teachers will find this book useful in meeting their needs from the view point of their examination. We shall consider our efforts amply rewarded if this book is appreciated by those for whom it is meant.

In spite of sincere efforts, some errors might have crept in the book at some places, which we hope shall be condoned.

We are very grateful to Shri. Dineshbhai Furia, Shri. Jigneshbhai Furia, our publishers; Mr. Malik Shaikh, Mrs. Nirja Sharma, Mr. Prasad Chintakindi and the entire staff of Nirali Prakashan, Pune for publishing this book.

We extend our good wishes to all students, teachers, and readers with the genuine hope that they will receive this book with the same degree of enthusiasm with which we have written it.

Pune   **Prof. S. D. GEET**
December 2013   **Mrs. Asmita A. Deshpande**

Syllabus ...

1. Framework of Human Resource Management

Introduction to HRM and Framework Nature of HRM, Scope of HRM, HRM: Functions and Objectives, HRM: Policies and Practices.

HRM and SHRM - Nature of SHRM, The Strategic Functions of HRM Understood and Implemented in the Company, Global Competitiveness and Strategic HR, Linkage of Organizational and HR Strategies.

Models of SHRM - The Integrated System Model, Devanna et. al - Strategic Human Resource Management "Matching Model".

2. HR Procurement

Job Analysis and Design - Job Analysis: introduction, Importance of Job Analysis, Purpose Of Job Analysis, Benefits of Job analysis, Competency Based Job Analysis, Job Design: Writing Job Description, Introduction, and Factors Affecting Job Design. Job Characteristics Model (Hackrnan and Oldham, 1976) of Effective Job and Job Satisfaction.

Human Resource Planning - The Need of Man Power Planning , What is Human Resource Planning, Definition, objectives, Importance, Benefits, the Process of Human Resource Planning; Preparing Manpower Inventory (Supply Forecasting)

Recruitment - Strategic Approach to Recruitment, Labour Markets and Recruitment, Geographic Labour Markets, Global Labour Markets, Industry and Occupational Labour Markets, Educational and Technical Labour Markets, Unemployment Rate and Labour Markets, Recruiting and Diversity Considerations, Employment Advertising, Recruiting Diverse Workers, Recruiting Source Choices: Internal vs. External - Internal: Organizational Database, Job postings, Promotions and Transfers, Current Employee Reference and Re-recruiting of former Employees and Applicants, External: College and University Recruiting., School Recruiting, Labour Unions, Employment Agencies and Headhunters, Competitive Sources, Media Sources, E-Recruiting Methods - Internet Job Boards, Professional Career Websites, Employer Websites Selection - Introduction to Selection Process, Selection Procedure.

3. Training and Development

Employee Training and Development Nature of Training, Training Process, Training Needs Assessment, Training Evaluation, Training Design, Implementing Training Programmes (Training methods), Implementing Management Development Programmes.

4. Employee Appraisal and Compensation

Performance - Definition, Why to Measure Performance, Use of Performance Data, Measurement Process, Performance Feedback, Compensation - Concept, Traditional Approach, Current trends in Compensation, Linking Compensation with Performance - Advantages and Problems, Team Based Incentives

5. Managing Employee Relations

Concept, Importance, Organizational Entry, Employee Status, Flexible Work Arrangement, Employee Surveys, Handbooks, Violations of Policy/Discipline, Organizational Exit, Termination, Resignation, Downsizing, Lay off Retirement.

Contents ...

1. Framework of Human Resource Management	1.1 - 1.34
2. HR Procurement	2.1 - 2.72
3. Training and Development	3.1 - 3.56
4. Employee Appraisal and Compensation	4.1 - 4.36
5. Managing Employee Relations	5.1 - 5.26
• **Case Studies**	C.1 - C.4

Chapter 1...

Framework of Human Resource Management

Contents ...

1.1 Introduction to HRM and Framework
    1.1.1 Definitions of Human Resource Managment
    1.1.2 Nature and Features of Human Resource Management
    1.1.3 Functions and Objectives of Human Resource Management
    1.1.4 Scope of Human Resource Management
    1.1.5 Importance of Human Resource Management
    1.1.6 HRM: Policies and Practices

1.2 Human Resource Management and Strategic Human Resource Management
    1.2.1 Meaning and Nature of Strategic Human Resource Management
    1.2.2 Global Competitiveness and Strategic HR
    1.2.3 Linkage of Organisational Strategy and HRM Strategy

1.3 Models of SHRM
    1.3.1 The Harvard Model or The Integrated System Model
    1.3.3 Devanna Model - Strategic Human Resource Management "Matching Model", Michigan Model

- Points to Remember
- Questions for Discussion
- Questions from Previous Pune University Examinations

Learning Objectives:

- To understand the Concept of HRM, its Nature and Features and the Importance of HRM
- To be able to discuss the Objectives and Scope of HRM
- To learn about SHRM, Global Competitiveness and Strategic HR
- To understand the Linkage of Organisations and HR Strategies
- To gain Knowledge of the Models of SHRM

Introduction

Human Resource Management is an evolving science which is concerned with the management of human resources.

The term 'Human Resources' can be thought of as the total knowledge, creative skills and abilities, talents, aptitudes and attitudes of an organisation's total workforce i.e. people at work as well as the values and beliefs of the individuals involved.

Human resources consist of inter-dependent, inter-related and interacting psychological, physiological, sociological and ethical components.

An organisation possesses various resources in the form of materials, machines, space, money, etc. These resources are required to be used in the most efficient manner for the success of an organisation. Use of these resources is done by employees working in the organisation. They may use the resources fully or partially. However, if the available resources are not used fully and properly, there will be wastage. As a result, sufficient returns will not be available to the owners.

Human resources are the most vital assets of an organisation. It is the human resources who make other resources moving. They perform various functions like production, research, finance, marketing, and so on by carrying out the relevant activities.

From the management's point of view, human resource is important because for engaging and maintaining the human resource, it has to spend money.

Performance of an organisation depends upon the quality of the employee efforts. To engage the best employees, the management must be ready to pay competitive remunerations and provide satisfactory working conditions along with various amenities. Such expenditure varies from 20% to 50% of the total cost incurred. Since such a large proportion of the cost is related to the human resource employed, all decisions relating to it has to be taken in a careful manner.

Efforts are required to be made for the use of this valuable resource in a proper way. If the productivity of the employees is increased through training and development programmemes, the labour cost can be reduced.

Further, while managing the human resources, attention should be given to team building. Employees work in groups and establish relationships with other members of the group. These relations can be formal or informal but they satisfy the social needs of the employees. Therefore, management should encourage such relationships and use them for creating team spirit which helps in increasing productivity of the employees.

Management's aim should be to get the best from the employees and for this purpose, handling of the employees should be done in an effective way. Success of the organisations, to a great extent, also depends upon the attitude of the management towards the employees.

Success in today's competitive business environment is increasingly a result of effective human resource management. Structure and technology can be duplicated. But the factor that can set apart an organisation is its human resource. Hence, human resource must be managed effectively.

To understand the framework of human resource management, let us first gain knowledge of the definitions, nature, importance, objectives and other aspects of Human Resource Management in this chapter.

1.1 Introduction to HRM and Framework

Human Resource Management, as a branch of management, is comparatively of recent origin. Though Human Resource Management activities have probably been performed since ancient times and human resource has always been a key source as a formal discipline, its roots are traceable to the period immediately following the Industrial Revolution. It can be said that the pioneering work of the masters of management like Peter Drucker, Douglas McGregor, etc., laid the formal foundation of Human Resource Management.

Human resource is the greatest asset to any organisation and all efforts are required to be made to develop the available human resource. An organisation must either have or develop an ability to effectively manage and develop its human resources. The concept of HRD has been gaining prominence and focus in management during the last three decades.

An employee in HRM is treated not merely as a worker or an economic resource but is considered as a social and psychological resource. HRM is thus the management of employees' knowledge, skills, abilities, attitudes and aptitudes, talents and creative abilities. They are very often used for mutual benefits of the organisation wherein they themselves work. They are treated as a profit centre and hence, their all-sided development is desired. From this point of view, HRM is a strategic management function which involves procurement of suitable human resources, training and development of their competencies, proper motivation and creation of vigour in them so that they become the part of the management team for the success and growth of the organisation.

In order to know more about HRM, let us consider some views presented by management experts and authorities. From the definitions stated below, you will come to know the nature and features of Human Resource Management.

1.1.1 Definitions of Human Resource Management

(1) **Prof. Cynthia D. Fisher, Lyle F. Schoenfeldt and James B. Shaw** state that, *"HRM involves all management decisions and practices that directly affect or influence the people or human resources who work for the organisation. In recent years, increasing attention has been devoted to how the organisations manage human resources. It is important to examine as to how organisation's employees enable an organisation to achieve its goals".*

(2) **According to Prof. Wendell L. French, University of Washington**, *"HRM is the term increasingly used for the philosophy, policies, procedures and practices related to the management of people working in an organisation".* He further makes clear that the usual way to describe human resources as it is practiced today is in process system view and the significance of the process-system view is that it – (i) takes in account the interdependence of all aspects of human resources management; and (ii) recognises the relationship between human resources activities and organisational goals. According to the process-system view, human resource management is the systematic planning, development and a network of inter-related processes affecting and involving all members of an organisation. These processes include human resources planning, job and work design, staffing, training and development, performance appraisal and review, compensation and reward, employee protection and representation, organisation improvement".

(3) **Prof. K. Aswathappa** makes it clear that, *"Human Resources Management is a management function that helps managers' recruit, select, train and develop members for an organisation. Obviously, HRM is concerned with people's dimension in organisation".*

(4) **According to Prof. George T. Milkovich and Prof. John W. Boudreau**, *"Human Resource Management is a series of decisions that affect the relationship between employees and employers; it affects many aspects and is intended to influence the effectiveness and abilities of employees and employers to achieve their objectives.*

(5) **Prof. C. B. Mamoria and Prof. S. V. Gankar** have stated a very simple and easily understandable definition of HRM which is as follows:

"Human Resource Management is concerned with the people who work in the organisation to achieve the objectives of the organisation. It concerns with the acquisition of appropriate human resources, developing their skills and competencies, motivating them for best performance and ensuring their continued commitment to the organisation to achieve its objectives". According to them, this definition applies to all types of organisations - industry, business, government, education, health or social welfare of the people.

(6) **According to Prof. Gary Dessler of the Florida International University**, all managers have to perform certain basic functions viz., planning, organising, staffing, leading, controlling etc. These functions, in fact, represent the management process. In his opinion, *"Human Resource Management is the process of acquiring, training, appraising and compensating employees and attending to their labour relations, health and safety and fairness concerns"*. Prof. Gary Dessler has pointed out certain important aspects of human resource management. Of course, there are many other aspects or topics which have also now become the part of the study of 'Human Resource Management'.

(7) **Ivancevich and Glueek** stated that, *"Human Resource Management is the function performed in organisations that facilitates the most effective use of people (employees) to achieve organisational and individual goals"*.

(8) **According to Dale Yoder**, *"The management of human resources is viewed as a system in which participants seek to attain both individual and group goals"*.

(9) **According to David Decenzo and Stephen Robbins**, *"Human Resource Management is concerned with the people dimension in management. Since every organisation is made up of people, acquiring their services, developing their skills, motivating them to high level of performance and ensuring that they continue to maintain their commitment to the organisation are essential to achieve organisational objectives. This is true, regardless of the type of organisation, government, business, education, health, recreation or social action"*.

(10) **According to Michael VP**, *"Human Resource Management is that part of management process which develops and manages the human elements of enterprise considering the resourcefulness of the people employed in organisation in terms of total knowledge, skills, creative abilities, talents, aptitudes and potentialities for actuating effectively"*.

(11) **Prof. L. M. Prasad** focuses attention on the employment and utilisation of human resources with a view that the organisation has the right people, at the right time and also at right place. According to him, *"HRM is concerned with competing for and competing on human resources. Competing for human resources involves recruitment and employing right personnel and competing on human resources involves developing, training and integrating personnel to achieve competitive advantages"*.

(12) **Prof. Guest** has developed four propositions-*strategic integration, high commitment, high quality and flexibility* - which he believes can be tested and can be used for creating more effective organisation. These propositions are defined by him as under:

- **Strategic integration** is defined as *the ability of organisations to integrate HRM issues into their strategic plans, to ensure that the various aspects of HRM cohere and for line managers to incorporate an HRM perspective into their decision-making.*

- **High commitment** is defined as *being concerned with both behavioural commitment to pursue agreed goals and attitudinal commitment reflected in a strong identification with the enterprise.*

- **High quality** refers to *all aspects of managerial behaviour, including management of employees and investment in high-quality employees, which in turn will bear directly on the quality of the goods and services provided.*

- **Flexibility** is seen *as being primarily concerned with what is sometimes called functional flexibility but also with an adaptable organisational structure with the capacity to manage innovation.*

The scope of Human Resource Management is quite large and increasing. It includes human resource or manpower planning, the selection and recruitment, development of all the employees, performance appraisal and review, compensation and rewards, employee protection and representation, organisational development, maintenance of cordial industrial relations, etc.

Human Resource Management is thus the management of employees with a human approach. Employees should be treated with respect and mutuality of interests of the management and the employees is to be ensured. Management and employees must work together for the success of the organisation.

1.1.2 Nature and Features of Human Resource Management

From the definitions of Human Resource Management stated above and the discussions so far, we come to know the nature and features of the Human Resource Management.

Human Resource Management definitely has a much broader scope than personnel management at the component level as well as in coverage at the organisational level.

HRM is a very important approach to the management of people at different levels. In other words, it refers to a set of programmemes, functions, activities, and so on, designed and carried out for maximising effectiveness of employees as well as the organisation.

Proper incentives, mutual involvement, timely guidance, training and advice, quick decision-making for career planning, development activities, etc. are very essential if human resource has to operate efficiently. Hence, human resources are required to be managed through the application of sound managerial principles. From this point of view, HRM is considered as a strategic approach to the acquisition, motivation, development and management of the human resources of the organisation. The points given below make clear the nature and scope of Human Resource Management.

1. **Human Resource Management is a Science**

   Human Resource Management is based on the principle and theories of management. It is a positive science as it is based on logical reasoning, certain principles and theories. It is not only a positive science but it also has a normative side. It will be useless unless it studies the causes which promote welfare of human resources. It is concerned with what should be done under given circumstances to make better management decisions and to achieve organisational goals most efficiently considering the welfare of the people employed. Value judgement cannot be neglected while taking certain decisions.

2. **The scope of the Human Resource Management is Vast and Increasing**

   The scope of HRM is really very vast. All major activities in the working life of the people employed, right from the time of their entry into an organisation until they leave the organisation come under the purview of HRM. Such activities are human resource or manpower planning, recruitment and selection, job analysis and design, training, orientation, placement, development, performance appraisal and job evaluation, remuneration of employees, motivation, welfare, safety and health of employees, industrial relations, etc. It is found that organisations, around the world are remodeling themselves as they have to respond to the challenges presented by the global economy. There is increased globalisation of the economy. Technological changes are taking place. Characteristics of workforce are also changing. All these and many such other aspects affect human resource practices and as a result, the scope of HRM is getting wider by the day.

3. **HRM is a Comprehensive Function**

   HRM covers all categories of employees employed at different levels. This implies that HRM applies to workers, supervisors, officers, managers and all other types of employees. It covers organised as well as unorganised employees and it applies to the employees in all types of organisations.

4. **HRM is Employee-Oriented**

   HRM is concerned with employees in attaining goals and objectives. It is also concerned with behavioural, emotional, social, economic, organisational aspects of employees. It is the process of bringing employees, other people and the organisation together so that the goals of each of them can be met.

5. **HRM is Individual-Oriented**

   HRM considers every employee as an individual so as to provide services and programmemes in order to facilitate employee satisfaction, development and growth. This implies that HRM is concerned with the proper development of human resources in suitable manner and is individual oriented.

6. HRM is a Staff Function

HRM is a responsibility of all line managers and a function of staff managers in an organisation. HR Managers do not manufacture or sell goods but they direct various organisational activities for the success, development and growth of an organisation by advising and managing the operating departments in the desired manner.

7. HRM is a Continuous Function or Process

HRM is a continuous and never ending process. George R. Terry, the renowned expert in the field of management, rightly pointed out that, *"It cannot be turned on and off like water from a faucet (i.e. tap); it cannot be practiced, only one hour each day or one day each week. Personnel management (or HRM) requires a constant alertness and awareness of human relations and their importance in everyday operations"*.

8. HRM is a Challenging Function

Management of human resources is not an easy task. It is a challenging job due to the dynamic nature of human resources. HRM aims at securing unreserved co-operation from all employees for attaining the pre-determined goals and objectives.

9. HRM is a Pervasive (i.e. tending to spread) Function

HRM is the central sub-function of an organisation. It is concerned with all types of functional management such as production management, marketing management, financial management, etc. All managers working in an organisation are involved with human resources function.

10. HRM is Development Oriented

Goals of employees consist of job security, job satisfaction, attractive salaries and fringe benefits, pride, status and recognition, opportunity for development, etc. HRM is definitely concerned with developing the potential of employees so that they can derive maximum satisfaction from their work and put in their best efforts, for their organisation.

11. HRM is a part of Management Discipline

It is beyond any doubt that HRM is an integral part of management discipline. HRM, being a branch of management science, draws heavily from management concepts, theories, principles and techniques and applies them in managing human resources.

12. HRM is Directed towards the Achievement of Goals and Objectives:

HRM is directed towards the achievement of organisational goals and objectives by providing tools and techniques of managing employees in the organisation properly and effectively. It is certain that the achievement of organisational goals and objectives depends largely on the quality of its human resources and the manner in which this quality is utilised in getting the things done.

1.1.3 Functions and Objectives of Human Resource Management

Objectives are pre-determined goals towards which individual or group activities in an organisation are directed. Every organisation has certain objectives and every part of an organisation should contribute directly or indirectly for attaining the same. Objectives determine the character and nature of an organisation and serve as the basis for whole-hearted voluntary co-operation and co-ordination among the employees.

As a matter of fact, objectives provide benchmarks or standards of evaluating performance. Objectives of HRM also are influenced by organisational objectives.

The primary or basic objective of HRM is to ensure the availability of a competitive and willing workforce to an organisation i.e. right people at the right time and at the right place and enhance effectiveness of the people employed by adopting suitable measures for the purpose of the attainment or accomplishment of organisational goals.

The above mentioned basic objective generates several other objectives of HRM such as meeting the needs, values, dignity etc. of the employees, proper staffing at all levels of the organisation, training and developing available human resources at all levels, creating high-performing work culture, improving quality of work life, and so on. Thus, the objectives of HRM are derived from the basic objectives of an organisation.

The important objectives of Human Resource Management are as follows:

(1) To create an able and motivated workforce and ensure its effective utilisation to accomplish various organisational goals.

(2) To establish and maintain suitable and sound organisational structure in order to secure integration of employees and groups and to create desirable working relationship amongst them for increasing the organisational effectiveness. For this purpose, efforts are required to be made to create a sense and feeling of belongingness and team spirit by encouraging the employees to make positive and valuable suggestions.

(3) To create an environment that would help maintain high morale and to encourage a value system that would foster trust and mutuality of interests.

(4) To provide training and education for developing human resources.

(5) To provide opportunities for participation, recognition, etc., and for a fair, acceptable and efficient leadership.

(6) To provide attractive incentives, monetary benefits, social security measures and welfare facilities, various non-monetary rewards, benefits, etc., in order to ensure the retention of competent employees.

(7) To adopt such policies which recognise merits and contributions by the employees.

(8) To ensure that there is no threat of unemployment by instilling confidence among the employees regarding stability of their employment.

(9) An organisation has to bear in mind its responsibility towards the society as a whole. The society may not desire to enforce reservation in hiring and the laws leading to discrimination affecting the society badly or if certain organisational decisions have some negative impact on the society, such decisions should be avoided. It should be the objective of an organisation to use the resources for the betterment of the society and the nation.

(10) To develop and maintain a quality work life which makes employment in the organisation a desirable, personal and social situation.

If we want to categorise the above mentioned objectives of HRM, that can be done in the following manner.

(a) Personal objectives
(b) Functional objectives
(c) Organisational objectives
(d) Social objectives

To ensure that there are right people, at the right time and at the right place, maximum employee development, development of desirable working relationships, effective utilisation of human resources are the primary or important objectives of HRM. How can they be achieved? Obviously, besides many other things, management has to create a conducive environment and provide necessary pre-requisites for attainment of the objectives of HRM. There should be effective utilisation of human resources through proper motivation and changing their attitudes towards the work and organisation. Human resources must be developed to meet the demands of the work effectively.

1.1.4 Scope of Human Resource Management

In order to attain the various objectives stated above, HRM has to perform certain functions and undertake important activities. Not only all major and important activities in the working life of a worker from the time of his or her entry into an organisation until he or she leaves the organisation comes under the purview of Human Resource Management; but many other activities, topics are also studied in HRM.

Human resource planning, job design, recruitment analysis, selection, training and development, appraisal, placement, assessment, proper motivation to the employees, maintenance of union-management relations, human resource accounting and audit, etc. are some of the important activities. This makes clear the scope of Human Resource Management, which is really very vast. The major topics, aspects which are generally included in the scope of HRM are shown in the figure from which we also get an idea about the activities and functions of HRM.

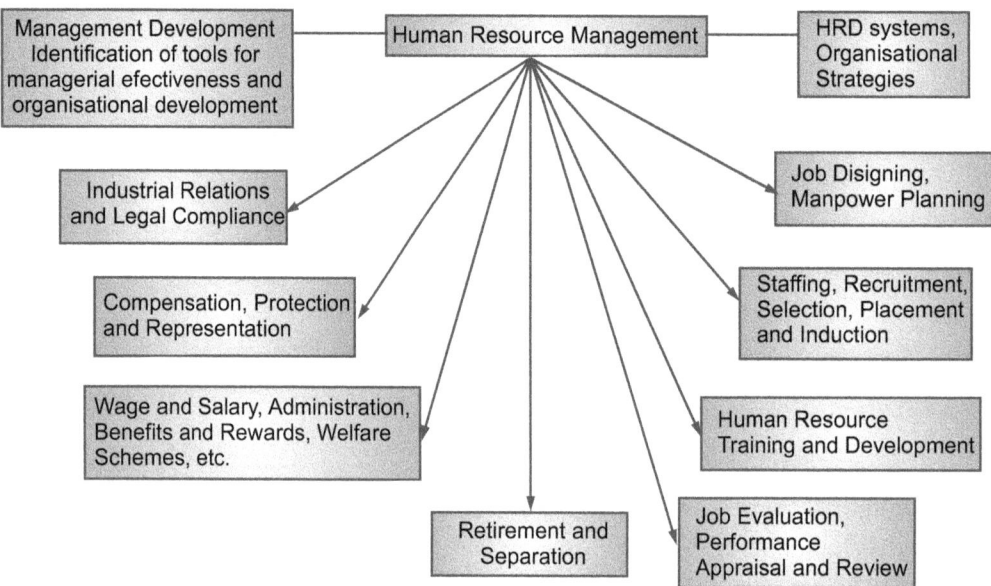

Fig. 1.1: Human Resource Management

1.1.5 Importance of Human Resource Management

Money, Men, Materials, Machines, Markets are very important Five M's, which are essential for carrying on the activities of production and selling the same in order to carry on the business of an organisation. The proper and efficient management of these Five M's is very essential for the success of an organisation. But, the management of men and human resources is most fundamental and is really a challenging task.

In a wider sense, human resources create organisations and make them survive and prosper. If human resources are neglected or not properly managed, the organisation is not likely to do well. The human resources of an organisation is considered as one of the largest investments and plays a very crucial role in the development process of an organisation at the micro-level and of the whole economy at the macro-level. For full and proper utilisation of natural resources, machines, technology, etc., efficient and committed manpower is very essential. Hence, successful human resource management is very essential for the growth and success of an organisation.

The importance of Human Resource Management is universally recognised from different standpoints and its role is continuously becoming very important in long-range planning and policy making activities from the viewpoint of enterprises and economic development of a country.

Human Resource Management helps the organisations in the public, private, and co-operative sectors in accomplishing their goals to effectively utilise the available human resources by systematic planning and control of a network of fundamental organisational processes, affecting and involving all organisational members. These processes generally include human resource planning, job and work design, job analysis, staffing, recruitment, training and development, compensation and reward, employee protection, etc. Efforts are made to develop positive attitude amongst the employees through proper and effective motivation. This leads to creating healthy work environment and promoting team work. All this helps the organisations to become successful in attaining their goals and flourish in a systematic way.

Social significance of Human Resource Management is evident since it maintains and increases the dignity of the employees by satisfying their social needs. This is done by utilising the resources to the optimum in an effective manner and paying employees the best rewards for their participation in the organisation. As a result, they get the psychological satisfaction and social status.

So far as economy is concerned, though it has plenty of natural and physical resources, they cannot be used profitably, efficiently for economic development if human resources are not managed properly. Human resources are basically responsible for transformation. It is observed that, lack of proper organisation of human resources comes in the way of development of less developed or backward economies. For utilising all the resources properly, Human Resource Management is essential. Human Resource Management is really a multi-sided approach from the beginning to the end. It is, in fact, a scientific process that enables the employees to improve themselves and their competency and capability to play their roles properly, so that the goals set are achieved more fully by meeting the needs of the employees to a great extent.

1.1.6 HRM: Policies and Practices

Human resource policies *are the formal rules and guidelines that businesses put in place to hire, train, assess, and reward the members of their workforce.* These policies, when organised and disseminated in an easily used form, can serve to anticipate many misunderstandings between employees and employers about their rights and obligations in the organisation.

Human Resource practices imply *the customary way of operations and behaviour, translating idea into action, and knowledge of how something is usually done. In simple terms, it is to apply principles or policies.*

Some methods utilised by human resources department staff are called "best practices," meaning the way an employment action is handled is the recommended way according to human resources experts. For example, a human resources best practice is conducting an HR audit each year to determine if human resources processes are helpful to the company.

Another best practice is providing new employees with a formal orientation session where they are fully aware of the company, its philosophy and mission. A company known for its human resources best practices is most likely the leader among its competition and typically has a high level of employee satisfaction.

Best practices in human resources are shared with other human resources practitioners as an industry-accepted way of doing business from the HR perspective.

Human Resources policies are generalised guidelines on employee management, adopted by consensus in an organisation to regulate the behaviour of employees and their managers or supervisors. As for the dichotomy between an HR policy and a procedure, they can be compared to a human being and the shadow. Both are inseparable and as shadows set the outlines of a human being, so do procedures set the outlines of an HR policy.

"HR policies may be defined as guidelines, procedures, codes and regulations adopted by management to guide workplace activities within acceptable limits, which are communicated through a summarised statement called policy statement and implemented through instructions referred to as policy directives."

The human resources department develops the introduction to the set of policies and guidelines and explains the importance of the policies. Policies about performance appraisals, fair employment practices, appearance and behaviour are just a few of the several policies contained in an employee handbook.

The handbook is distributed to new employees on the first day of work and is typically discussed during informal or formal orientation sessions. Employers expect employees to fully understand the policies; a signed form to acknowledge the employee has received and understands the employment policies is contained in the employee's personnel file.

From the above definitions and explanations, it is quite clear that HR policies outline what and how HR professionals undertake their day to day activities in the workplace. Because every HR action and activity in the workplace today is highly regulated and has legal, human rights and discriminatory implications, it is important that such actions be regulated and directed strictly. This is what makes HR policies very important and necessary in every business environment today.

Another reason why HR policies are extremely important in the workplace today is that it sets the direction an organisation wants to take in the management of its employees. Business management practice requires that an organisation adopts a distinct approach towards managing employees and getting the best out of them. So surely, a solid HR policy is a must for every business today. Unfortunately, most HR practitioners pass off their Conditions of Service or Employee Manuals or Handbooks as HR Policies. These documents should or are rather, derivatives of the comprehensive collection of all HR Policies (HR Policy Manual). Contracts of Employment, Conditions of Service, Employee Handbooks are all or should all come from the HR Policy.

In HR Operations, policies are developed to cover areas of the HR function which are considered strategic to the achievement of specific HR and organisational objectives. These may include HR Planning and Outsourcing, Recruitment, Training and Development, employment Contracts Negotiations and Administration, Employee Performance and Exit/Termination Process Management.

In HR Administration, the services functions of HR become the focus of policy making. HR Services such as employee welfare (Health and Safety) including annual leave administration, Employee Attendance, Pensions fund Management, Logistics Administration, Cleaning and Sanitation. Sometimes, the function also covers transportation administration, rest house management and protocol services.

In HR Governance, policies are developed to focus on compliance and enforcement of the various policies developed. Policies are also put in place under HR Governance to evaluate performance in accordance with agreed objectives and set targets for the HR function as a strategic business unit as well as the business as a whole. It is based on this information that HR audit systems are developed.

Importance of HRM Policies Practices:

Policies serve several important functions:

- Communicate values and expectations for how things are done at your organisation.
- Keep the organisation in compliance with legislation and provide protection against employment claims.
- Document and implement best practices appropriate to the organisation.
- Support consistent treatment of staff, fairness and transparency.
- Help management to make decisions that are consistent, uniform and predictable.
- Protect individuals and the organisation from the pressures of expediency.

Areas where policies are commonly established:

Organisations commonly have written policies in the following areas:

- Code of Conduct
- Confidentiality
- Conflict of Interest
- Working Conditions
- Attendance
- Hours of Operations
- Termination (Voluntary and Involuntary)
- Recruitment
- Compensation
- Performance Management
- Learning and Development
- Benefits and Eligibility
- Overtime
- Privacy
- Employee Information
- Bereavement Leave
- Compassionate Leave
- Vacation

- Sick Leave, Short Term Disability, Long Term Disability
- Maternity, Parental, and Adoption Leave
- Unpaid Leave
- Family Leave
- Grievance/Conflict Resolution
- Formal Complaint Process
- Disciplinary
- Discrimination and Harassment/Respectful Workplace
- Health and Safety
- Accident Reporting
- Workplace Violence
- Alcohol and Drug Use Policy
- Use of Company Equipment
- General Policy on the Review and Update of Organisation Policies

A successful policies and practices strategy does more than draw boundaries; it also recognises and addresses people's needs.

There are many different types of people, and not surprisingly, they react differently to the need for policies and practices based on those differences. For example, some people prefer there be a written policy for everything, while others favour having no policies at all and would leave everything open to interpretation as situations arise. Neither of these extremes contributes to a work environment that's conducive to high productivity levels. The answer is found in between, with the right number and types of policies and practices that are focused on a primary goal – improving individual performance in the workplace.

So how can an organisation make sure that the employees have clear expectations and are treated fairly as they work to help build the organisation? The answer is found in the way four key elements related to the development and deployment of policies and practices are addressed: roles, rules, consequences and tools.

Roles

People like to have a clear understanding of their role in a company as well as the roles of others. Every successful team has well-defined positions for its members: Everyone knows what he or she is to do, how to do it and how their performance can impact those around them. In business, this means you need to have clear reporting structures that spell out who's in charge and how tasks are to be accomplished in the organisation.

This approach applies not only to intradepartmental structures, but also to company-wide or interdepartmental projects. In addition, role definition is a foundational part of establishing clear performance expectations for each employee.

Rules

Managers and employees need to share a clear understanding of what is and what is not acceptable behaviour within the company. Having a clear set of behavioral expectations is critical. Setting clear and specific behavioural standards in the form of rules establishes a framework for spotting and addressing violations of those standards.

Consequences

It's important that consequences for violations of behavioural standards are clearly stated so that employees know what to expect and have fair warning of those expectations.

Tools

Tools address the question of how you support the people in your company who manage other employees. When faced with a specific personnel issue, what resources are available to them? Do they have an employee handbook or a policy guide? What about regular training in company policies and practices, coupled with simple, easy-to-use forms to guide them when dealing with particular issues? Are you giving them a clear directive on working with your human resources personnel or legal representatives? Are your resources available online?

Human resources policies are therefore vital to any organisation because they provide structure for the human resources department and guidelines for employment activities. Without human resources policies, it would be extremely difficult to justify employment or business decisions. Human resources leadership is initially responsible for creating the policies and later discussing the policies with executive leadership. Human resources practices are the method used to conduct any type of employment action.

1.2 Human Resources Management and Strategic Human Resource Management

There are various types of business organisations which carry on different types of business activities. These business activities are carried on with a view to attain certain objectives of the concerned business organisations. Of course, one of the important purposes is to plan various business activities properly. Every organisation has to adopt certain strategies for its proper and smooth development. Besides, other factors, development of human resources are much needed. Human Resource Management plays a very important role in that respect.

There are different approaches to HRM which look at human resources from different angles. The traditional approach to HRM gives importance to employee relations and considers that the responsibility for human resource management programmeme rests with the staff specialists in an organisation. But, strategic human resource management has a different approach. First, let us try to be acquainted with the meaning of 'Strategic Human Resource Management'.

1.2.1 Meaning and Nature of 'Strategic Human Resource Management'

With reference to a company or a corporation and its activities, 'strategy' means its long-term plan or activities for balancing its internal strengths and weaknesses with its external opportunities and threats to maintain a competitive advantage. For executing strategic plan, certain actions are required and they need to be managed systematically. There should be strategic management for achieving these objectives.

Strategic management, in simple words, is *the process of identifying and executing the company's or organisation's mission by matching properly its capabilities with the requirements or with the demands of its environment*. Strategic management implies the process of formulating, implementing and also evaluating various business strategies to achieve organisational objectives. Obviously, human resource strategies are certain or specific actions an organisation pursues to achieve its goals or objectives through its HRM function.

According to **Prof. Gary Dessler**, *"strategic human resource management means formulating and executing HR systems i.e. HR policies and activities that produce the employee competencies and behaviours the organisation needs so as to achieve its strategic aims"*.

This implies that various HR programmemes, activities, policies etc. should be integrated within a larger framework for achieving the strategic goals of an organisation. This is what exactly is accomplished under strategic human resource management.

Some of the important aspects which make the nature of strategic Human Resource Management clear are enumerated as follows:

(a) Strategic human resource management has an integrated approach and it takes into consideration short, medium and long period for overall development of human resources. From this point of view, it can be said that strategic human resource management is the process of formulating, developing, executing suitable HR programmemes and activities, certain policies as well as practices, improving HR systems considering the organisational strategies and goals or objectives. The important goal or objective of the HR strategy is to build and to develop a committed, competent workforce.

(b) Strategic human resource management considers the implications of business strategy for all the HR systems within the organisation and translates the role that the HR system must play in achieving organisational goals and objectives. Specific approach, processes, actions, programmemes etc. may not be the same in all organisations. But all HR systems, programmemes, policies etc. are required to be integrated within a broader framework for attaining the objectives of an organisation. The 'integration' is important in the strategic human resource management.

(c) Organisational strategies are formulated by the core team and generally HR persons/managers work as the members of the team. Thus, they participate in deciding the organisational strategy. They also suggest the structure, systems, processes, skills etc., required for carrying on HR activities successfully. HR executives/managers assume more strategic planning responsibilities and hence, they have to acquire the new skills. They really need to have an in-depth understanding of the values, policy etc. of their organisations. No doubt, strategy formulation and execution role of HR managers/executives is very important.

(d) In strategic HRM, the function of managing and developing human resource is performed by the managers who interact with line managers. In traditional HRM approach, the function of managing, developing the human resources is carried on by the staff specialists in an organisation. This means in strategic HRM, line managers have a very significant role to play.

Activity	Recap the meaning, benefits, measures and concerns with the practice of both strategic integration of HRM into the business strategy and devolvement of HRM to line managers.

The Strategic Functions of HRM Understood and Implemented in the Company

There are significant functions to be performed by the HR department with the Strategic Management Process. HRM is in a unique position to supply competitive intelligence that may be useful in strategy formulation. Details regarding advanced incentive plans used by competitors, opinion survey data from employees, elicit information about customer complaints, information about pending legislation etc. can be provided by HRM. Unique HR capabilities serve as a driving force in strategy formulation.

HRM supplies the company with a competent and willing workforce for executing strategies. It is important to remember that linking strategy and HRM effectively requires more than selection from a series of practice choices. The challenge is to develop a configuration of HR practice choices that help implement the organization's strategy and enhance its competitiveness.

The main strategic functions of HRM can be classified into two categories:

(i) HR functions in formulation of strategy.

(ii) HR Functions in implementation of the strategy.

(i) HR functions in formulation of strategy: Strategy is formulated by environmental scanning. With the help of environmental scanning, both the threats and opportunities that prevail in the external environment can be identified. In this connection HR functions can help in locating such opportunities as well as threats for the organisation. Moreover, HRM should supply competitive intelligence as are necessary for the formulation of strategy. Different incentive plans of competitors, opinion survey data from employees, pending legislation etc. information can be supplied by the HRM. The success and viability of strategy mostly depend on the position of existing human resource. That is why, HRM can arrange necessary training, accounting, and also can determine the driving force in Strategy formulation.

(ii) HR Function in implementation of the Strategy: A quality strategy can fail, if no attention is paid by the HRM. There are mainly three common problems that arise in implementing any Strategy.

(a) Disruption of social and political structures.

(b) Failure to match individual's aptitudes with the implementation task, and

(c) Inadequate top management support for implementation activities.

HRM is to be observed whether in time of implementation of Strategy any employee opposes this or not. Moreover, some new power, status and authority relationship are requested by the managers of different levels. HRM should maintain this relationship and fix the authority and responsibilities amongst employees as required.

HRM is to issue some important guidelines for better human relationships to make the implementation of strategy more meaningful. Transfer, Promotion, job enlargement and job enrichment, communication, coordination, cooperation along with necessary control are the different functions to be performed by HRM during the time of implementing the strategy.

1.2.2 Global Competitiveness and Strategic HR

The globalisation of business has meant that more organisations now operate across borders with ties to foreign operations, international suppliers, vendors, employees and other business partners. A global presence can range from importing and exporting to operating as a MNC.

By competitive advantage, we mean that a firm or business unit has higher than average profits for firms in its market.

Global Framework: Mastering the global complexities of managing human resources is important not only for HR results but also for the overall success of the organisation. Companies operating globally must deliver basic HR services while also overcoming various operational, cultural and organisational obstacles. Even organisations that operate in domestic market face pressure from foreign competitors. Technology advances have eliminated many barriers to operating on a global scale.

Having a global HR mind set means looking at HR issues from an international perspective using ideas and resources throughout the world and ensuring openness to other cultures and ideas. To compete on an international scale the organisation needs expertise to administer all HR activities in a wide range of nations. Policies and practices should be established to address the unique demands for operating in a global context.

One of the keys to successful competition in the global market is the effective deployment of human resources to achieve a competitive advantage. Much of the research on the role of human resources in global competitiveness has focused on management. The effectiveness of management techniques across cultures and the difficulties of adjustment both in the work place and in the social environment have been extensively examined. The role of the remainder of the firm's work force in achieving competitive advantage in the global marketplace has received much less attention.

Recent research in the strategic management area has focused on the role of heterogeneous firm resources in achieving and sustaining competitive advantage. This emerging paradigm is called the resource-based view of the firm and has become increasingly popular for explaining why firms differ in performance. According to this view, the internal resources of the firm are responsible for competitive advantage and are the source of sustained competitive advantage.

While it has been demonstrated that resources in and of themselves contribute positive returns to organisations, it is the interaction of resources and strategy that seem to form the basis of sustainable competitive advantage. Barney developed a model that demonstrates that, for a resource to be the source of sustained competitive advantage, it must create value (V) for the firm; it must be rare (R); it must be inimitable (I); and it must be nonsubstitutable (S).

Applying Barney's VRIS framework of sustained competitive advantage, Wright, McMahan, and McWilliams (1994) demonstrate that human resources defined as the total pool of human capital under the control of the firm have the highest probability among all resources of being the source of sustained competitive advantage for the firm. This is because human resources are more likely than other resources to be inimitable and non-substitutable, as well as being valuable and rare. We use this argument to support our first point, that a firm should focus on its entire pool of human resources, as outlined below.

Managers in transnational firms should recognise the critical importance of human resources rather than attempting to rely heavily upon capital and technology for success. They must truly be transnational, striving for global integration with local responsiveness. Managers in transnational firms should recognise the value of having access to multiple human resource pools. These expanded pools provide greater opportunity to locate qualified personnel capable of helping the firms achieve their objectives in a global environment. Human resource professionals should help managers develop awareness of cultural diversity both through training and also through direct experience on international assignments. Human resource professionals should also develop training programmes for all employees on cultural diversity so that they are able to better deal with diversity and change. Those individuals should get involved in organisations in countries in which they operate – Chambers of Commerce, policy-formulating governmental bodies, powerful civic organisations, and the like. Performance assessments should be restructured to include evaluations of effectiveness in adapting to and performing within the country in which the manager operates.

Managers in transnational firms and human resource professionals should recognise that HRM strategies will have local variations depending upon the laws and customs of differing countries. The design and management of employee benefit and compensation programmes, for instance, are highly likely to necessitate local variation as are programmes dealing with safety and health. Employee privacy and rights issues are also likely to vary from one country to another. The impact of the shadow work force and the use of temporary help may become even more complicated as personnel are able to cross national boundaries and become more mobile.

There has been a void in knowledge and practice where global corporate strategy and human resource management intersect. Hopefully, focusing on the model presented in this paper will enable both researchers and practitioners to fill that void. Researchers might investigate, for instance, the specific impact of multiple human resource pools. Are the benefits derived from having simply more than one pool or are numerous pools required? Is involvement, as suggested by Lawler, necessary in every country in which a firm operates or only in those in which it is compatible with local cultures? These and other specific research questions can readily be derived from the model. The role of technological learning that takes place in transnational human capital pools is largely supported only through case studies and merits stronger empirical research. The answers to such questions would go a long way towards improving the practice of human resource management in transnational organisations.

That research, however, will need to be different from that to which most management scholars are accustomed. Rouse and Daellenbach have shown very clearly that research methods dealing with the resource-based view will need to be crafted very carefully particularly when one is investigating the concept of sustainable competitive advantage. While much strategic management research relies on secondary sources of information from large sample, multi-industry, single time-period samples, those approaches are not applicable to studying sustainable competitive advantages. Because the sample is so critical, they propose a four-step selection process. Step One is to select a single industry. Step Two is to "cluster firms by strategic type or group within the industry selected", and to validate the clustering. Step Three involves comparisons of performance indicators within these strategic groupings. Step Four then involves careful internal analysis of similarities and differences between high and low performers within each group. Research done using this framework will likely shed more light on the role of human resources in organisations.

This paper, then, sheds light on the importance of a firm's human resources for achieving competitive advantage in a global marketplace. It points to the fact that human resources are a potential source of sustainable competitive advantage, and one over which managers have influence. Further research and observation will refine and clarify the model presented here so that both the theory and practice of transnational human resource management will continue to develop and improve.

1.2.3 Linkage of Organisational Strategy and HRM Strategy

A well-researched and presented organisational strategy is a valuable blueprint for how an organisation is going to be successful. An effective strategy sets a clear vision and ambition for the organisation while identifying the necessary resources required to deliver it, including the people. Linking the organisation's HR strategy to the organisational strategy of the organisation makes good business sense for a number of reasons.

1. **Strategic Alignment of HR:** HR departments sometimes are left to deal with only administrative functions, such as recruitment, performance management, training and compensation. These functions are important, but on their own, they form no part of how an organisation plans for the right level of human resources to deliver on its plans and ambitions. Empowering your HR department to add value to your business strategy ensures it undertakes its functional activities in a manner that supports growth and success.

2. **Delivering the Strategy:** An effective HR strategy with clear links to the business strategy enables the organisation to align its activities better with its human resources. An HR department that understands the demands of the organisation's business strategy can help ensure that the organisation has the right people in place to deliver on the organisation's ambitions and support growth. HR departments integrated into the senior strategic management team can work across the organisation ensuring that human resource requirements are considered equally with other organisational investments.

3. **Effective Training and Development**: Organisations are affected by a huge range of external and internal factors that together can change the nature of individual job roles or place new demands on individuals skill sets. An HR strategy linked to the organisational strategy is better placed to anticipate any such changes and therefore can put in place a targeted training and development plan to help the organisation more quickly adapt to new circumstances.

4. **Improved Recruitment and Retention:** Employees who feel better supported in their jobs tend to be happier and more productive. Furthermore, organisations with a positive reputation in the jobs market for taking care of its workforce face fewer barriers to effective recruitment. Taken together, these factors are important elements in illustrating why HR strategy must link to organisational strategy. With recruitment and retention being two key areas where monetary value can be assigned, a more stable and better-trained workforce means improved operating profits.

5. **HR Drives Strategy**: A mature approach to HR strategy places it at the center of understanding an organisation's overall capacity and capability. Having a clear concept of employees and their different skills can help the organisation to see where the organisation has potential for development and growth and help structure the organisation to take advantage of emerging opportunities. Organisations that have reached this point in their development see HR as a key driver of strategy and integral to their future success, rather than as a simple administrative function that ensures everyone gets paid on time.

All elements of the organisational strategy have implications for human resources, as illustrated in the table below. The challenge for management is to identify and respond to these HR challenges:

Examples of Key Strategy Issues	Possible Human Resource Implications
What markets should the business compete in?	What expertise is required in these markets? Do existing management and employees have the right experience and skills?
Where should the business be located to compete optimally?	Where do we need our people? How many do we need?
How can we achieve improvements in our unit production costs to remain competitive?	How productive is the workforce currently? How does this compare with competitors? What investment in the workforce (e.g. training, recruitment) and their equipment is required to achieve the desired improvement in productivity?
How can the business effect cultural change?	What are the current values of the workforce. How can the prevailing culture be influenced/changed to help implement a change programmeme?
How can the business respond to rapid technological change in its markets?	What technological skills does the business currently possess? What additional skills are needed to respond to technological change? Can these skills be acquired through training or do they need to be recruited?

The strategic fit or the hard variant of HRM

1.3 Models of SHMR

There are a good number of models that have been postulated by various scholars to describe the HRM concept.

However, as shall be seen these various models either fall under the soft or the hard approach of HRM.

1.3.1 The Harvard Model or the Integrated System Model

The Harvard Model was postulated by Beer et al (1984) at Harvard University. The authors of the model also coined it the map of HRM territory.

The Harvard model acknowledges the existence of multiple stakeholders within the organisation. These multiple stakeholders include shareholders of various groups of employees, government and the community at large.

The recognition of the legitimacy of these multiple stakeholders renders this model a neo-pluralist model.

This model emphasises more on the human/soft side of HRM.

Basically this is because this model emphasizes more on the fact that employees like any other shareholder are equally important in influencing organisational outcomes.

In fact the interest of the various groups must be fused and factored in the creation of HRM strategies and ultimately the creation of business strategies.

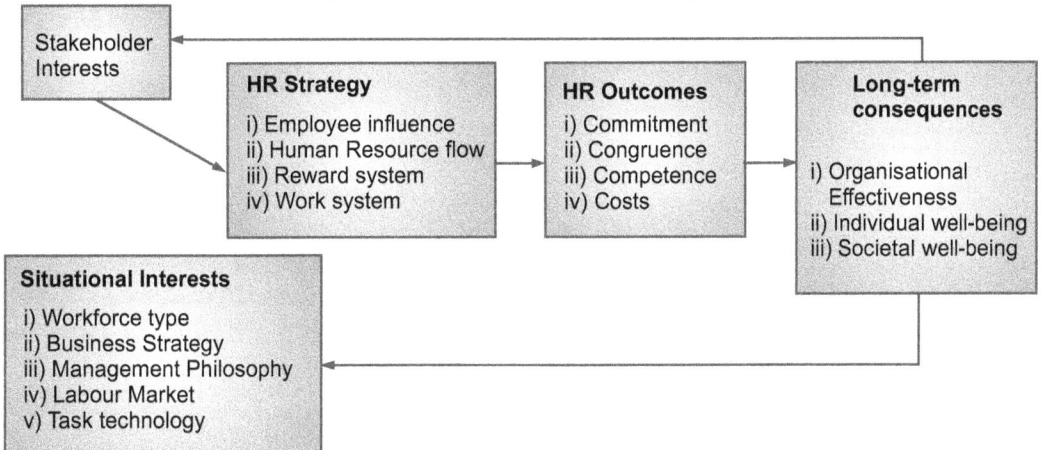

Fig. 1.2: Harvard Model

- A critical analysis of the model shows that it is deeply rooted in the human relations tradition.
- Employee influence is recognised through people motivation and the development of an organisation culture based on mutual trust and team work.
- The factors above must be factored into the HR strategy which is premised on employee influences, HR flows, reward system etc.
- The outcomes from such a set up are soft in nature as they include high congruence, commitment, competencies etc.
- The achievement of the crucial HR outcomes has got an impact on long term consequences, increased productivity, organisational effectiveness which will in turn influence shareholder interests and situational factors hence making it a cycle.
- It is thus important to note that the Harvard model is premised on the belief that it is the organisation's human resources that give competitive advantage through treating them as assets and not costs.

1.3.2 Devanna Model - Strategic Human Resource Management "Matching Model", Michigan Model

- The Michigan model was propounded by Fombrun Tichy and Devanna (1984) at the Michigan Business School.
- They also named this model a matching model of HRM.
- Precisely, the matching aspect of this model demonstrates that the model is inclined towards the harder side of HRM.
- This is because the matching model emphaises more on "tight fit" between the HR strategy and the buisness strategy.
- It demands that available human resources must be matched with jobs in the organisation.
- The HR strategy must be highly calculative in terms of the quantity of the human resources required to achieve the objectives enshrined in the business strategy.
- Business strategy takes the central stage in this model hence human resources are taken like any other resource which must be fully utilised together with the other resoruces to achieve organisational objectives.

(Evans and Lorange, 1989) argue that the Michigan model is based on the "product market logic" which demands that to gain high profits labour must be obtained cheaply, used sparingly, developed and exploited fully.

The Fomburn Matching Model of HRM

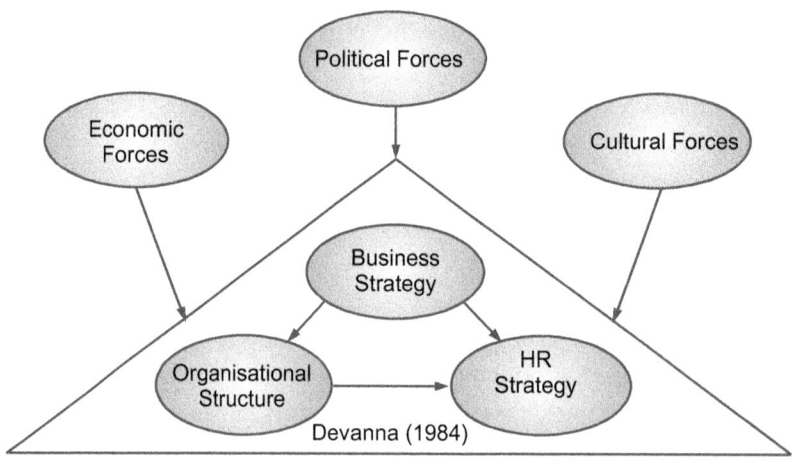

Fig. 1.3: Matching Model of HRM

The point of departure in the Michigan Model is the pre-eminence and pre-dominance of a business strategy, which must strictly be achieved by the available resources regardless of whether, they are able to do so or not.

In fact the business strategy must be achieved through minimum labour costs enhanced by structural re-organisation, Performance Related Pay and staff reduction.

The model held that the HR systems and the organisation structure should be managed in a way that is congruent with the organisational strategy. They further explained that there is a human resource cycle which consists of four generic processes or functions that are performed in all organisations. These are:

1. **Selection**: Matching available human resources to jobs
2. **Appraisal**: Performance management
3. **Rewards**: The reward system if one of the most under-utlitised and mishandled managerial tools for driving organisational performance; it must reward short as well as long-term achievements, bearing in mind that business must perform in the present to succeed in the future.
4. **Development**: Developing high quality employees.

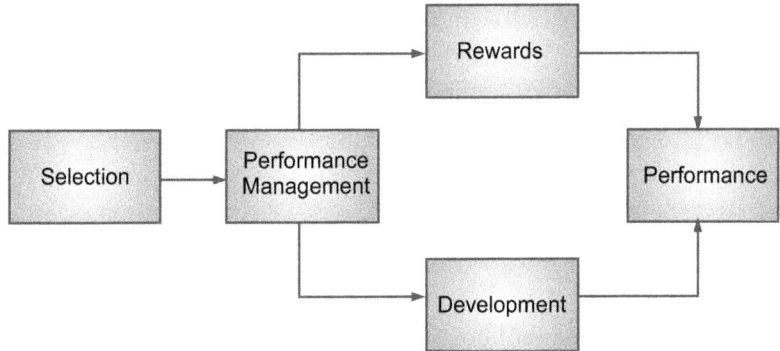

Fig. 1.4: The Human Resource Cycle

Fombrun et al.'s (1984) 'matching model' highlights the 'resource' aspect of HRM and emphasises the efficient utilisation of human resources to meet organisational objectives. This means that, like other resources of organisation, human resources have to be obtained cheaply, used sparingly and developed and exploited as fully as possible. The matching model is mainly based on Chandler's (1962) argument that an organisation's structure is an outcome of its strategy. Fombrun et al. expanded this premise in their model of strategic HRM, which emphasises a 'tight fit' between organisational strategy, organisational structure and HRM system. The organisational strategy is pre-eminent; both organisation structure and HRM are dependent on the organisation strategy. The main aim of the matching model is therefore to develop an appropriate 'human resource system' that will characterise those HRM strategies that contribute to the most efficient implementation of business strategies.

The matching model of HRM has been criticised for a number of reasons. It is thought to be too prescriptive by nature, mainly because its assumptions are strongly unitarist. As the model emphasises a 'tight fit' between organisational strategy and HR strategies, it completely ignores the interest of employees, and hence considers HRM as a passive, reactive and implementationist function. However, the opposite trend is also highlighted by research. It is asserted that this model fails to perceive the potential for a reciprocal relationship between HR strategy and organisational strategy. Indeed, for some, the very idea of 'tight fit' makes the organisation inflexible, incapable of adapting to required changes and hence 'misfitted' to today's dynamic business environment. The matching model also misses the 'human' aspect of human resources and has been called a 'hard' model of HRM. The idea of considering and using human resources like any other resource of an organisation seems unpragmatic in the present world.

Despite the many criticisms, however, the matching model deserves credit for providing an initial framework for subsequent theory development in the field of strategic HRM. Researchers need to adopt a comprehensive methodology in order to study the dynamic concept of human resource strategy. Do elements of the matching model exist in different settings? This can be discovered by examining the presence of some of the core issues of the model. The main propositions emerging from the matching models that can be adopted by managers to evaluate scenario of strategic HRM in their organisations are:

- Do organisations show a 'tight fit' between their HRM and organisation strategy where the former is dependent on the latter? Do specialist people managers believe they should develop HRM systems only for the effective implementation of their organisation's strategies?
- Do organisations consider their human resources as a cost and use them sparingly? Or do they devote resources to the training of their HRs to make the best use of them?
- Do HRM strategies vary across different levels of employees?

Points to Remember

- **HRM** involves all management decisions and practices that directly affect or influence the people or human resources who work for the organisation. In recent years, increasing attention has been devoted to how the organisations manage human resources. It is important to examine as to how organisation's employees enable an organisation to achieve its goals.

- **Nature and Features of Human Resource Management**
    1. Human Resource Management is a science
    2. The scope of the Human Resource Management is vast and increasing
    3. HRM is comprehensive function
    4. HRM is employee-oriented
    5. HRM is individual-oriented
    6. HRM is a staff function
    7. HRM is a continuous function or process
    8. HRM is a challenging function
    9. HRM is a pervasive (i.e. tending to spread) function
    10. HRM is development oriented
    11. HRM is a part of management discipline
    12. HRM is directed towards the achievement of goals and objectives

The important objectives of Human Resource Management are as follows:

(1) To create an able and motivated workforce and ensure its effective utilisation to accomplish various organisational goals.

(2) To establish and maintain suitable and sound organisational structure in order to secure integration of employees and groups and to create desirable working relationship amongst them for increasing the organisational effectiveness. For this purpose, efforts are required to be done to create a sense and feeling of belongingness and team spirit by encouraging the employees to make positive and valuable suggestions.

(3) To create an environment that would help, maintain high morale and to encourage a value system that would foster trust and mutuality of interests.

(4) To provide training and education for developing the human resources.

(5) To provide opportunities for participation, recognition, etc., and for a fair, acceptable and efficient leadership.

(6) To provide attractive incentives, monetary benefits, social security measures and welfare facilities, various non-monetary rewards, benefits, etc., in order to ensure the retention of competent employees.

(7) To adopt such policies which recognise merits and contributions by the employees.

(8) To ensure that there is no threat of unemployment by instilling confidence among the employees regarding stability of their employment.

(9) An organisation has to bear in mind its responsibility towards the society as a whole. The society may not desire to enforce reservation in hiring and the laws leading to discrimination affecting the society badly or if certain organisational decisions have some negative impact on the society, such decisions should be avoided. It should be the objective of an organisation to use the resources for the betterment of the society and the nation.

(10) To develop and maintain a quality work life which makes employment in the organisation a desirable, personal and social situation.

- *Strategic human resource management* means formulating and executing HR systems i.e. HR policies and activities that produce the employee competencies and behaviours the organisation needs so as to achieve its strategic aims.

- *Models of SHRM:*

    1. Harvard Model

    2. Matching Model

    Harvard model is a soft HRM model and focuses on the employee as well as other agencies.

- **Matching model:**

    There four generic processes or functions that are performed in all organisations. These are:

    1. ***Selection***: Matching available human resources to jobs.

    2. ***Appraisal***: Performance management.

    3. ***Rewards***: The reward system if one of the most under - utlitised and mishandled managerial tools for driving organisational performance; it must reward short as well as long-term achievements, bearing in mind that business must perform in the present to succeed in the future.

    4. ***Development***: Developing high quality employees.

Questions For Discussion

1. What is Human Resource Management? Outline its objectives.

2. Define Human Resource Management and explain the nature and importance of Human Resource Management.

3. Explain the objectives of Human Resource Management. What is required to achieve those objectives?

4. Explain the nature and scope of Human Resource Management and trace its evolution in brief.

5. Explain the models of SHRM.

6. Distinguish between Personnel Management and Human Resource Management. Explain the role of H.R. Manager.

7. Explain the structure of Human Resource Department.

8. Explain linkage of organisational strategy and HRM strategy

10. "Human Resource Management" is a basic management function which pertains to all levels and types of Management". Elucidate.

11. What is 'Strategic Human Resource Management'? Explain the nature of "Strategic Human Resource Management".

12. Write short notes on:

    (a) Meaning and importance of HRM

    (b) Evolution of HRM

    (c) "Strategic Human Resource Management" and "Human Resource Management".

    (d) Matching model

    (e) Linkage of organisational strategy and HRM strategy

Multiple Choice Questions (MCQs)

1. What is the meaning of the acronym HRM?

    (a) Human Relations Management

    (b) Humanistic Resource Management

    (c) Humane Resource Management

    (d) Human Resource Management

2. Which of the following terms was also used before the language of modern HRM.

    (a) Labour Relations

    (b) Personnel Management

    (c) Industrial Management

    (d) All of the above

3. Which of the following is not a function normally performed by HR department?

    (a) Accounting

    (b) Recruitment and selection

    (c) Pay and reward

    (d) Training and development

    (e) Employee relations

4. Which of the following statements is false?

    (a) Organisations are now less hierarchical in nature.

    (b) Organisations have been subject to a raft of organisational change programmemes.

    (c) Organisations have adopted more flexible norms.

    (d) Organisations are now generally focusing upon domestic rather than international markets.

ANSWERS

| 1. (d) | 2. (d) | 3. (a) | 4. (d) |

Questions From Previous Pune University Examinations

1. Discuss the importance of Human Resource Management. **M.B.A. April 2006**

Ans. Refer Article 1.1.5 of this chapter.

2. What is Human Resource Management ? **M.B.A. April 2007**

Ans. Refer Article 1.1.1 of this chapter.

3. Define Human Resource Management. **M.B.A. April 2009, 2010**

Ans. Refer Article 1.1.1 of this chapter.

4. Define Human Resource Management and Elaborate its importance.

   M.B.A. December 2009

Ans. Refer Articles 1.1.1 and 1.1.5 of this chapter.

5. Explain the Nature, Objectives and Scope of HRM. **M.B.A. December 2010**

Ans. Refer Articles 1.1.2, 1.1.3 and 1.1.4 of this chapter.

6. Define HRM. Explain the various Functions of HRM. **M.B.A. April 2011**

Ans. Refer Articles 1.1.1 and 1.1.3 of this chapter.

7. Explain the concept of HRM. **M.B.A. April 2012**

Ans. Refer Article 1.1.1 of this chapter.

✳✳✳

Chapter 2...
HR Procurement

Contents ...
2.1 Job Analysis and Design
    2.1.1 Introduction and Definition of Job Analysis
    2.1.2 Importance of Job Analysis
    2.1.3 Purpose/Objectives of Job Analysis
    2.1.4 Benefits of Job Analysis
    2.1.5 Competency Based Job Analysis
    2.1.6 Job Design – Importance and Benefits
    2.1.7 Writing Job Description
    2.1.8 Factors Affecting Job Design
    2.1.9 Job Characteristics Model (Hackman and Oldham 1976)
2.2 Human Resource Planning – Definitions
    2.2.1 Objectives of Human Resource Planning
    2.2.2 Advantages and Importance of Human Resource or Manpower Planning
    2.2.3 Limitations of Human Resource or Manpower Planning
    2.2.4 Process of Human Resource Planning and Estimation of Human Resources
    2.2.5 Manpower Estimation
    2.2.6 Preparing Manpower Inventory
2.3 Recruitment
    2.3.1 Definitions of Recruitment
    2.3.2 Features of Recruitment
    2.3.3 Objectives or Purposes of Recruitment
    2.3.4 Strategic Approach to Recruitment
    2.3.5 Labour Markets and Recruitment
    2.3.6 Recruiting and Diversity Considerations
    2.3.7 Employment Advertising
    2.3.8 Recruiting Source Choices/Sources of Recruitment
    2.3.9 Methods or Techniques of Recruitment
    2.3.10 E-Recruiting Methods
2.4 Selection
    2.4.1 Meaning of Selection and Selection Process
    2.4.2 Importance of Selection
    2.4.3 Essentials of Selection Process
    2.4.4 Selection Procedure/Process
    2.4.5 Barriers and Limitations of Selection Process
- Points to Remember
- Questions for Discussion
- Questions from Previous Pune University Examinations

Learning Objectives:
- To learn about the Meaning of certain terms relating to the Job such as a Job, Job Analysis, Job Description, Job Specification, Job Design and Job Evaluation
- To gain knowledge of the Definitions of Human Resource Planning and its Need or Objectives
- To be aware of the Advantages or Importance and Limitations of Human Resource Planning
- To understand the Human Resource Planning Process
- To be able to discuss the Meaning and Objectives of Manpower Estimation
- To understand the Meaning, Features and Objectives of Recruitment, the Meaning and Importance of Selection and understand the Selection Process

Introduction

In order to have adequate and well qualified human resources on a scientific basis, a standard should be established in advance, with which applicants can be compared. This standard should make clear the minimum acceptable qualities necessary for adequate performance of the job duties and responsibilities to determine human abilities and skills required for execution.

Decisions concerning human resources requirements are not only confined to the human resource department but should also consider the requirements of other departments, and hence human resource planning is required to be done.

In today's modern era of resource constraints, organisations must efficiently manage their activities by procuring and retaining the best of their employees and avoiding the employment of excess human capital in their operations.

The first operative function of human resource management is procurement. It is concerned with procuring and employing people who possess necessary skill, knowledge and aptitude. Under its purview you have job analysis, human resource or manpower planning, recruitment, selection, placement, induction and internal mobility.

The chapter is thus divided into four sections i.e. job analysis and design, human resource or manpower planning, recruitment, and selection.

2.1 Job Analysis and Design

It is understood that it is essential for organisations to undertake manpower estimation, or manpower/human resource planning for effective, efficient, proper utilisation of the employees.

Employees in any organisation are recruited, retained, retrenched or retired considering the volume of jobs, tasks, opportunities of expansion, growth and such other factors. But what is meant by 'job', 'task', 'job analysis', 'job design' etc.? These terms are explained below.

2.1.1 Introduction and Definition of Job Analysis

To clearly understand the meaning of job analysis it is essential first to understand what a "job" is?

A job can be defined as a collection or aggregate of tasks, positions, duties and responsibilities which as a whole are regarded as a regular assignment to individual employees. This implies that the nature of jobs is not similar everywhere.

When total activities are divided and grouped into packages, it is called a job. Every job has certain definite task or tasks based upon some standard trade specifications within a job. A job may consist of positions which are similar as to the kind and level of work.

So now that we know what a job is, let us understand what we mean by job analysis. In simple terms, job analysis may be understood as a process of collecting information about a job. The process of job analysis results in two sets of data:

(i) Job description and

(ii) Job specification.

These data are recorded separately for references.

A few definitions on job analysis are quoted below:

- *Job analysis is defined as the process or procedure of gathering information systematically in order to determine the duties, responsibilities, abilities, skill requirements of a job and also the kind of person who should be employed for it.*

- *Job analysis is the systematic study of jobs to identify the observable work activities, tasks, and responsibilities associated with a particular job or group of jobs.*

- *Job analysis is the process of studying and collecting information relating to the operations and responsibilities of a specific job. The immediate products of this analysis are job descriptions and job specifications.*

- *Job analysis is a systematic exploration of the activities within a job. It is a basic technical procedure, one that is used to define the duties, responsibilities and accountabilities of a job.*

- *A job is a collection of tasks that can be performed by a single employee to contribute to the production of some products or service provided by the organisation. Each job has certain ability recruitments (as well as certain rewards) associated with it. Job analysis is the process used to identity these requirements.*

Job analysis is important from the point of view of manpower planning, recruitment and selection, job re-engineering, wage and salary administration. Job analysis involves detailed examination of the:

(1) tasks (performance elements) that make up a job (employee role),
(2) conditions under which they are performed, and
(3) what the job requires in terms of aptitudes (potential for achievement), attitudes (behaviour characteristics), knowledge, skills, and the physical condition of the employee.

2.1.2 Importance of Job Analysis

Job analysis is an essential ingredient in designing a sound human resource programmeme. Job information gathered from a job analysis may be used for the following purposes:

(1) **Organisation and Manpower Planning:** Job analysis is helpful in organisational planning, for it defines labour needs in clear terms. It coordinates the activities of the work force and facilitates the division of work, duties and responsibilities. Thus, it is an essential element of manpower planning because it matches jobs with them.

(2) **Recruitment and Selection:** Job analysis indicates the specific job requirements of each job i.e. skills and knowledge. In this way, job analysis provides a realistic basis for hiring, training, placement, transfer and promotion of personnel. Basically, the goal of job analysis is to match the job requirements with a worker's aptitude, abilities and interests.

(3) **Training and Development:** Job analysis determines the levels of standard of job performance. Job analysis provides the necessary information to the management of training and development programmes. It helps to determine the content and subject matter of training courses. It also helps in checking application information, interviewing, weighing test results and in checking references.

(4) **Wage and Salary Administration:** Job analysis is the foundation for job evaluation. By indicating the qualifications required for doing a specified job and the risks and hazards involved in its performance, it helps in salary and wage administration.

(5) **Performance Appraisal:** Job analysis helps in establishing clear cut standards which may be compared with the actual contribution of each individual. Job analysis data provide a clear cut performance for every job.

(6) **Job Re-engineering:** Job analysis provides information which enables the management to change jobs in order to permit their being manner by personnel with specific characteristics and qualifications. This takes two forms - industrial engineering activity and human engineering activity. Industrial engineers may use the job analysis information in designing the job by making the comprehensive study. It helps in time study and motion study and work measurement. Human engineering activities such as physical, mental and psychological are studied with the help of job analysis.

(7) Health and Safety: Job analysis provides an opportunity for identifying hazardous and unhealthy conditions so that corrective measures may be taken to minimise the possibility of accidents and sickness.

2.1.3 Purpose/Objectives of Job Analysis

Purpose of Job Analysis

Job Analysis plays an important role in recruitment and selection, job evaluation, job designing, deciding compensation and benefits packages, performance appraisal, analysing training and development needs, assessing the worth of a job and increasing personnel as well as organisational productivity.

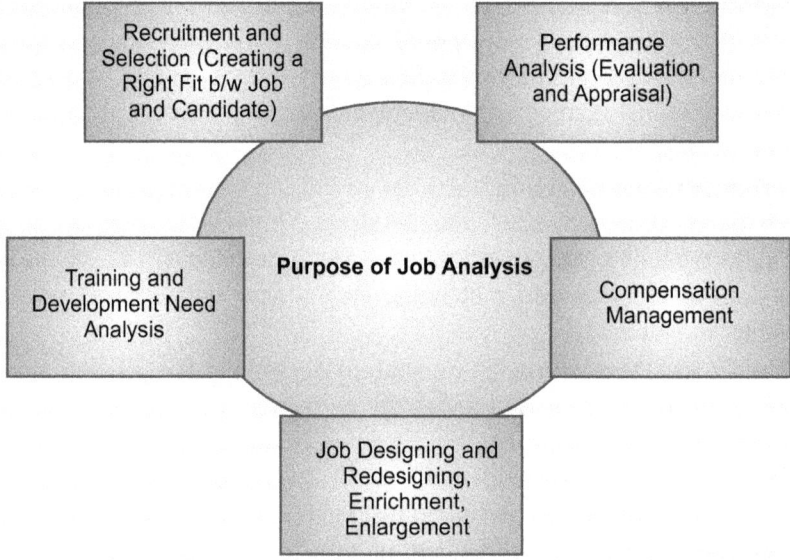

Fig. 2.1

- **Recruitment and Selection:** Job Analysis helps in determining what kind of person is required to perform a particular job. It points out the educational qualifications, level of experience and technical, physical, emotional and personal skills required to carry out a job in desired fashion. The objective is to fit a right person at a right place.

- **Performance Analysis:** Job analysis is done to check if goals and objectives of a particular job are met or not. It helps in deciding the performance standards, evaluation criteria and individual's output. On this basis, the overall performance of an employee is measured and he or she is appraised accordingly.

- **Training and Development:** Job Analysis can be used to assess the training and development needs of employees. The difference between the expected and actual output determines the level of training that need to be imparted to employees. It also helps in deciding the training content, tools and equipments to be used to conduct training and methods of training.

- **Compensation Management:** Of course, job analysis plays a vital role in deciding the pay packages and extra perks and benefits and fixed and variable incentives of employees. After all, the pay package depends on the position, job title and duties and responsibilities involved in a job. The process guides HR managers in deciding the worth of an employee for a particular job opening.

- **Job Designing and Redesigning:** The main purpose of job analysis is to streamline the human efforts and get the best possible output. It helps in designing, redesigning, enriching, evaluating and also cutting back and adding the extra responsibilities in a particular job. This is done to enhance the employee satisfaction while increasing the human output.

Therefore, job analysis is one of the most important functions of an HR manager or department. This helps in fitting the right kind of talent at the right place and at the right time.

Objectives of Job Analysis

Its objectives include:

(a) determination of the most efficient methods of doing a job.

(b) enhancement of the employee's job satisfaction.

(c) improvement in training methods.

(d) development of performance measurement systems.

(e) matching of job-specifications with the person specifications in employee selection.

Comprehensive job analysis begins with the study of the organisation itself, its purpose, design and structure, inputs and outputs, internal and external environments, and resource constraints. It is the first step in a thorough understanding of the job and forms the basis of job description which leads to job specification. Job analysis is also called human resource audit, job study, or occupational analysis.

2.1.4 Benefits of Job Analysis

The following are the benefits of job analysis.

- **Organisational structure and design:** Job analysis helps the organisation to make suitable changes in the organisational structure, so that it matches the needs and requirements of the organisation. Duties are either added or deleted from the job.

- **Recruitment and selection:** Job analysis helps to plan for the future human resource. It helps to recruit and select the right kind of people. It provides information necessary to select the right person.

- **Performance appraisal and training/development:** Based on the job requirements identified in the job analysis, the company decides a training programme. Training is given in those areas which will help to improve the performance on the job. Similarly when appraisal is conducted we check whether the employee is able to work in a manner in which we require him to do the job.

- **Job evaluation:** Job evaluation refers to studying in detail the job performance by all individual. The difficulty levels, skills required and on that basis the salary is fixed. Information regarding qualities required, skilled levels, difficulty levels are obtained from job analysis.

- **Promotions and transfer:** When we give a promotion to an employee we need to promote him on the basis of the skill and talent required for the future job. Similarly when we transfer an employee to another branch the job must be very similar to what he has done before. To take these decisions we collect information from job analysis.

- **Career path planning:** Many companies have not taken up career planning for their employees. This is done to prevent the employee from leaving the company. When we plan the future career of the employee, information will be collected from job analysis. Hence job analysis becomes important or advantageous.

- **Labour relations:** When companies plan to add extra duties or delete certain duties from a job, they require the help of job analysis, when this activity is systematically done using job analysis, the number of problems with union members reduce and labour relations improve.

- **Health and safety:** Most companies prepare their own health and safety, plans and programmes based on job analysis. From the job analysis company identifies the risk factor on the job and based on the risk factor safety equipments are provided.

- **Acceptance of job offer:** When a person is given an offer/appointment letter the duties to be performed by him are clearly mentioned in it, this information is collected from job analysis, which is why job analysis becomes important.

2.1.5 Competency Based Job Analysis

Competency is the combination of knowledge, skills, abilities, values and interest. The use of the term competency as applied to the world of work is most commonly thought to have been first used by **David McClelland**, a psychologist in the early 70s.

At that time, he argued that conventional tests of intelligence and abilities did not predict job performance or success in life and that they were biased against different groups. He invited the term competencies to overcome these defects, suggesting that they made possible the development of valid and unbiased predictors of performance.

His approach included interviewing superior performers, identifying what they did differently from average performers and using the competencies identified for selection purposes. Competencies included motivation such as achievement, orientation, traits and specialised knowledge or skills.

A competency is a measurable skill. In the job analysis process, a competency is a specific and measurable quality that an individual who performs a role must possess. Generally, identifying the competencies tied to each job is the first step in the job analysis process. Often, both the individual who currently holds the job as well as the people who oversee the worker within the position work together to determine which competencies are necessary for success in the position.

An encompassing definition that shows competency as support for job analysis can be seen in the following: Competency is an individual's actual performance in a particular situation. Competency describes how well that individual integrates knowledge, skill, attitudes and behaviour in delivering care according to expectations.

Competencies can fit into an assortment of different categories. Common competencies include oral communication skills, a competency that would be highly important for someone for whom making presentations was a requirement. Customer service is another common workplace competency, particularly when the position involves dealing in a face-to-face manner with customers.

During the job analysis process, competencies are ranked from most to least important. Generally after identifying the competencies, those conducting the job analysis rank each competency and use these rankings to determine which competencies the individual who holds the position must possess and which are more optional in nature and, as a result, are simply preferable, not completely requirements.

Purpose of Competency based Job Analysis

Companies can elect to perform job analysis for an assortment of reasons. The most common reason a company may elect to perform an analysis of this type is to determine if duties that an individual who holds a certain position currently has should be tied to this position or if, instead, they should be attached to another position. For example, if a job analysis shows that the person who holds a set position doesn't necessarily need to possess customer service skills, duties that involve dealing directly with customers may not be appropriate for the individual who holds this job.

Therefore it can be said that the most consistent, valuable method is competency-based job analysis. Practical knowledge and experience are obviously critical to success in many jobs, but they're only part of the picture.

Competencies allow us to take a step back and get to the heart of what will really make an employee successful. Rather than focusing purely on responsibilities and requirements, they address more fundamental personality traits, motivators and behaviours.

The distinct benefits of creating competency-based job descriptions are that they:
- Tend to address the best indicators of success.
- Enhance manager's flexibility in assigning work.
- Lengthen the life of a job description.
- Allow firms to group jobs requiring similar competencies using a single description.

2.1.6 Job Design - Importance and Benefits

Job design means to decide the contents of a job. It fixes the duties and responsibilities of the job, the methods of doing the job and the relationships between the job holder (manager) and his superiors, subordinates and colleagues.

A job design is the division of the total task to be performed into the manageable and efficient units, e.g., positions, departments and divisions and it is done to provide for their proper integration. Actually, it is the sub-division of total work which can be either in horizontal scale or vertical scale.

When sub-division is done on a vertical scale, authorities at the higher levels of the organisation are entrusted the responsibilities of supervising more people or employees in the organisation. They are also responsible for co-ordination of sub-groups, planning etc. When the sub-division of work is done on a horizontal scale, different tasks across the organisation are performed by different people.

A job design can be described as a deliberate attempt to structure the technical aspects of work and it encompasses the organising components of the tasks to be performed as well as the interaction patterns among the work-group members in order to get the job done properly and effectively.

The important objectives of the job design process are motivation and maximum operational efficiency, satisfaction of employees and creating suitable atmosphere to get the job done successfully.

Importance of Job Design

Job design is a very important in human resource management. If the jobs are designed properly, then highly efficient managers will join the organisation. They will be motivated to improve the productivity and profitability of the organisation. However, if the jobs are designed badly, then it will result in absenteeism, high labour turnover, conflicts, and other labour problems.

Well designed and clearly defined job roles are critical for successful:

1. **Job evaluation:** Information about the design of the job is needed for job evaluation, which is the process of comparing the job with other jobs in an organisation to determine the appropriate grade.

2. **Recruitment and selection:** The process gives you a better understanding about the job that needs to be filled and helps:
   - the selection panel identify the job requirements (selection criteria), write the job advertisement, develop interview questions, and assess the best applicant for the job
   - job applicants to decide if they should apply for the job and to prepare for the selection process.

3. **Career planning and development:** The information helps employees to understand the requirements of their role, gain insight into the requirements of other roles in the organisation and identify the capabilities needed for their chosen career paths.

4. **Performance management:** Clearly defined roles allow managers and staff to develop shared understanding of work performance expectations. Capability benchmarks help them identify and meet their professional development needs.

5. **Reward and recognition:** Clearly defined capability benchmarks make it easier to recognise work performance which is above expectations.

6. **Workforce planning:** When aggregated, all the individual roles in the organisation should meet the organisation's capability needs.

7. **Work allocation planning:** Managers can ensure that the work relates to the organisation's core business and is correctly allocated.

8. **Decisions on training investments:** Individual and organisational training are better targeted.

9. **Ensuring workforce safety:** The information may help identify hazardous conditions, unhealthy environments or unsafe work practices/processes which need to be addressed. It may also be used to identify return to work solutions as part of a rehabilitation plan.

10. **Workforce equity and diversity:** The process may also identify ways of improving workforce equity.

Benfits of Job Design

Good job design increases the value of the position to the organisation, engages the worker and reduces individual and organisational risk. It leads to greater organisational effectiveness and efficiency and better results from employees. Key benefits include:

Organisational Benefits	Employee benefits
1. Increased productivity and efficiency	1. Greater clarity of work role, purpose and accountabilities
2. Less need for close staff supervision, checking and control	2. Shared understanding of work expectations with supervisor
3. More effective work teams	3. Good team cohesion as roles, relationships and resources are clearly defined
4. Skilled, flexible, responsive and able workforce to meet work requirements	4. Varied work and challenges, opportunity to develop work skills, flexibility and experience
5. Targeted training to maximise value from training investment	5. Targeted training to meet current and future job needs
6. Improved talent management and succession planning	6. Better career pathways and developmental opportunities
7. Safer and healthier workplace	7. Safer and healthier workplace Support for work/life balance
8. Improved employee attraction, engagement and retention	8. Increased job satisfaction and engagement

2.1.7 Writing Job Description

Job description is *a broad, general, and written statement of a specific job, based on the findings of a job analysis*. It generally includes duties, purpose, responsibilities, scope, and working conditions of a job along with the job's title, and the name or designation of the person to whom the employee reports.

Job description is one of the broad areas of job analysis while the other is job specification. Job specification gives details relating to the candidate who is supposed to perform duties on the job, such as qualifications, experience, abilities, skills etc. While job description gives details of the job in respect of duties, responsibilities, etc.

Job description is a brief and compact written statement of duties, responsibilities and it is based on job analysis which gathers, assembles and analyses the factual information about a specific job. In other words, job description is a systematic, summarised record about the specific job. Such description gives an indication about the physical, mental and other general requirements required for performing the job. It also makes clear what is to be done, how it is to be done and why it is to be done. Its basic objective is to differentiate it from other jobs and to set its outer limits. Job description helps the management to establish assessment standards and objectives.

According to **Edwin B. Flippo**, *"The first and immediate product of job analysis is the job description. As its title indicates, this document is basically descriptive in nature and constitutes a record of existing and pertinent job facts"*.

While **Maurice W. Cuming** makes it clear that, *"Job description is a broad statement of the purpose, scope, duties and responsibilities of a particular job"*.

From the above stated definitions and discussion done, we can define job description as the organised, factual and written statement specifying the duties, responsibilities, requirements of a particular or a specific job prepared on the basis of job analysis.

Contents or Components of Job Description

A job description usually contains the following information:

(a) Job Identification:

This includes the job title, alternative title, department and division, plant and code number of the job. The job title helps to identify the job and department and division indicate the name of the department, its place, whether maintenance, mechanical or any other department.

(b) Job Summary:

It is a brief write-up what the job is all about. In fact, it is a quick capsule explanation of the job in one or two sentences.

(c) Job Duties and Responsibilities:

This portion of the job description gives a comprehensive list of duties to be performed. It is regarded as the heart of the job description. Job duties also make clear the job activities. Responsibilities related to the custody of cash, supervision, training to subordinates are also described in this part.

(d) Relation to other jobs:

This section makes clear the vertical relationship of work flow and procedures and also the location of the job in the organisation by indicating the job immediately below or above it in the job hierarchy.

(e) Supervision:

This section is related to the supervision making clear the number of employees to be supervised alongwith their job titles, the extent and degree of supervision involved i.e., general, intermediate or close supervision.

(f) Information about machines, tools and equipments, materials:

In this part, information relating to major type or trade name of the machines, tools, equipments and raw materials used is given.

(g) Working Conditions:

It specifies the conditions under which the employees have to work i.e. heat, cold, dust, moisture, fumes, etc. Because of this, job holders get an idea about the environment in which they have to work.

(h) Hazards:

Many jobs are hazardous involving the risks of accidents. Hazardous conditions are particularly noted making clear the nature of risks of life, limbs as well as the possibilities of their occurrence.

From the above discussion, we come to know about the contents of a job description. But to remember them easily, the points to be considered relating to the job are enlisted below:

1. Title of the Job.
2. Alternative title, if any.
3. Organisational location of the job.
4. Designation of a immediate supervisor and a subordinate, and supervision given and received.
5. Definitions of job purposes and job duties.
6. Definitions of unusual terms, if any.
7. Extent and limits of authority.
8. Relation to other jobs.
9. Additional responsibility requirements.
10. Materials tools and equipments etc., required as per nature of the job.
11. Complete list of duties to be performed according to daily, hourly, weekly, monthly, etc., estimated time to be spent on each duty.
12. Working conditions i.e. location, time, accuracy, various types of hazards, etc.
13. Salary levels i.e., pay, D.A. and other allowances, bonus, methods of payment, etc.
14. Training and developmental facilities.
15. Promotional chances and channels.

Process of Writing a Job Description

A job analyst writes the job description and for that purpose, he consults the workers concerned or both, workers and supervisors. First, preliminary draft is prepared, then it is shown to the employees concerned and after their comments, suggestions, the final draft is prepared. For writing the job description any one or a combination of two or more methods mentioned as follows can be used:

(a) For the purpose of required information, suitable questionnaire is asked to be filled in by the immediate supervisor.

(b) Job analyst may gather necessary information pertaining to the job from the worker, and

(c) Job analyst observes the actual work when the processes done by the worker and on that basis, he completes the job description.

It should be noted that job descriptions are not perfect reflections of the jobs, they are based on certain variables. Even when, final draft of job description is prepared, it should be reviewed systematically. A job tends to be dynamic and hence a job description can quickly go out of date. Job descriptions are therefore required to be constantly revised and kept up-to-date.

Guidelines for Writing a Job Description

As already made clear, a job description is an important document which provides organisational information i.e., location in structure, authority, etc., and functional information i.e., what activities pertain to the specific job. From the job description, one comes to know the scope of job activities, major responsibilities, positioning of the job in the organisation. A job description makes clear what the worker must do to meet the demands of the job. It is the description of the job and not of the job holders.

According to some experts, job descriptions must be written in detail and in terms of work flow. While others feel that the job descriptions should be written in terms of goals or results to be achieved. There is always a view that duties and responsibilities must also be included in the job descriptions. Thus, how to write the job description seems to be a subjective issue depending upon the needs of the organisation. But to study the topic 'Job Description', let us consider its following two aspects:

[A] Important guidelines for writing a job description or characteristics of a good job description, and

[B] How to write a job description.

Important Guidelines for Writing Job Description:

There is no particular format of writing a job description. Some experts like Dale have developed certain guidelines for writing the job description.

Important guidelines are given below.

(1) The job description should make clear the nature, scope etc., of the job including all important relationships.

(2) It should be brief, factual and precise. Moreover, active verbs should be used to give clear picture of the job avoiding opinions.

(3) There should be proper job title suggesting the nature of job.

(4) In the job description, primary, secondary and other related duties and responsibilities should be clearly defined and explained.

(5) It should include comprehensive job summary. Specific words should be used to show kinds of work, degree of complexity, degree of skills, abilities required, various possible problems, hazards, degree and type of accountability, etc.

(6) Job description should be easily understandable and there should not be any sort of ambiguity.

(7) Job requirements should be clearly stated in the job description.

(8) The extent of supervision should be clearly stated.

(9) The reporting relationship should be clearly indicated.

(10) It should make clear the opportunities for career development.

(11) Utility of the job description in meeting the basic requirements should be examined from the extent of understanding the job by reading the job description by the new employees.

(12) There can be changes in the nature of the job. Considering the changes, the job description should be modified and made up-to-date from time to time.

How to Write a Job Description:

Valerie, Grant and British Institute of Management have stated in "Personnel Administration and Industrial Relations" and "Job Evaluation": "A Practical Guide for Managers – 1970" respectively, point-wise fairly typical pattern of writing the job description generally used by many companies.

Accordingly, the following points are considered while writing a job description:

(1) Each major task or responsibility pertaining to the job is stated in a separate paragraph.

(2) The paragraphs are numbered properly and arranged in a logical order, task sequence or importance.

(3) Sentences begin with an active verb such as 'types letters', 'interviews the candidates', "Collects, sort out routes and distributes the mails", etc.

(4) Accuracy and simplicity are emphasised rather than an elegant style.

(5) Brevity is usually considered as an important aspect but it is largely conditioned by the type of job being analysed and the need for accuracy.

(6) Examples of work performed are quoted in order to make the job description explicit.

(7) Job descriptions, particularly when they are used as the bases for training, often incorporate details of which may be encountered in operator tasks and safety check-points.

(8) Statements of opinion such as "dangerous situations are encountered" are avoided.

(9) When job descriptions are written for supervisory jobs, the main factors such as manning, cost control, etc., are identified and listed. Each factor is then broken down into a series of elements with a note on the supervisor's responsibility.

In the British Institute of Management's Publication "Job Evaluation: A practical guide for Managers (1970)", following four guidelines of writing the job description are given:

(a) Give a clear, concise and readily understandable picture of the whole job;

(b) Describe in sufficient detail each of the main duties and responsibilities;

(c) Indicate the extent of direction received and supervision given and

(d) Ensure that a new employee understands the job if he reads the job description.

No doubt, there are many difficulties in writing the job description. It may not be hundred per cent correct. But it is certain that it is useful method of providing necessary information for making decisions in personnel activities. It is used for job evaluation, providing safety measures, employee evaluation, improvements in the job, etc.

2.1.8 Factors Affecting Job Design

A well-defined job will make the job interesting and satisfying for the employee. The result is increased performance and productivity. If a job fails to appear compelling or interesting and leads to employee dissatisfaction, it means the job has to be redesigned based upon the feedback from the employees.

Broadly speaking the various factors that affect a job design can classified under three heads. They are:

1. Organisational Factors
2. Environmental Factors
3. Behavioural Factors

1. **Organisational Factors**: Organisational factors that affect job design can be work nature or characteristics, work flow, organisational practices and ergonomics.

   - **Work Nature:** There are various elements of a job and job design is required to classify various tasks into a job or a coherent set of jobs. The various tasks may be planning, executing, monitoring, controlling etc. and all these are to be taken into consideration while designing a job.

- **Ergonomics:** Ergonomics aims at designing jobs in such a way that the physical abilities and individual traits of employees are taken into consideration so as to ensure efficiency and productivity.
- **Workflow:** Product and service type often determines the sequence of work flow. A balance is required between various product or service processes and a job design ensures this.
- **Culture:** Organisational culture determines the way tasks are carried out at the work places. Practices are methods or standards laid out for carrying out a certain task. These practices often affect the job design especially when the practices are not aligned to the interests of the unions.

2. **Environmental Factors**: Environmental factors affect the job design to a considerable extent. These factors include both the internal as well as external factors. They include factors like employee skills and abilities, their availability, and their socio economic and cultural prospects.

   - **Employee availability and abilities:** Employee skills, abilities and time of availability play a crucial role while designing of the jobs. The above mentioned factors of employees who will actually perform the job are taken into consideration. Designing a job that is more demanding and above their skill set will lead to decreased productivity and employee satisfaction.
   - **Socio economic and cultural expectations:** Jobs are nowadays becoming more employee centered rather than process centered. They are therefore designed keeping the employees into consideration. In addition the literacy level among the employees is also on the rise. They now demand jobs that are to their liking and competency and which they can perform the best.

3. **Behavioural Factors**: Behavioural factors or human factors are those that pertain to the human need and that need to be satisfied for ensuring productivity at workplace. They include the elements like autonomy, diversity, feedback etc. A brief explanation of some is given below:

   - **Autonomy:** Employees should work in an open environment rather than one that contains fear. It promotes creativity, independence and leads to increased efficiency.
   - **Feedback:** Feedback should be an integral part of work. Each employee should receive proper feedback about his work performance.
   - **Diversity**: Repetitive jobs often make work monotonous which leads to boredom. A job should carry sufficient diversity and variety so that it remains as interesting with every passing day. Job variety / diversity should be given due importance while designing a job.

- **Use of Skills and Abilities**: Jobs should be employee rather than process centered. Though due emphasis needs to be given to the latter but jobs should be designed in a manner such that an employee is able to make full use of his abilities and perform the job effectively.

2.1.9 Job Characteristics Model (Hackman and Oldham 1976)

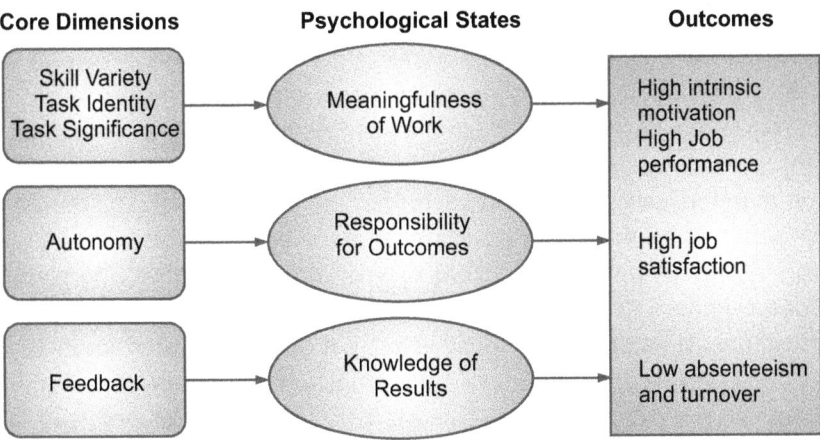

Fig. 2.2: Job Characteristics Model

The *job characteristics model* is one of the most influential attempts to design jobs with increased motivational properties. Proposed by Hackman and Oldham, the model describes five core job dimensions leading to three critical psychological states, resulting in work-related outcomes.

1. **Skill** variety refers to the extent to which the job requires a person to utilise multiple high-level skills. A car wash employee whose job consists of directing customers into the automated car wash demonstrates low levels of skill variety, whereas a car wash employee who acts as a cashier, maintains carwash equipment, and manages the inventory of chemicals demonstrates high skill variety.

2. **Task identity** refers to the degree to which a person is in charge of completing an identifiable piece of work from start to finish. A Web designer who designs parts of a Web site will have low task identity, because the work blends in with other Web designers' work; in the end it will be hard for any one person to claim responsibility for the final output. The Web master who designs an entire Web site will have high task identity.

3. **Task significance** refers to whether a person's job substantially affects other people's work, health, or well-being. A janitor who cleans the floors at an office building may find the job low in significance, thinking it is not a very important job. However, janitors cleaning the floors at a hospital may see their role as essential in helping patients get

better. When they feel that their tasks are significant, employees tend to feel that they are making an impact on their environment, and their feelings of self-worth are boosted.

4. **Autonomy** is the degree to which a person has the freedom to decide how to perform his or her tasks. As an example, an instructor who is required to follow a predetermined textbook, covering a given list of topics using a specified list of classroom activities, has low autonomy. On the other hand, an instructor who is free to choose the textbook, design the course content, and use any relevant materials when delivering lectures has higher levels of autonomy. Autonomy increases motivation at work, but it also has other benefits. Giving employee's autonomy at work is a key to individual as well as company success, because autonomous employees are free to choose how to do their jobs and therefore can be more effective. They are also less likely to adopt a "this is not my job" approach to their work environment and instead be proactive (do what needs to be done without waiting to be told what to do) and creative. The consequence of this resourcefulness can be higher company performance. For example, a Cornell University study shows that small businesses that gave employees autonomy grew four times more than those that did not. Giving employees autonomy is also a great way to train them on the job. For example, Gucci's CEO Robert Polet points to the level of autonomy he was given while working at Unilever PLC as a key to his development of leadership talents. Autonomy can arise from workplace features, such as telecommuting, company structure, organisational climate, and leadership style.

5. **Feedback** refers to the degree to which people learn how effective they are being at work. Feedback at work may come from other people, such as supervisors, peers, subordinates, and customers, or it may come from the job itself. A salesperson that gives presentations to potential clients but is not informed of the clients' decisions has low feedback at work. If this person receives notification that a sale was made based on the presentation, feedback will be high.

The relationship between feedback and job performance is more controversial. In other words, just the presence of feedback is not sufficient for employees to feel motivated to perform better. In fact, a review of this literature shows that in about one-third of the cases, feedback was detrimental to performance.

In addition to whether feedback is present, the sign of feedback (positive or negative), whether the person is ready to receive the feedback, and the manner in which feedback was given will all determine whether employees feel motivated or demotivated as a result of feedback.

According to the job characteristics model, the presence of these five core job dimensions leads employees to experience three psychological states: They view their work as meaningful, they feel responsible for the outcomes, and they acquire knowledge of results. These three psychological states in turn are related to positive outcomes such as overall job satisfaction, internal motivation, higher performance, and lower absenteeism and turnover. Research shows that out of these three psychological states, experienced meaningfulness is the most important for employee attitudes and behaviours, and it is the key mechanism through which the five core job dimensions operate.

Are all five job characteristics equally valuable for employees? Hackman and Oldham's model proposes that the five characteristics will not have uniform effects. Instead, they proposed the following formula to calculate the motivating potential of a given job:

MPS = ((Skill Variety + Task Identity + Task Significance) ÷ 3) × Autonomy × Feedback

According to this formula, autonomy and feedback are the more important elements in deciding motivating potential compared to skill variety, task identity, or task significance. Moreover, note how the job characteristics interact with each other in this model. If someone's job is completely lacking in autonomy (or feedback), regardless of levels of variety, identity, and significance, the motivating potential score will be very low.

Note that the five job characteristics are not objective features of a job. Two employees working in the same job may have very different perceptions regarding how much skill variety, task identity, task significance, autonomy, or feedback the job affords. In other words, motivating potential is in the eye of the beholder. This is both good and bad news. The bad news is that even though a manager may design a job that is supposed to motivate employees, some employees may not find the job to be motivational.

The good news is that sometimes it is possible to increase employee motivation by helping employees change their perspective about the job. For example, employees laying bricks at a construction site may feel their jobs are low in significance, but by pointing out that they are building a home for others, their perceptions about their job may be changed.

Do all employees expect to have a job that has a high motivating potential? Research has shown that the desire for the five core job characteristics is not universal. One factor that affects how much of these characteristics people want or need is growth need strength. Growth need strength describes the degree to which a person has higher order needs, such as self-esteem and self-actualization. When an employee's expectation from his job includes such higher order needs, employees will have high-growth need strength, whereas those who expect their job to pay the bills and satisfy more basic needs will have low-growth need strength.

Not surprisingly, research shows that those with high-growth need strength respond more favourably to jobs with a high motivating potential. It also seems that an employee's career stage influences how important the five dimensions are. For example, when employees are new to an organisation, task significance is a positive influence over job satisfaction, but autonomy may be a negative influence.

2.2 Human Resource Planning - Definitions

Human Resource Planning determines the human resource needs of the whole organisation and also of each of its departments for a given period in future to accomplish various activities, functions and operations envisaged in connection with the achieving the organisational goals and objectives. Human Resource Planning is the predetermination of the future courses of action from a number of alternatives for procuring, managing, motivating, compensating, career and succession planning, promoting and separating the human resources of an organisation.

Human Resource Planning or Manpower Planning involves identifying staffing needs by analysing properly the available human resources and determining what additions and/or replacements are required in order to maintain the staff of the desired size and quality. It can be at different levels and for different purposes. At the national level, manpower planning is done by the Government for economic development, such as population projections, educational facilities, etc. Such manpower planning is also known as macro-level planning.

Definitions:

Following are some definitions of 'HRP' or 'MPP' which throw light on different aspects of human resource or manpower planning.

(1) Lean C. Megginson:

"Human Resource Planning is an integrated approach in performing the planning aspects of the personnel function in order to have a sufficient supply of adequately developed and motivated people to perform the duties and tasks required to meet organisational objectives and satisfy the individual needs and goals of organisational members".

(2) E. B. Geisler:

"Manpower planning is the process - including forecasting, developing and controlling – by which a firm ensures that it has the right number of people and the right kind of people, at the right places, at the right time doing work for which they are economically most useful".

(3) Eric W. Vetter:

"Manpower planning is the process by which management determines how the organisation should move from its current manpower position to its desired manpower position. Through planning, management strives to have right number of and the right kind of people at the right place at the right time, doing things which result in, both the organisational and the individual, receiving maximum long run benefits".

(4) Wendell French:

"Human Resource Planning is the process of assessing the organisation's human resources needs in the light of organisational goals and making plans to ensure that a competent, stable work force is employed".

(5) Leap and Crino:

"Human Resource Planning includes the estimation of how many qualified people are necessary to carry out the assigned activities, how many people will be available, and what, if anything, must be done to ensure that personnel supply equals personnel demand at the appropriate point in future".

(6) Decenzo and Robbins:

"Human Resource Planning is the process by which an organisation ensures that it has the right number and kind of people, at the right place, at the right time, capable of effectively and efficiently completing those tasks that will help the organisation to achieve its overall objectives".

(7) Coleman:

Human Resource or Manpower Planning is *"the process of determining manpower requirements and the means for meeting those requirements in order to carry out the integrated plan of the organisation".*

(8) Strainer:

"Manpower Planning is *"strategy for the acquisition, utilisation, improvement and preservation of an enterprise's human resources. It relates to establishing job specifications or the quantitative requirements of jobs determining the number of personnel required and developing sources of manpower".*

(9) Gordon MacBeath:

"Manpower planning involves two stages. The first stage is concerned with the detailed planning of manpower requirements for all types and levels of employees throughout the period of the plan and the second stage is concerned with Planning of manpower supplies to provide the organisation with the right types of people from all the sources to meet the planned requirements".

(10) James J. Lynch:

Manpower planning is *"The integration of manpower policies, practices and procedures so as to achieve the right number of the right people at the right jobs at the right time".*

Human Resource Planning is a continuous process of identifying human resource requirements for an organisation in terms of quality and quantity. It is a strategy for the acquisition, utilisation, improvement and preservation of an organisation's human resources. It cannot be rigid or static. It requires modifications, review and adjustments according to the needs of an organisation in the changing business environments. Planning activities focus on the future. These consider how an organisation should move from its current human resources condition to achieve its human resource objectives.

Human Resource Planning helps to establish the links between the organisation's overall strategies and its human resource strategies. It is mainly concerned with how to integrate all human resource decisions into a coherent overall resource strategy.

Characteristics of Human Resource Planning:

From the definitions stated above and the discussion done so far, we come to now certain characteristics of Human Resource Planning which are as follows:

(a) Human resource planning is an important process and its integrated approach helps the management in many ways. Through proper and effective human resource planning, management strives to have right number of and right types of employees at the right place and at the right time for attaining the goals and objectives of the organisation.

(b) Human resource planning helps to identify the human resources needs in the light of organisational goals.

(c) Human resource planning paves the way for an effective motivational process.

(d) Human resource planning takes into account likely possibility of new developments and extends plans to cover the changes during the given long period.

(e) Human resource planning also provides the base for developing skills and talents.

It is found that human resource planning means different things from the view point of different experts in the field of management. However, general agreement exists on its ultimate objectives i.e. the most effective and efficient placement of scarce human resources in the interest of employees as well as of their organisation.

2.2.1 Objectives of Human Resource Planning

Human resource planning is undertaken to achieve the overall objectives of an organisation. Some of the important objectives which the human resource planning is expected to fulfil are explained below.

1. To use the human resources to the optimum level:

The human resource planning should ensure optimum utilisation of the human resource currently employed in the organisation. This is expected to be done by providing sufficient work to each employee and by assigning the work according to the skills and abilities of the persons working in the organisation.

2. To provide employees having technical skills to face the changes expected to take place in the future:

Constant changes take place in the technological field and accordingly an organisation has to use new techniques in its operation. For this purpose, persons who have acquired new skills are needed by the organisation. Human resource planning is carried out with the objective of deciding the skills which will be needed in the future and either training the present employees to acquire the new skills or obtain new employees who possess the new skills.

3. **To ensure that the human resources are made available as and when required:**

   Employees are needed in various departments of the organisation to perform different functions. They may be needed to fill up the vacancies which arise in the organisation as well as for the additional posts created due to expansion programmes or modernisation or diversification programmes. Human resource planning is expected to anticipate the number of employees needed, the kind of employees needed and when they will be needed and make arrangements for supplying the employees from different sources.

4. **To determine the recruitment level and training needs:**

   An organisation needs persons to work at different levels. Unskilled, semi-skilled, skilled and highly skilled employees needed by the organisation are recruited in different ways. Human resource planning should decide which category of the employees will be needed and make arrangements for recruitment of the required employees. It is also expected to find out the level of skills and abilities possessed by the present employees and decide what type of training should be given to them to make them competent to face the fast changing future.

5. **To provide a basis for management and organisation development programmes:**

   To face increasing competition and changes which take place in technology and other fields, organisation has to plan management and organisational development programmes. Human resource planning is expected to provide the basic information by using which of these programmes can be prepared and implemented.

6. **To draw attention to trouble spots as far as the human resource is concerned:**

   When information about the present employees is studied for the purpose of manpower planning, attention is drawn to those sections or departments where the required type of people are not easily available in adequate number. Management takes special care in such cases to overcome the deficiency.

   Similarly, human resource planning also brings to the notice of the management those employees who from the organisation's point of view are indispensable.

7. **To avoid redundancy and redeployment of the existing employees:**

   It's the business plan that directs Manpower planning. Process of Human Resource Planning does not find whether some products are to be discontinued. These are strategic decision. Manpower planning is done based on such decisions and not vice-versa. Due to such changes, some jobs which are being done at present may be required to be eliminated and the persons performing these jobs may become redundant. Process of manpower planning can identify such positions and management can arrange to retrain such employees and redeploy them for the new jobs.

8. **To ensure career planning of every employee and prepare succession programmes for the organisation:**

Human resource planning is not only for the benefit of the organisation but is also expected to benefit the employees working in the organisation. Employees have expectations of getting opportunities of working at more responsible and higher positions. Human resource planning helps to provide human resources not only from outside but also from within the organisation.

Posts at higher level may be filled up by promoting the employees working at lower level. Employees are given information about the promotion opportunities and the eligibility criteria for such promotions. Managerial vacancies are filled up by selecting and developing suitable persons from the organisation and for this purpose succession programmes are prepared.

9. **To control the costs and increase the productivity of human resources:**

It is one of the important objectives of the human resource planning to retain the desired employees longer and keep them functioning more productively and at reasonable cost. Human resource planning attempts to make efforts to reduce labour costs, recruitment and replacement costs.

By keeping an inventory of existing human resources in the organisation properly by skills, levels, training, educational qualifications, work experience, salaries and wages, etc., it becomes possible to utilise the existing resources more efficiently and productively. Manpower additions are thus controlled and this leads to control of wage and salary costs.

The above mentioned objectives underline the importance of human resource planning.

2.2.2 Advantages and Importance of Human Resource or Manpower Planning

Manpower planning is a very important tool and technique of human resource management. It basically aims at maintaining and improving the ability of an organisation to attain the goals of an organisation by developing and utilising properly its human resources. V. S. Narayanrao explained the practical utility and importance of manpower planning in "Manpower Planning Companies", accordingly –

(1) At the national level, it is generally done by the government and covers various items like population projections, economic development programmes, educational facilities, occupational distribution and growth, industrial and geographical mobility of human resources.

(2) At the sector level, it can be done by the Central and State Governments covering the manpower needs of various sectors such as industry, agriculture, service sector.

(3) At the industry level, it may cover manpower forecast for specific industries e.g., heavy industries, engineering, consumer goods industries, public utility industries, etc.

(4) At the industrial unit level i.e., micro level, it may cover its manpower needs for its various departments and for different types of personnel.

Thus, Manpower Planning plays an important role at both the micro as well as the macro level. It is found today that more complex technologies are functioning in economic, social, business environments. As a result, the organisations face shortages of the right type of human resources. Manpower planning enables to get the right type of personnel in the organisation. Besides this, following points also throw light on the advantages and manpower planning:

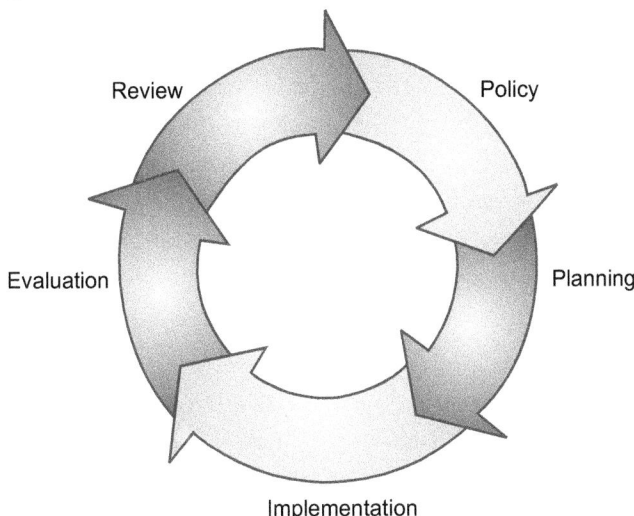

Fig. 2.3: Human Resource Planning

(1) Manpower planning involves forecasting of manpower requirements in an organisation and helps the management in anticipating personnel shortages and surpluses and also to develop the ways to avoid or correct problems before they become serious. Further, forecasting of long-range manpower requirements is helpful in forecasting the compensation costs involved in that connection.

(2) A proper and systematic forecasting of human resource requirements helps an organisation to determine proper sources and methods of recruitment. Further, an organisation can also adopt a proper selection procedure depending upon the needs of the jobs. Proper tests can be designed for the purpose of selecting the right candidates for the right jobs. Thus, importance of manpower planning is immense in recruiting and selecting of the personnel.

(3) From the view point of training and development, the importance of manpower planning is definitely great. Manpower planning ensures training of employees in an organisation. Training involves imparting of knowledge and developing attitudes, skills, social behaviour, etc., of the employees. Manpower planning identifies the training needs of the personnel of an organisation before hand so that necessary arrangements and training programmes can be chalked out accordingly to give training to the employees. Training helps the organisation to utilise its human resources to the optimum. Manpower planning is not only important from the view point of an organisation but it also helps the employees of an organisation in developing and in the application of skills, abilities, knowledge which affect their capacity positively as for as efficiency, earnings, etc., are concerned.

(4) So far as performance appraisal is concerned, manpower planning plays an important role in that area too. Performance appraisal refers to identification of strengths and weaknesses of the employees of an organisation relating to their jobs. It is conducted to know whether the existing human resources possess the necessary qualities and qualifications as per the requirements of the jobs. Manpower planning makes available necessary strategies to correct the weaknesses of the employees by making the proper arrangements for corrective training, retraining, orientation programmes. As a matter of fact, all these are inter-related activities.

(5) Importance of manpower planning is none-the-less in respect of controlling the labour costs. Efforts are made in manpower planning to assure the timely and sufficient supply of labour, thus, avoiding the shortages and surpluses of labour which leads to save and control labour costs.

(6) Manpower planning facilitates career development of employees. Career development refers to upward movement of the personnel employed in an organisation. Taking into consideration the long range plans of the organisation, a career path of an employee can be projected along with what is expected from him in terms of competence levels. The employees can then plan their career accordingly within the organisation. The clarity plays a significant role in enhancing the levels of motivation of employees – a very important role of Manpower Planning.

(7) Manpower Planning if done properly and systematically, problems of low productivity, absenteeism, inter-deparmental conflicts, resistance to change, etc., can be tackled and solved efficiently. The effort leads to higher productivity and efficiency levels, thus stressing on the importance of this major function under HR organisation.

Thus, it can be said that manpower planning definitely helps to increase the prospects of an organisation in managing its resources in a better way and coping more effectively with dynamic situations.

2.2.3 Limitations of Human Resource or Manpower Planning

Though manpower planning is an important tool in the hands of management and is quite useful, it suffers from uncertain limitations. These limitations basically arise from the uncertainty of predictions, methods used, etc. Important limitations of manpower planning are as follows:

(a) The most important inherent limitation of manpower planning lies with the forecasting. Future is uncertain and changes in technology, economic conditions, political situations, working conditions and business environments, etc., cannot always be anticipated accurately and long-range forecasts cannot be made accurately. As the degree of uncertainty varies, so does the style, the scope and efficacy of manpower planning change.

(b) Management can predict as to how many vacancies can be created in future with a reasonable degree of accuracy resulting from retirements. But deaths and resignations of the employees cannot be predicted and hence, it becomes very difficult to anticipate as to which particular employee will be required to be replaced. In that respect, planning may not be done accurately and certain steps cannot be taken as far as new recruitments are concerned.

(c) Another important difficulty in manpower planning arises on account of top management. Sometimes, top management remains reluctant and does not support because of inherent uncertainty. The over cautious approach on the part of the top management may lead to frustration in the personnel concerned involved in manpower planning.

2.2.4 Process of Human Resource Planning and Estimation of Human Resources

Manpower planning is described as a process. It is a continuous process in the sense that the work of estimating demand for and supply of employees is required to be carried on as long as the organisation carries on its business. The process of manpower planning is one of the most important, crucial, complex and continuing managerial functions. It entails consideration of several steps with relevant input before the estimation of manpower requirements can be arrived at and also involves, the identification of the source of supply to meet the requirements, taking into consideration various constraints.

Manpower planning process seeks to ensure that the people with right fit in the required number are placed at the right time in the organisation. From this point of view, **G. Stainer** suggested nine strategies for human resource planning which are stated as follows.

(a) Collection, maintenance and interpretation of relevant information regarding human resources.

(b) Periodical review of manpower objectives and requirements.

(c) Development of procedures and techniques to determine the requirements of different types of manpower over a period of time.

(d) Development of measures for the utilisation of manpower alongwith independent validation, if possible.

(e) Employment of suitable techniques for the effective allocation of work with a view to improve manpower utilisation properly.

(f) Conducting surveys for determining the factors hampering the contribution of individual as well as of the groups in the organisation for modifying or removing those handicaps.

(g) Development and employment of methods of economic assessment of human resources, reflecting its features as an income generator and cost.

(h) Evaluation of the procurement, promotion, retention, etc., of the effective manpower resources in relation to the forecast of manpower requirements of the organisation.

(i) Analysis and controlling of organisational processes and structure for encouraging maximum individual and group performance without incurring excessive costs.

These strategies also throw light on the objectives of manpower planning and we can get an idea from these points about the steps involved in the manpower planning.

The process of manpower planning begins with the determination and review of the objectives of organisation. This enables the management to estimate the manpower requirements and internal supply of human resources. **W. S. Wickstorm** suggested that the manpower planning consists of a series of activities such as –

(1) forecasting of future manpower requirements.

(2) making an inventory of present manpower resources and also assessing the extent to which these manpower resources are employed optimally.

(3) anticipation of manpower problems by projecting the present resources into the future and making comparison with the estimation of human requirements in order to determine their adequacy, both qualitatively and quantitatively.

(4) planning for the programmes of selection, training, development, utilisation, promotions, etc., in order to ensure adequate manpower supply in the future.

Prof. R. S. Davar suggested the following important steps involved in the process of manpower planning:

(1) anticipation of manpower requirements for the organisation.

(2) proper planning of job requirements and descriptions.

(3) analysis of skills required in order to determine the nature of manpower needed.

(4) selection of adequate and suitable sources of recruitment.

Dr. P. Subba Rao pointed out following eight steps of process of human resource planning.

(a) Analysis of organisational plans.

(b) Demand forecasting – Forcasting of overall human resource requirements in accordance with the organisational plans.

(c) Supply forecasting – Obtaining the data and information about the present inventory of human resources and forecasting of the future changes in the human resource inventory.

(d) Estimation of net human resources or manpower requirements.

(e) In case of future surplus, plan for redeployment, retrenchment and lay-off.

(f) In case of future deficit, forecasting of the future supply of human resources from all sources with reference to plans of other companies.

(g) Plan for recruitment, development and internal mobility if future supply is more than or equal to net human resource requirements.

(h) Plan to modify or adjust the organisational plan if the future supply is expected to be inadequate with reference to future net requirements.

Prof. P. Subba Rao further makes it clear that all the steps of manpower planning are interdependent and sometimes, certain steps can be processed simultaneously. For example, steps 'a' and 'h' mentioned above can be undertaken simultaneously.

The persons who perform manpower planning work have to decide the period for which the plan should be prepared. Manpower planning can be done for:

(1) Short term such as one year or so.

(2) A medium term which is for more than one year but upto five years.

(3) For a long term which is for a period of more than five years, ten years or upto fifteen years.

It is regarded that manpower planning for a very long period of time does not serve much purpose. Manpower planning is generally done for a period of five to seven years with a break-up given for each year. While doing the manpower planning the following important steps are expected to be completed.

[A] Analysis of the objectives of the organisation in relation to the human resource planning:

Objectives of the organisation act as a guideline for estimating the demand for manpower in the future. The objectives should be stated in clear terms so that the work expected to be done for achieving the objectives can become clear to the people involved in man-power planning. Hence, the process of manpower planning should start with analysing the organisational plans into production plan, technological plan, expansion and diversification plan, marketing and sales plan, etc., and further, each plan should be analysed into sub-units as per requirements.

Analysis of organisational plans helps in estimating the demand for manpower as it gives the idea about the quantum of future work activities. It is to be done to relate future manpower needs to the future organisational needs so as to maximise the future returns on investment in manpower or human resources.

If the objectives are stated in terms of market share to be obtained or the type of product to be manufactured and the volume in which it is to be manufactured, it becomes possible for the planners to estimate the manpower which will have to be employed in various departments and sections to complete the expected production. Objectives decided in terms of expansion, modernisation and diversification programmes also enable the planners in preparing a proper manpower plan.

If the organisation is small, manpower planning can be done to cover the entire unit. But, if it is large, manpower planning is done for separate departments or units or by class of employees at each level or at a cluster of levels.

[B] Forecasting future human resource needs [Estimating manpower requirements]:

The concept of 'Forecasting future human resource needs' implies estimating the manpower requirements or estimating the need and demand for manpower for the fixed period for which the manpower planning activity is undertaken.

When manpower planning is done, the person in charge has to find out the requirements of human resources in order to undertake various activities. The human requirements forecast must be both in terms of quantity as well as quality. While doing so, forecasting supply of manpower is also required to be considered to adjust demand of human resources with its supply.

The following figure gives us an idea about the importance of the demand for and supply of the manpower function:

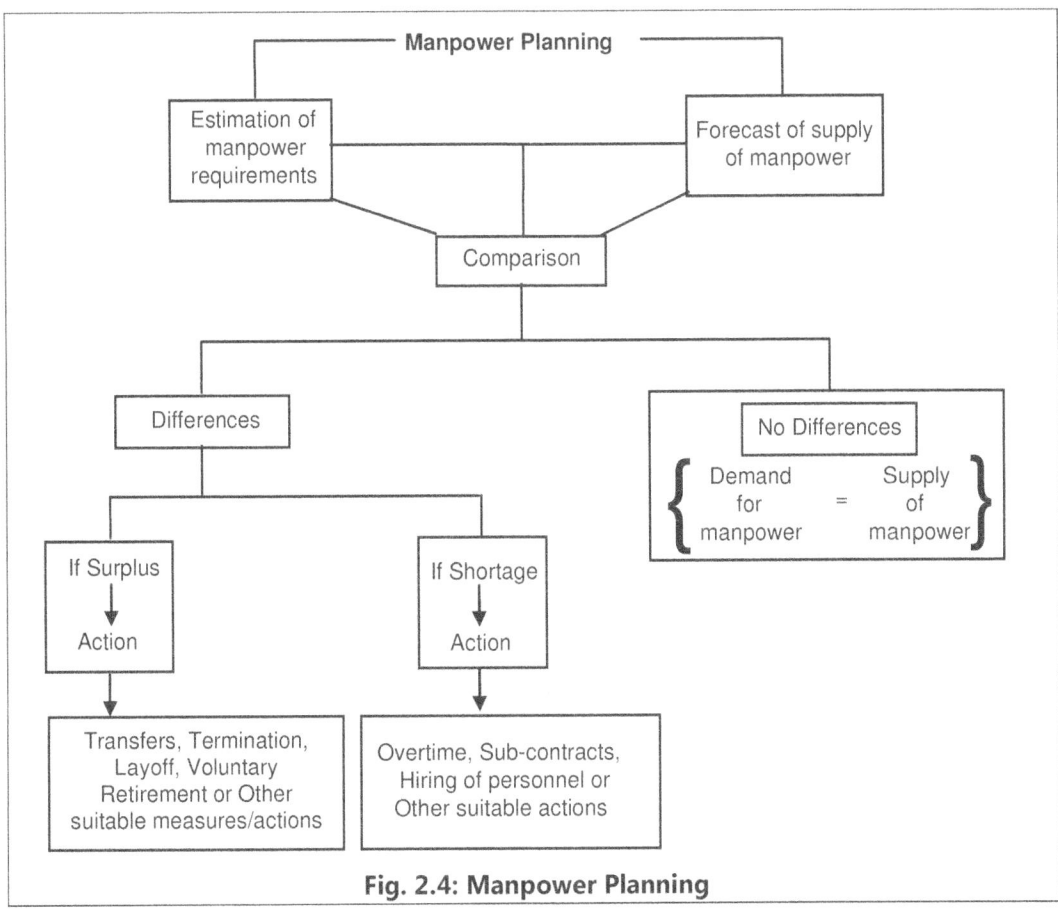

Fig. 2.4: Manpower Planning

While forecasting or estimating manpower requirements, the existing job design and analysis is required to be reviewed thoroughly keeping in mind the future required capabilities, knowledge, skills, etc., of the present employees. If required, various jobs are redesigned considering the organisational and unit-wise plans and programmes, quantum of future work, activities, tasks, etc.,

After analysis and estimation of the objectives of the organisation, in the light of expected changes in the process of production, job designs, etc., the requirements of human resources for the existing departments of the organisation as well as for new vacancies are found out.

The demand for the employees depends upon the objectives of the organisation. It becomes necessary to estimate the future demand for the product or products which the organisation is manufacturing. The demand for the product itself is affected by many factors such as the degree of competition faced by the organisation, likes and dislikes of the customers, state of the economy, policies of the Government in respect of imports and exports, etc.

Once the demand for the product of the organisation is decided, in the light of it, the number of employees needed for manufacturing the required quantity is calculated. Need for employees is also required to be decided by considering the type of technology which the organisation intends to use in its work. Technology changes at a very rapid rate and, therefore, it becomes difficult to know what will be its effect on the number of employees which the organisation will need.

Along with the external factors, internal factors like budget constraints, level of production, policies of management regarding new products to be introduced, labour intensive or capital intensive methods of production to be adopted, future organisational structure planned by the management also affects the demand for the manpower and due consideration of these factors also becomes necessary on the part of persons doing demand forecasting for the manpower.

Techniques of Forecasting the Manpower Demand:

For forecasting the demand for the manpower, the following techniques are used:

1. Managerial judgement
2. Ratio-trend analysis
3. Work study techniques
4. Delphi techniques
5. Statistical techniques.

(1) Managerial Judgement:

In managerial judgement technique, the managers of the various departments come together and after considering the future volume of work decides how many and what type of persons will be needed by the organisation.

There are two different ways in which this technique can be used. In the 'top-down' way, the top managers prepare the forecast for the number of employees needed for the unit as a whole and then they discuss these estimates with the departmental heads and their subordinates to see whether any modification is necessary in the estimate prepared by them. In the second approach, which is known as 'bottom-up' approach, the estimates about employees is demanded from the foreman or supervisors of the sections and departments and their heads consider the estimates, make necessary changes and forward them to the top managers for their consideration.

(2) Ratio-Trend Analysis:

In ratio-trend analysis technique, use is made of certain ratios calculated for the previous period and then they are applied to the future period for determining the number of employees which will be needed by the organisation. The ratios may be ratio of units produced to number of employees or the ratio of sales value to number of employees. While using this technique, necessary modification in the ratio may be required to be made in the light of changes in the technique and method of production. You will get an idea about ratio-trend analysis method of forecasting or estimating the manpower requirement in respect of foremen.

Table 2.1: Ratio Trend Analysis

Particulars	Period	Production and number of Foremen
Production level	2010-2011	3,000
Present number of supervisors i.e. Ratio 5 : 3000 (1 : 600)	2010-2011	Five
Estimation of production	2011-2012	12,000
Number of Supervisors required assuming other things constant	2011-2012	Twenty

(3) **Work Study Techniques:**

Work study technique is used for demand forecasting when it is possible to fix standard time for producing one unit of the product and the type of labour which is needed for doing that work.

For the unit or for the department a production budget is prepared to decide production of how many units is to be completed. Then, the standard time in terms of labour hours is decided by using work study method. For producing the units as given in production budget how many total labour hours will be needed are calculated. Then, how many labour hours will be available if one employee is appointed is calculated and while deciding these hours, allowance is made for absenteeism, overtime and idle time on the part of the employee. Total labour hours required for completing the planned production divided by manhours available per employee will give the number of employees needed.

(4) **Delphi Technique:**

In Delphi Technique, a group of experts, who work independently without getting in touch with each other so that options are not influenced, are asked to submit the estimates of manpower required. The members of HRP team who work as intermediaries collect and summarise all the options and with mentioning individual name report the findings to the experts. In light of the feedback, experts review there estimates and modify them and send back to the members of MRP team who again summarises and submit report. This process continues and experts begin to reach a common ground as their opinions begin to match. The agreement reached by the experts is the final forecast of manpower demand.

It must be remembered that the experts do not have any interaction with each other and the final forecast is reached only through the summarisation and feedback provided by the human resource planning team.

Some organisations make use of sophisticated statistical techniques for forecasting demand for the manpower. Time series analysis, regression analysis and econometrics models are some of the statistical techniques used for this purpose.

When forecast for manpower demand is prepared it should not merely give information about the total number of employees needed in future but the sub division of this total number according to the type or category of the employees should also be given. Thus, how many skilled workers, semi-skilled workers and unskilled workers will be needed, how many employees will be needed to operate machines, to work in the office and to perform various other jobs should become clear to the management from the forecast prepared for manpower demand.

It should be also remembered that while determining the human resources requirements, the expected losses likely to occur through labour turnover i.e., retirements, transfers, deaths, quits, promotions and demotions, disabilities, dismissals, lay-offs and other such separations are required to be considered. On the other hand, positive changes in the qualities, capabilities gained by the employees resulting from experiences, training, etc., also need to be considered. When new lines of production, new projects are started, that too influences the demand estimates of human resources. All these factors affect the estimation of manpower requirements.

[C] Forecasting supply of manpower:

After completing the second step of demand forecasting, planners doing manpower planning have to forecast the supply of manpower. The first step in supply forecasting is to consider the present manpower available with the organisation. For this purpose manpower inventory is prepared.

(i) Manpower inventory: Manpower inventory is the data collected about the present employees of the organisation. Information about all the employees is collected with reference to the department in which the employee is working, his status or position, age, sex, qualifications, experience, training programmes completed, pay-scale, skills possessed, abilities and capabilities, etc., This information is classified in a proper way to enable the planners to understand how many employees are available with the organisation at present.

(ii) Manpower audit: Manpower audit is carried out to find out how the present employees are utilised. The manpower audit points out the information about the performance of the employees and whether the skills and abilities of the present employees are fully utilised or not. It also enables the planners to identify the employees who can be developed for undertaking more responsible jobs in the future. Information about absenteeism of the employees, productivity of the employees also becomes available through manpower audit and this information can be used by the management for improving the performance of the employees.

[D] Comparing demand forecast with supply forecast:

The total number of employees needed as calculated by demand forecast is compared with the total supply of manpower expected to be available in the plan period. Such a comparison may show that there is shortage of manpower or there is excess manpower available with the organisation. The persons doing manpower planning would find out what is the position of manpower in the organisation so that accordingly, necessary plans can be prepared for meeting that situation.

[E] Preparing plans and programmes:

On the basis of the information available from the 4th step mentioned above, the planners have to prepare a plan and a programmeme. If there is shortage of manpower, plans are prepared for recruitment and selection of the new employees. For this, the sources of recruitment are decided and information available about prospective employees is obtained. Depending upon the type of person to be selected, an adequate selection programmeme is prepared and implemented.

If instead of shortage of manpower it is found that there is excess manpower available, arrangement is made to redeploy the surplus employees by providing training to them so, that they can perform the new jobs satisfactorily or schemes like 'golden handshake' are prepared and the equilibrium between the demand for and supply of manpower is achieved. Plans are also prepared for full utilisation of the human resource available. Transfer of employees, training of employees and career development plans for the employees are prepared with the objective of making proper and full use of the abilities of the employees and also to help employees get job-satisfaction, one of leading factors of retention.

[F] Execution of the plans and evaluation of the manpower planning:

The plans prepared for obtaining additional employees or for reducing the excess number of employees is implemented. The effectiveness of the entire manpower planning is evaluated by finding out whether manpower planning has enabled the organisation to achieve the objectives as per expectations. In case the objectives are not satisfactorily realised, manpower plans may be required to be modified or the organisational objectives may be altered.

Thus, in the human resource planning process, there is forecast of personnel needs i.e., employees needed, assessment of the supply factors through various personnel-related programmes. Of course, the HRP process is definitely influenced by the overall organisational goals and objectives as well as the environment of business.

The HRP process can be summed up as follows:

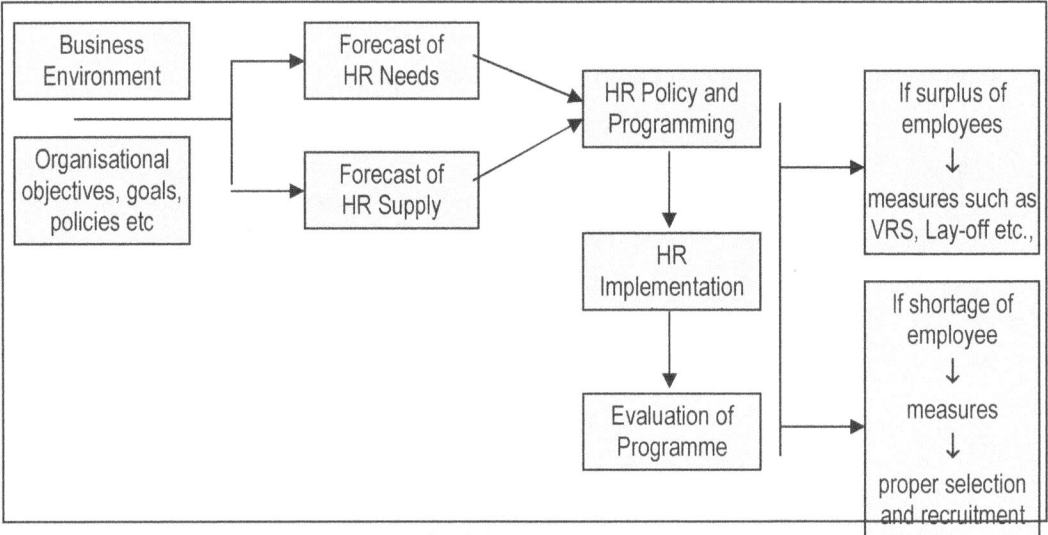

Fig. 2.5: HR Process

2.2.5 Manpower Estimation

It is very essential for the management to estimate the structure of its organisation at a given point of time. For this estimation, the number, type, qualifications, qualities etc., of the employees needed must be determined. In fact, many environmental and other factors affect this determination of manpower. Important factors amongst them are business forecast, development, expansion and growth of the organisation itself, management philosophy and policy, government policy, design and structural changes, product and human skills mix, competition etc., Manpower estimation is very important in the human resource or manpower planning process

It has already been made clear that the objectives of an organisation are decided and defined by the top management. The role of human resource department is to subserve the overall objectives by ensuring the availability and optimum utilisation of human resources. Therefore, manpower estimation is required to be done properly which involves the estimation of the quantity and quality of right type of people or human force. It is obvious that the basis of the manpower estimation should be the annual budget and also long-term corporate plan. For this purpose, certain techniques such as managerial judgement, ratio-trend analysis, Delphi technique can be used. We have already studied these techniques in brief while studying the HR planning process.

The main dimensions of HR planning, estimation of manpower are as follows:

(a) Total number of employees presently available and their types, nature of work, wages etc.

(b) A detailed job-description for each position of employee working in different departments.

(c) Age distribution, qualifications, experience etc., of the employees.

(d) Estimation of short, medium and long-term manpower needs.

Manpower estimation can help an organisation to retain the desired employees longer and keep them functioning more efficiently and more productively at a reasonable cost. Specifically, it can help to achieve the following objectives:

(i) To make available the human resource in adequate quantity and of required quality.

(ii) To reduce recruiting and replacement costs.

(iii) To reduce labour costs associated with attrition.

(iv) To improve employee morale and satisfaction.

(v) To control unnecessary expansion, or rapid expansion or reduction in workforce.

(vi) To monitor staffing and retention policies.

(vii) To focus on training resources properly.

Manpower estimation definitely helps an organisation to manage its human resources in a better way and more effectively with dynamic situations. It should be noted that all organisations, especially those which have a high labour turnover must systematically do their short-terms, medium-term as well as long-term manpower estimation and human resource planning. Further, in order to meet the changing conditions, periodical reviews and adjustments are also necessary.

In order to achieve effective HRP by doing manpower estimation properly, the duties involved and the skills required for performing all the jobs in an organisation, necessary information is required to be collected in respect of various jobs to be performed. Hence, job analysis becomes essential. Job analysis refers, in simple language, to the process of collecting information about a job. The job analysis process results in two sets of data i.e., (a) Job description, and (b) Job specification which is then used to carry out job evaluation. Let us see what each of these terms refers to in the next point.

2.2.6 Preparing Manpower Inventory

"Manpower Inventory involves the classification of characteristics of personnel in an organisation, in addition to counting their number."

The term 'inventory' is often used in relation to counting of tangible objects like raw materials, goods in progress, or finished products, etc. In manpower inventory, the items are intangible.

It involves cataloguing the characteristics of personnel in the organisation, besides counting their number. Both present and future characteristics of personnel are recorded in the manpower inventory. It involves the following steps:

1. The first step in manpower inventory is to decide who should form a part of it. Generally, inventory is prepared for persons working on important posts—the executives and some persons from the operative staff are covered in it. From operative staff only those persons are included in inventory who have the potential of taking up higher responsibility posts.

2. After determining the persons to be included in manpower inventory, the second step is to collect information about them. Some information may be collected from records while some may be collected through interview or talks with the concerned persons.

The factual information such as age, experience, education, health, appraisal reports, attitude, etc. will be noted from the records. The brief interviews with persons will help in understanding his caliber, attitude, aspirations, motives, etc.

A summary statement of information is prepared about each person and is kept ready for consultation. The information will help management to find out the suitable persons in the organisation for taking up senior positions in future. This will also enable management to determine whether persons from outside will be required in future or not.

3. The next step in manpower inventory is to appraise the talent catalogue. The present and future capabilities of persons are assessed. Some scale is prepared for appraising the persons.

Besides appraisal tests, remarks about persons are also given. The remarks may relate to their talent, decision-taking ability, training required, specific limitations, etc. Besides appraisal tests, specific remarks are useful in picking up persons for future positions.

The manpower inventory will enable manager to know the present and future potentialities of all individuals and their suitability for various jobs.

2.3 Recruitment

Recruitment is the development and maintenance of adequate and efficient manpower sources. It is a very important process of attracting candidates who have required skills, abilities, qualities etc. to meet the job vacancies in an organisation. The function of recruitment is to locate the sources of manpower to meet job requirements.

In simple words, the term 'recruitment' implies the services of certain required persons for certain jobs. It is a process of obtaining information about the people who are willing to offer their services to the organisation for performing the jobs available in the organisation and it helps to develop and maintain adequate manpower sources. As a matter of fact, the first stage in the selection process is to make the available vacancies known to the people and the opportunities that the organisation offers. In response to this knowledge, potential applicants apply for the jobs and from among them, most suitable ones are then selected.

2.3.1 Definitions of Recruitment

Some of the definitions of 'Recruitment' are as follows:

(a) Edwin B. Flippo:

"Recruitment is the process of searching for prospective employees and stimulating to apply for jobs in the organisation".

(b) Dale Yoder:

"Recruitment is a process to discover the sources of manpower to meet the requirements of the staffing schedule and employ effective measures for attracting the manpower in adequate numbers to facilitate effective selection of an effective working force".

(c) William B. Werther and Keith Davis:

"Recruitment is the process of finding and attracting capable applicants for employment. The process begins when new recruits are sought and ends when their applications are submitted. The result is a pool of applications from which new employees are selected".

(d) S. Lord:

"Recruitment is a form of competition. Just as corporations compete to develop, manufacture, and market the best product or service, they must also compete to identify, attract and hire the most qualified people. Recruitment is a business, and it is a big business".

This definition takes into consideration the competitive nature of finding out most qualified people. The recruitment is important and a big business activity. It is concerned with the identification of possible sources of recruiting the most qualified employees.

(e) Dale S. Beach:

"Recruitment is the development and maintenance of adequate manpower resources and it involves the creation of a pool of available labour upon whom the organisation can depend when it needs additional employees".

(f) William F. Glueck:

"Recruitment is that set of activities which an enterprise uses to attract job candidates who have the abilities and attitudes needed to help the enterprise achieve the objectives".

(g) Plumbley:

"Recruitment is a matching process and the capacities and inclinations of the candidates have to be matched against the demands and rewards inherent in a given job or career pattern".

2.3.2 Features of Recruitment

From the above mentioned definitions stated by the experts in the field of human resource management, we come to know the following important points so far as the recruitment is concerned.

(1) Recruitment is an important process of attracting applicants with certain capabilities, skills, attitudes etc., to job vacancies in an organisation.

(2) Recruitment helps to develop and maintain adequate manpower resources.

(3) Recruitment helps to create a pool of applicants from which new employees can be selected.

(4) Recruitment is a matching process.

(5) Recruitment lays foundation for selection of employees.

(6) Recruitment is a two-way process. It helps both i.e., a recruiter and a recruitee. A recruiter gets a choice as to whom to recruit from among the pool. While a recruitee also can decide whether he should apply for the job in the organisation considering his abilities, future prospects and his expectations.

(7) Recruitment helps to identify, attract and hire the most qualified people for an organisation.

2.3.3 Objectives or Purposes of Recruitment

There are various objectives or purposes of recruitment. Following are some of the important objectives or purposes of recruitment:

(1) To attract candidates having the desired qualities and qualifications to meet the organisation's present and future needs.

(2) To create a pool of candidates with minimum cost.

(3) To fill the vacancies created in the organisation due to promotions, termination, transfers, retirements etc., as well as due to expansion, diversification etc.,

(4) To help the selection process to become successful.

(5) To ensure that the candidates will not leave the organisation atleast in the short period once they are selected.

(6) To create and develop organisational and individual effectiveness in short as well as in the long-run and also to develop an organisational culture which may help attract the competent people towards the organisation.

(7) To help evaluate the effectiveness of various recruitment techniques and sources for various types of job applicants.

2.3.4 Strategic Approach to Recruitment

The market is short of qualified and experienced employees (demand does not match with the offer). Young talents are not loyal with the organisation; they want to mix their career with their free time activities and they prefer being hired only for the interesting projects. The critical roles are often not filled within the reasonable time, and the company realises financial losses or limits its growth. The organisation often fights for talents, and its' under constant pressure to offer highly competitive packages. The costs of recruitment are huge, and top management wants a significant cost cut.

Employee recruiting is the process of identifying and attracting people to work for an organisation. The basic goals of recruiting are to communicate a positive image of the organisation and to identify and gain the interest and commitment of people who will be good employees. A strategic approach to recruiting helps an organisation become an employer of choice and thereby obtain and keep great employees who produce superior goods and services.

The recruitment strategy connects all important recruitment components and HR components, as the organisation realises its strategic goals. The recruitment strategy defines the unique mix of:

- Position of the organisation on the job market
- Recruitment Channels to be used for attracting candidates
- Recruitment Style of the Organisation
- Differentiators from Competitors on the job market
- Recruitment Processes and Procedures
- Recruitment Metrics Visit Creative HRM for more information.

The Recruitment Strategy:

- Allows the organisation to staff vacancies using the optimum mix of channels, processes and adverts
- Allows to optimise the recruitment costs by utilizing channels and processes, which contribute most
- Differentiates the organisation from competitors and help building the position of the employer of the first choice
- Identifies critical internal resources and builds the critical momentum for the retention programmes. Visit Creative HRM for more information.

There are two approaches used in business today:

- **Broad scope**, which represents a set of work skills that a lot of people have.
- **Targeted scope**, which represents a set of skills that only a few people have.

Fig. 2.6: Types of Business Strategies Approaches

Broad skill scope strategy focuses on attracting a large number of applicants. This approach makes sense when a lot of people have the characteristics needed to succeed in the job. Organisations using the Bargain Labourer HR strategy would use this approach to hire a large number of non-specialised employees, who often stay with the company for only short periods of time. Organisations with the Loyal Soldier HR strategy seek to keep employees for longer periods, but, the employees do not need specialised skills to succeed.

Targeted skill scope strategy seeks to attract a small group of applicants who have a high probability of possessing the characteristics that are needed to perform the specific job. This approach is used when you are looking for a very limited number of applicants with a very specific or rare set of skills.

The business strategy is a key document, which drives everything in the organisation. The recruitment strategy has to reflect:

- Strategic growth areas.
- Plans for new products and services introduction.
- Estimated development of the workforce.
- Geography and future plans of the company.
- Costs allocated to employees and the growth of employee related costs.

The recruitment strategy has to analyse the current organisation and all gaps in the staffing area. Most organisations do not have the optimum composition of the workforce; the recruitment strategy has to address this issue. The gap analysis in the recruitment strategy:

- Identifies critical and missing roles in the organisation.
- Formulates the tactics for the recruitment of critical roles for the company.

The recruitment strategy defines the basic recruitment processes and procedures. The strategy defines the recruitment metrics to be used for the measurement of the performance of recruiters and other employees involved. The recruitment processes are important, because:

- Managers have to be trained in job interviewing
- The organisation has to define the common approach and each job interview should follow the defined standard by Human Resources.

2.3.5 Labour Markets and Recruitment

Labour markets are the external supply pool from which organisations attract their employees. A labour market is seen as segmented if it "consists of various sub-groups with little or no crossover capability". Segmentation can result in different groups, for example men and women, receiving different wages for the same work.

A labour market can be understood as the mechanism through which human labour is bought and sold as a commodity and the means by which labour demand (the number and type of available jobs) is matched with labour supply (the number and type of available workers). As such, the labour market constitutes the systematic relationship that exists between workers and work organisations.

In order to achieve its strategic objectives, a fundamental concern for an organisation is to ensure that it has the right people with the right skills, knowledge and attributes in the appropriate positions. A tight labour market exists when demand for employees exceeds the supply of people with appropriate qualifications.

The labour force population includes all individuals available for selection, if all possible recruitment strategies are used. The group available for selection using a particular recruiting approach is called the applicant population. The applicant pool consists of all individuals who are actually evaluated for selection.

The labour market components are:

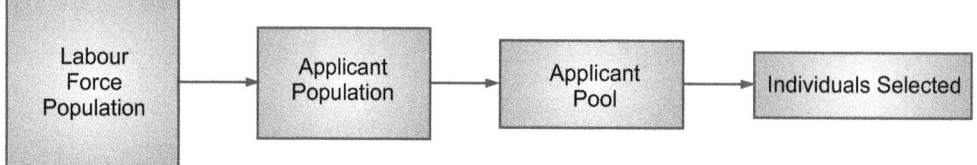

Fig. 2.7: Labour Market Components

There are many ways to identify labour markets, including by geographical area, type of skill, and educational level. Some labour market segments might include managerial, clerical, professional and technical, and blue collar. Classified differently, some markets are local, others regional, and others national; and there are international labour markets as well. Labour markets can be segmented into:

- Georgraphic labour markets.
- Global labour markets.
- Industry and Occupational labour markets.
- Educational and technical labour markets.

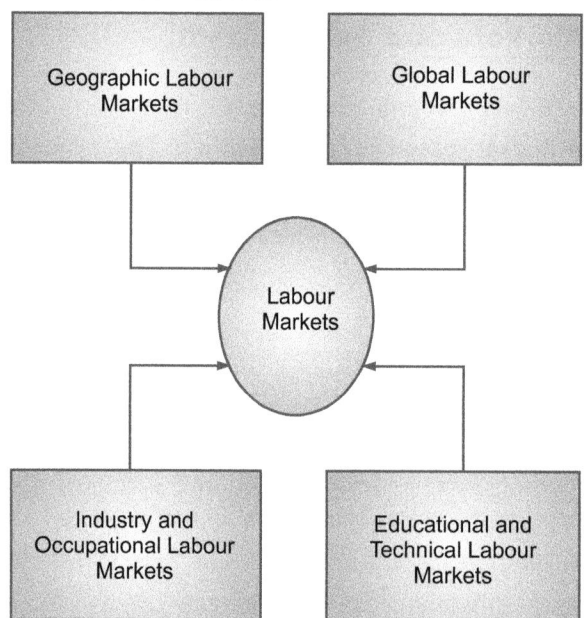

Fig. 2.8: Segmentation of Labour Markets

Geographic Labour Markets: A common way to classify labour markets is based on geographic location. Markets can be local, area or regional, national or international. Local and area labour markets vary significantly in terms of workforce availability and quality and changes in geographic labour market may force changes in recruiting efforts. For instance, if a major employer locates in regional labour markets other existing area employers may see a decline in their numbers of applicants. Geographic markets require different recruiting considerations. For example attempting to recruit locally for a job market that is a national competitive market will result in disappointing applicant rates.

Global Labour Markets: Many companies are expanding export work to overseas labour market as it is much more advantageous. Companies in USA are outsourcing to India, China etc as labour is cheaper. The use of internet has resulted in global jobs being recruited in many places, but often recruiting employees for global assignments requires different approaches from those used for typical recruiting efforts in the home country. The recruiting process must consider variations in culture laws and language.

Educations and Technical Labour Markets: Another way to look at labour markets is by considering the educational and technical qualifications that define the people being recruited. Employes may need individuals with specific licenses, certifications or educational backgrounds. Some examples in shortages in specific labour markets include certified auto mechanics, network certified computer specialists.

Industry and Occupation Labour Markets: Labour markets can be classified by industry and occupation. Depending on economic and industry aspects, recruiting emphasis can be changed. For example in the next few years in USA the positions of nurses and customer service representatives are going to have the biggest increase. These figures say that recruiting will be more difficult in filling these jobs during the next few years. Recruiting for smaller firms can be difficult.

2.3.6 Recruiting and Diversity Considerations

"Diversity" refers to the variety of personal experiences, values and world views that arises from differences in culture and circumstance. Such differences include race, ethnicity, gender, age, religion, language, abilities/disabilities, sexual orientation, socioeconomic status and geographic region, among others.

To ensure the selection of diverse talent, HR policies and practices should be reviewed carefully to identify barriers and opportunities for improvement. Working towards increased and enhanced workplace diversity is not difficult or complicated– it's about having solid HR practices.

A broad range of factors applies to recruiting diversity. Many employers have expanded efforts to recruit workers from what are nontraditional labour pools. Nontraditional diverse recruitees for certain jobs may include:

- Older workers over 40 years of age.
- Single parents.
- Workers with disabilities.
- Persons with different racial/ethnic backgrounds.

The growth in racial/ethnic workforce diversity means that a wider range of potential employment sources should be utilised. Individuals with disabilities are another group of potential resources.

Recruiting Diverse Workers

A workforce that is diverse, as well as engaged and talented is best suited to overcome business problems and, taking the current economic climate into consideration, therefore better equipped to ride out a recession. The success of diversity works on the principle that everyone is different, and therefore will have a different way of approaching a problem. So if diversity helps organisations to be more competitive, encouraging a diverse applicant pool and the fairest process of assessment to identify top minority talent is what all organisations should aim to do. While there can be no standard approach to achieving this end, there are a few things organisations can look to do as important first steps.

A good starting point that organisations often overlook is ensuring regular auditing of their recruitment processes. Organisations should constantly challenge themselves opening up procedures to the scrutiny of independent experts, listening to the feedback and, importantly, acting on it.

Psychological and Cultural Barriers

Some organisations may not have difficulty in attracting top talent initially, but are still failing to achieve a diverse workforce ultimately. This can be due to the hidden problem of minority culture and candidates' confidence at assessment, which can ultimately leads to minority candidates not performing to the best of their ability.

Business psychologists have identified that there is a widespread belief within minority groups that assessment centres are not fair to them, which leads to a number of good candidates withdrawing applications early or attending the centre with a very low level of belief which then leads to underperformance. This issue is combined with cultural beliefs within minority groups, that hard work and not drawing attention to themselves are key to success. This can all seriously undermine a candidate's performance and lead to organisations unwittingly underestimating the true potential of the individual.

Investment in assessment awareness programmes for potential applicants is one way to overcome this issue. It involves training applicants in the rules of engagement at assessment centres, helping them to indentify situations and behaviours that will undermine their ability to perform Being aware of the pitfalls enables candidates from minority groups to approach the assessment centre with a much more positive and effective mindset. It can also create a very strong feeling of "perceived fairness".

Mystery Applicant Programme

Another way of assessing the fairness of an organisations' recruitment process is to implement a "mystery applicant" programmeme. The programmeme works by organisations submitting CVs with identical content but with the names changed to suggest differing ethnic backgrounds of applicants. This process can successfully identify any issues early on and give organisations the chance to raise their level of internal awareness and professionalism in a discreet and effective manner.

Assessor Pools

Finally, organisations can improve by aiming to have a diverse assessor pool. Business psychologists have noted that the emotional impact of the first meeting between the assessor group and a minority candidate cannot be underestimated. At some stage in all application procedures, applicants are introduced to their assessors but in most organisations these assessor groups are often white, male, and middle-aged. Psychologists refer to this emotional reaction as "white juror syndrome" and can give an instant negative emotional response in some applicants, along the lines of; 'this organisation is not like me.'

One way organisations are tackling these issues is by ensuring that internal assessors are 'buddied' with external independent and experienced assessors from a wide range of minority groups. While these highly-trained and experienced assessors are a rare commodity, they can add immense value to a selection process. Their inclusion allows a fairer environment for assessment, which should be what every organisation is aiming to create.

There is so much that can be done to encourage a more diverse workforce. If organisations could all make some of these small changes it could result in a much larger positive changes to the diversity of their workforce.

2.3.7 Employment Advertising

The best techniques for writing effective job advertisements are the same as for other forms of advertising. The job is your product; the readers of the job advert are your potential customers. The aim of the job advert is to attract interest, communicate quickly and clearly the essential (appealing and relevant) points, and to provide a clear response process and mechanism. Design should concentrate on clarity or text, layout, and on conveying a professional image. Branding should be present but not overbearing, and must not dominate the job advert itself.

The items to include in an effective job advert. The list is loosely in order but this is in no way prescriptive - use a sequence that works best.

- Job title.
- Employer or recruitment agency/consultancy.
- Job base location.
- Succinct description of business/organisation/division activity and market position and aims.
- To whom the position reports - or other indication of where the role is in the structure.

- Outline of job role and purpose - expressed in the 'second-person' (you, your, etc.).
- Indication of scale, size, responsibility, timescale, and territory of role.
- Outline of ideal candidate profile - expressed in 'second-person'.
- Indicate qualifications and experience required (which could be incorporated within candidate profile).
- Salary or salary guide.
- Whether the role is full-time or permanent or a short-term contract (if not implicitly clear from elsewhere in the advert).
- Other package details or guide (pension, car etc.).
- Explanation of recruitment process.
- Response and application instructions.
- Contact details as necessary, for example, address, phone, fax, email, etc.
- Job and or advert reference (advert references help you analyse results from different adverts for the same job).
- Website address.
- Corporate branding.
- Quality accreditations, for example in the UK, Investor in People.
- Equal opportunities statement.

Information on the Job and on the Application Process:
- Job title and responsibilities.
- Location of job.
- Starting pay range.
- Closing date for application.
- Whether or not to submit a resume and a cover letter.
- Whether or not calls are invited.
- Where to mail application or resume.

Information on the Organisation:
- Years of experience.
- Three to five key characteristics of successful candidates.

Information on the Organisation:
- That it is an EEO employer.
- Its primary business.

Fig. 2.9: Employee Advertising

2.3.8 Recruiting Source Choices/ Sources of Recruitment

For all types of recruitment, the important question pertaining to the policy matter is to decide the extent to which the emphasis is to be given to inside and outside sources and whether there should be centralised recruitment if an organisation is large having business centres widely spread. Generally, it is found that insurance companies, banks, multi-national corporations resort to centralised recruitment. Considering the suitability of method – centralised or decentralised – and the merits, limitations, etc., of the method, the organisation decides and develops the suitable sources of recruitment.

It is very essential for an organisation to have full and proper knowledge of various manpower supply and appropriate methods of tapping them. These sources of manpower supply do not remain constant but they vary from time to time. These sources of manpower supply or sources of recruitment refer to the areas of recruitment from which the potential employees can be attracted to make applications for the jobs or vacancies to be filled in. These sources are broadly divided into two groups i.e., (1) Internal sources, and (2) External sources.

(1) Internal Sources of Recruitment:

The internal sources of recruitment refers to sources from within an organisation and these are the most obvious sources. Whenever vacancies occur, suitable employees already employed in an organisation are promoted, upgraded, transferred or sometimes demoted. Sometimes, retired managers and other employees are also invited to fill the vacancies; especially for a short duration (leave-vacancies). Promotions and transfers are considered good sources of recruitment.

Thus, from among the present permanent or temporary employees, retrenched or retired employees, recruitment can be done. Recruitees can be considered even from amongst the dependents of deceased, disabled, retired and present employees.

Advantages of Internal Sources of Recruitment:

An organisation recruiting employees from internal sources has certain advantages. Some of them are given below:

(a) It is time saving and economical too as no advertisement is required to be given for the jobs in external media. Cost of selection is reduced.

(b) It helps to reduce the executive turnover.

(c) The internal candidates are well versed with policies, rules and regulations of the organisation, and as a result, cost of training, induction, orientation, period of adaptability to the organisation etc., can be reduced considerably.

(d) It helps to improve the morale and motivation of employees of the organisation and to develop loyalty towards the organisation and a sense of responsibility.

(e) As the management has better knowledge of the strengths and weaknesses of its employees, proper decisions can be taken to promote or to transfer or to demote and thereby, the chances of making wrong decisions are considerably reduced.

(f) It encourages the employees to work hard, sincerely and to put efforts to get promotions.

Disadvantages of Internal Sources of Recruitment:

Though there are certain advantages of recruitment from internal sources, it also suffers from some important disadvantages as mentioned below:

(i) This source of recruitment limits the scope for selection and further, there is possibility of not finding the personnel of required qualities within the organisation.

(ii) It prevents the suitable candidates from outside with innovative ideas, fresh and constructive thinking and dynamism from entering the organisation.

(iii) If the present employees are promoted or transferred to other posts, their posts fall vacant and filling their vacancies may be difficult and then one has to meet the requirement from external sources.

(iv) There can be bias or some sort of partiality in promoting or transferring the employees from within the organisation which may have adverse effects on the functioning. Further, it leads to generate a feeling of discontent among the employees who are hurt or not promoted. Unhealthy competition for promotions or transfers negatively affects the morale, performance, motivation etc., of the employees.

It should also be noted that excessive dependence on internal source is dangerous as too much consumption of even sugar tastes bitter and causes harm to the health.

(2) External Sources of Recruitment:

The external sources of recruitment refer to all such sources which are outside the purview of an organisation. Important external sources are as below.

(a) Advertisements

(b) Campus interview

(c) Management consultants

(d) Recommendation by present employees

(e) Government and private employment exchanges

(f) Labour or trade unions

(g) Professional organisations

(h) Casual applicants

(i) Walk-in-interviews

(j) Deputation and leasing

(k) Head Hunting – It means when the employees of other organisations are attracted to join the organisation

(l) Foreign sources

(m) e-recruitment through job portals and job-fairs

Advantages or Merits of External Sources of Recruitment:

(i) It helps to attract and introduce new blood in the organisation which makes the organisation more dynamic through the inflow of innovative ideas, fresh thinking, drive etc.

(ii) The best candidates can be selected. It offers wider scope for the selection of employees as there is a possibility that a large number of candidates with the requisite qualities, qualifications and experience may apply for the jobs advertised.

(iii) Employees can be selected without pre-conceived ideas, partiality or reservations.

(iv) Labour costs can be minimised by selecting the employees on minimum pay scales.

(v) This source proves to be more economical if experienced, well-trained candidates are selected.

Disadvantages or Demerits of External Sources of Recruitment:

(a) It sometimes proves to be expensive if advertisements are required to be done on a large scale and also because of heavy costs of making arrangements for interviews, tests etc.,

(b) It is a time consuming and involves lengthy selection process.

(c) The task of attracting, contacting and evaluating the potential employees is somewhat difficult and strenuous.

(d) It creates unhappiness among the existing employees who feel that they are qualified and fit for the jobs but no opportunity is given. It does not help to develop the loyalty among the existing employees.

(e) As newly recruited employees are not familiar with the policies, practices, procedures, environment etc., of the organisation, they take some time to adjust themselves. If they take more time to adjust or if they cannot adjust themselves, valuable time is wasted and costs also increase.

The importance of internal and external sources of recruitments as well as the merits or advantages and demerits or disadvantages of internal and external sources have been made clear above. As far as internal sources and external sources of recruitment are concerned, we come to know that every organisation has a number of alternative sources for recruitment purposes.

However, it should be noted that the best source is to tap the internal one first and then the external one. But, in practice, the choice of internal or external source to a large extent depends upon various factors. Amongst them, nature of jobs, skills and capabilities required, time available for skills and capabilities required, time available for selection, costs involved, policy and practices of an organisation, situations prevailing in the labour market are very important factors.

Types of Internal Recruiting

Internal sources include personnel already on the pay-roll of the organisation. Whenever any vacancy arises, somebody from within the organisation may be looked into, following are the internal sources of recruitment. Organisations consider the candidates from this source for higher level of jobs due to availability of most suitable candidates for jobs relatively or equally to external sources, to meet the trade union demands and due to the policy of the organisation to motivate the present employees.

(1) **Promotion:** Promotion means shifting of an employee to a higher position carrying higher responsibilities, facilities, status and salaries. Various positions in an organisation are usually filled up by promotion of existing employees on the basis of merit or seniority or a combination of these.

(2) **Transfer:** Transfer refers to a change in job assignment. It may involve a promotion or demotion, or no change in terms of responsibility and status. A transfer may be either temporary or permanent, depending on the necessity of filling jobs. Promotion involves upward mobility while transfer refers to a horizontal mobility of employees.

(3) **Ex-employees:** Ex-employee means persons who have even worked in the enterprise and have left the organisation and now eager to return. Such employees having good record may be preferred. They will require less initial training.

(4) **Employee recommendations:** In order to encourage existing employees, some concern have made a policy to recruit further staff only from the applicants introduced and recommended by employees or employees' union. Other conditions being equal, preference will be given to friends and relatives of existing employees.

Types of External Recruiting

1. **Advertising:** Advertising in newspapers and periodicals is one of the most important methods of recruitment. This is specially so in case of recruitment of management and technical personnel. The company needing manpower advertises details about the job, requirements, salary perquisites, duties and responsibilities etc. The advantage of advertising is that all details about the job can be given in

advertisement to allow self-screening by the prospective candidates. Advertisement gives the management a wider range of candidates from which to choose. Its disadvantage is that it brings large number of applications whose screening costs may be quite heavy.

2. **Employment Agencies:** There are government as well as private employment agencies providing a nation-wide or area-wise service in matching personnel demand and supply. In India, there are employment exchanges and employment and guidance bureau which provide a range of service. In some cases, compulsory notification of vacancies to the employment exchange is required by law. Employment seekers get themselves registered with these exchanges. The employment exchanges bring the job-givers in contact with job-seekers. Employment exchanges are well regarded particularly in the field of unskilled, semi-skilled and skilled operative jobs. However, in the technical and professional area, private consultancy firms provide recruitment facilities. In metropolitan cities, there are several such agencies prominent among them are Tata Consultancy Service, A.F. Ferguson and Company, ABS Consultants etc.

3. **Gate Hiring:** In a country like ours, where there is a large number of unemployed people, it is usual to find job-seekers thronging the factory gates. Whenever workers are required, the people who are available at the gate, are recruited in necessary number. This method can be used safely for unskilled workers. In some industries, a large number of workers work as *badli* or substitute workers. Whenever a permanent worker is absent, a substitute is employed in his place from among the people at the gate.

4. **Educational Institution:** Direct recruitment from colleges and universities is prevalent for the recruitment of higher staff in western countries but not in India. Many big organisations maintain a close liaison with educational institutions for recruitment to various jobs. Various recruiting groups develop systematic formal university recruiting programmes. They hold preliminary on-campus interviews and select some students for final interview mostly at their offices.

5. **Labour Unions:** In many organisatios, labour unions are regarded as a source from which to recruit manpower. This facilitates increasing the sense of cooperation and in developing the better industrial relations. But sometimes trade unions support a candidate who is not suitable for the job and not acceptable to management. This weakens the labour relations.

6. **Field Trips:** At interviewing team makes trips to towns and tides which are known to contain the kinds of employees required by the enterprise. Arrival dates and the time and venue of interview are advertised in advance.

2.3.9 Methods or Techniques of Recruitment

Various recruitment sources already studied indicate when and where the human resources can be procured while recruitment methods or techniques throw light on how various sources are to be tapped. Recruitment methods are in fact the media or means by which an organisation can contact prospective employees and help to provide necessary information, to exchange ideas and also to stimulate the potential employees to apply for the jobs.

An organisation can use different types of methods to stimulate internal as well as external candidates. Prof. J. D. Dunn and Prof. E. C. Stephens summarised the recruitment methods into three broad categories which are discussed below:

[A] Direct Methods:

Under these methods, job seekers are contacted directly through educational institutions by way of campus interviews. Usually, placement bureaus or offices of the educational institutions provide assistance in invited job seekers, make arrangements for interviews. Sometimes, recruitees are attracted to attend seminars, conventions at some suitable centres. Some business organisations directly solicit the information with a view to recruit required personnel from the concerned professors about the students having outstanding records. We generally find campus interviews being conducted for M.B.A. students or Engineering students, more than any other field.

[B] Indirect Methods:

Advertisements in publications such as newspapers, trade journals, magazines, technical and professional journals etc., are among the most frequently used indirect methods of recruitment. We also find advertisements for recruitment on radio and television. Advertisements have proved to be very useful for recruiting blue collar and white collar personnel as well as scientific, technical and professional employees. Of course, the choice of media, timing, place of the advertisements, appeals to job seekers etc., determine the efficiency of advertisements. It is essential to draft and design an advertisement in such a way that it should give proper and clear-cut idea about the organisation, location, nature of job, job requirement and a subtle hint on remuneration.

[C] Third Party Methods:

Private employment agencies, public employment exchanges, employee referrals, trade unions etc., are the mediums through which employees can be recruited. These organisations or institutions are included in the third party methods. In fact, they work as mediators between job seekers and business organisations in order to bring them together. Private agencies charge certain fees for the services they render.

Out of the methods and sources of recruitment mentioned above, a proper method and source is required to be adopted by the organisation. Selection of the best candidate is possible only when maximum number of suitable candidates apply for the post and hence, it is necessary that the method and source of recruitment used should become successful in attracting all such candidates to the organisation. It is also important to decide when the process of recruitment should be started. Depending upon the time required to receive the information from the candidates and the time needed to complete the selection procedure, the recruitment work must begin sufficiently in advance. If the total time required for the recruitment and selection procedure is say two months and if the post is to be filled at the beginning of September, it is obvious that the process of recruitment must be started in July.

2.3.10 E-Recruiting Methods

E-recruitment is a rapidly growing trend that is being adopted by a wide range of organisations. HR teams globally are trying to achieve the same goal: to simplify all recruitment related tasks.

E-recruitment or online recruitment makes use of technology to carry out the various recruitment processes. It helps enhance and streamline workflow of the hiring process, enabling a more automated and efficient process. The strongest candidates become more apparent, and the HR team can then concentrate their efforts on these individuals.

Definition of E-Recruitment

E-recruitment includes those practices and activities carried on by the organisation THROUGH INTERNET with the primary purpose of identifying and attracting potential employees.

E-recruitment eliminates most of the manual recruitment processes that are time consuming and hamper productivity of recruiters. Recruiter's time is spent on the candidates that have the best fit for both the company and the particular role that they are applying for.

Types of E-Recruitment

There are various types of e-recruitment that can be implemented for the purpose of recruitment automation. The following are the most common and popular.

E-Recruitment Software

E-recruitment software is currently the most popular method that can be used to automate recruitment. The main features are that it automates the recruitment process, eliminating the manual administration, e.g. screening of candidates that do not need the basic criteria required, ranking of candidates to highlight the strongest applicants, automatic communication at each stage of the process, tracking of each applicant's progress, reporting etc.

The recruiters are now able to concentrate on the strongest candidates, and the mundane, administrative tasks are automated, such as emailing successful and unsuccessful candidates, sifting through each application, informing the relevant managers etc. Communication lines are improved hugely.

Online Recruitment through Social Networking

Recruitment through social networking is the latest development in e-recruitment. Recruiters are increasingly leaning towards this with the type of use of social media. It has helped leverage communication between candidates and recruiters that was otherwise limited to just interviews and formal discussions. MySpace, Facebook, LinkedIn, etc. are some of the most commonly used networking sites where recruiters can find a pool of prospective candidates, especially passive ones. LinkedIn in particular is seen as a highly credible forum for recruiting as it used by professionals for networking, and provides a great opportunity for organisations to advertise roles.

The growth in the internet has led both employers and employees to use internet recruiting tools. Of the many recruiting sites using special software, the most common ones are internet job boards, professional / career websites and employer websites.

Internet job boards: Numerous internet boards such as monster and Naukri provide places for employers to post jobs or search for candidates. Job boards offer access to numerous candidates. Some internet locations allow recruiters to search for one website to obtain search links to many other major job sites. Applicants can also use these websites to do one match and then send their resumes to all jobs they are interested.

Professional / Career website: Many professional associations have employment sections at their websites. A number of private corporations maintain a specialised career or industry website to focus on IT, engineering, medicines and other areas. Use of these websites may limit somewhat recruiters search time and efforts.

Employer website: Despite the popularity of job boards and association job sites, many employers have learned that their own websites can be effective and efficient when recruiting candidates. Employers include employment and career information on their websites. IT is important for the recruiting and employment portions of an employer website to be seen as part of the marketing efforts of the firm.

2.4 Selection

Once the potential applicants are identified, the next step is to evaluate their qualifications, qualities, experiences, capabilities etc., and make a selection. From this point of view, selection refers to the process of offering jobs to the desired applicants.

The selection phase is complicated, lengthy and time consuming. The management has to make necessary efforts to select the people who are fit for the jobs. Selection of candidates implies a scrutiny of candidates to ascertain how far each one measures up to the demands of the job and then a comparison of what each candidate has to offer against the specification of that job and the person needed to fill it. It is matching the candidates to the requirements or choosing a right person for the right job.

Selection is that stage in the staffing process in which applicants are divided into two classes i.e., (1) those who will be offered employment, and (2) those who will not be. As more candidates generally are rejected than hired, the selection process is called a rejection process. For this reason, selection process is very often described as a negative process.

2.4.1 Meaning of Selection and Selection Process

With reference to selection of employees, selection means choosing a few from those who apply. It is the picking up of applicants or candidates with requisite qualifications and qualities to fill jobs in the organisation.

In the process of selection, unsuitable candidates are eliminated and the most suitable candidates are selected to perform the jobs. Hence, selection is defined as the process which enables to differentiate between applicants in order to identify those candidates with a greater likelihood of success in a job or jobs.

Prof. P. Subba Rao states that, "The objective of the selection decision is to choose the individual who can most successfully perform the job from the pool of qualified candidates", and "The selection procedure (process) is the system of functions and devices adopted in a given company to ascertain whether the candidates' specifications are matched with the job specifications and requirements or not".

He further states that, "The selection procedure cannot be effective until and unless:

(1) Requirements of the job to be filled, have been clearly specified (Job analysis etc.,)

(2) Employee specifications (physical, mental, social, behavioural etc.,) have been clearly specified.

(3) Candidates for screening have been attracted. A breakdown in any of these processes can make the best solution system ineffective".

2.4.2 Importance of Selection

Selection through various techniques that are reliable and proper ensures a better choice of employees. Selection of employees is a very crucial, complex and continuing function. If right employees are selected to perform right jobs, the employee contribution and commitment can reach a optimum level and employee-employer relations remain congenial. Capable, skilled employees are the valuable assets of an organisation. Systematic and well-planned section selection helps an organisation to derive following advantages:

(1) It becomes possible for an organisation to build a desirable culture and suitable norms in the organisation through proper selection of newcomers.

(2) The employees get satisfied when they feel that their capabilities, skills etc., are properly utilised when selection is done through internal sources.

(3) Right candidates in the right place help to increase the productivity, reduce the costs and make the organisation successful.

(4) Proper selection facilitates proper placement i.e., fitting the right employee for the right job considering his skills and capabilities. Further, it facilitates training. If newly recruited employees lack in certain areas, suitable training programmes can be organised for them.

(5) Proper selection facilitates optimum use of available resources – both the physical as well as human resources. When proper candidates are selected, various resources are handled and utilised properly.

(6) Proper selection results in job satisfaction and improved morale of the employees. Employees feel a sense of belonging towards their organisation.

(7) Proper selection helps to reduce the employee turnover. When candidates are selected properly, they may get adjusted easily to the new environment in an organisation and hence, do not wish to leave it.

2.4.3 Essentials of Selection Process

Selection process should be scientific and well planned. Selection process to become successful should fulfil the following requirements:

(1) The personnel department should find out the exact number of employees to be selected based on scientific analysis of work-load and work-force.

(2) Some executives must be vested with the authority of selection.

(3) Some standard of personnel must be fixed with which the prospective employees can be compared. In other words, comprehensive job description and job specification must be available for this purpose.

(4) Employee specifications i.e., physical and mental qualities, qualifications etc., must be clearly specified.

(5) Suitable tests, interview methods should be used considering the requirements.

(6) Sufficient target population must be available so that required number of employees can be selected.

(7) Cost of selection must be minimum and the process of selection should not be unnecessarily lengthy.

2.4.4 Selection Procedure/Process

Different organisations follow different selection procedures because there is difference in size and nature of job requirements. Hence, an uniform and elaborate selection procedure is neither advisable nor feasible to fill up all the posts in a given organisation as situational dynamics are different in each case. The cost incurred for selection procedure is also responsible for selecting a particular selection procedure, e.g. the cost which an organisation is ready to incur for selecting a top manager is always more but the organisation may not be ready to spend the same amount for selecting a person who is to be appointed as a clerk in the organisation.

The following process of selection can be mentioned as a scientific and widely used selection process:

1. Initial screening interview
2. Application blank or application form
3. Written test and other selection tests
4. Comprehensive interview
5. Medical examination
6. Checking of references
7. Final employment decision
8. Placement.

Let us consider the above steps briefly.

1. Initial screening interview: This step is also known as *conducting preliminary interview*. When there are a large number of applicants for a post, it becomes necessary to reduce the number by conducting initial screening interview. Generally, a receptionist or some officer who is connected with the selection work receives the applicants and gives them information about the job for which the person is to be selected and he also asks them a few questions to find out whether the applicant is suitable for the post or not. The objective of this preliminary interview is to 'weed out' those applicants who are not suitable for the post and thereby reduce the burden on the persons who have to complete the remaining stages in the process of selection. Questions which are asked in such interview are related to qualifications, age, experience, job interests of the applicant etc., and on the basis of information provided by the applicant, the suitability of the applicant for the post is decided. Those who are regarded as suitable are required to undergo the subsequent steps in the selection procedure. The receptionist or the officer conducting the preliminary interview should be an experienced person and he should take care to see that desirable candidates are not rejected in this step.

2. Application blank or application form: Application blank or application form is a device used in the selection process for getting detailed information about the prospective applicant. The receptionist or the officer who conducts the preliminary interview makes available the application blanks to those applicants who are selected by him as the promising candidates. The application blank contains questions seeking information about the applicant about the following points:

(a) **Biographical Data:** Full name, date of birth, place of birth, local address, permanent address, height, weight, identification marks, sex, marital status, nationality, physical disability; if any etc.

(b) **Educational Qualifications:** Education completed, name of examining body, year of passing, marks secured, special subjects at the examination, professional qualification etc.

(c) **Work Experience:** Experience possessed, type of job or jobs done, name of the organisation in which the previous jobs held, number of years experience, nature of duties and responsibilities, pay drawn, reason for leaving the previous job.

(d) **Extra-curricular Activities:** Participation in games, competitions, membership of N.C.C. or N.S.S., hobbies, membership of any social or cultural bodies etc., training programmes attended.

(e) **Other Information:** Family background, parents, brothers and sisters, posts held by them, expectations about salary, any illnesses experienced, or any legal cases involved in, languages known, references of previous employers, or respectable persons from the society not related to the applicant etc.

The applicant is required to fill up the information in the application blank in his own handwriting. The application blank also provides space where the applicant is required to affix his recent photograph which helps in finding out whether the appearance of the applicant is suitable for the post and also in identification of the applicant at the time of the interview. The information available from the application blank is considered in deciding the suitability of the applicant and also at the time of interview for obtaining more information from the applicant. Usually, there is an instruction given to the applicant in the application blank that the information given by the applicant should be correct and if later on such information is found to be false, the services of the applicant will be terminated immediately.

3. Written test and other selection tests: After studying and comparing the information which becomes available from the applications submitted by the applicants, either all of them or some of them are called for the written test. The purpose of the written test is to bring the applicants who may have passed the examination from the different universities, at different times on the same platform and judge them in respect of intelligence and ability. Written tests may be tests where the candidates are required to write essay type of answers or they may be objective type of tests. Command over the language of expression, power of expression, knowledge of the particular subject can be tested through the essay type of answers written by the candidates and on the basis of it, the suitability of the candidates for the particular post can be decided. Objective type of tests helps in judging the intelligence level and understanding capacity of the candidates.

In addition to the written test, these days many more tests are conducted by the organisations for selecting the most suitable candidate. These tests are known as psychological tests and include aptitude test, achievement test, personality test and interest test. Aptitude test may be conducted in the form of mental or intelligence test or mechanical aptitude test or skill test.

(a) Mental or intelligence test enables judging the intelligence quotient of the candidate and provide information about mental capacity, memory power, reasoning ability and capacity of perception.

(b) Mechanical aptitude test helps in determining the capacity of the candidate to learn a particular type of mechanical work. The manual dexterity, perceptual speed and the capacity for spatial visualisation of a candidate is judged with the help of this test.

(c) Skill tests are conducted to measure a candidate's ability to do a specific job. Certain jobs need the use of particular muscular movements and co-ordination of such movements. Skill tests point out the extent to which these abilities are possessed by the candidate.

(d) Achievement tests or experience tests are used to find out how much skill or knowledge is acquired by the candidate from his previous job. A person who has already performed a certain job in some other organisation becomes familiar with the procedure and technique of performing it. He can operate a machine at a certain speed and can use mechanical equipment with ease and familiarity. The level of his skill and knowledge about the job can be ascertained by providing him with the experience test. A dictation test can be given to a candidate who is being considered for the post of a stenographer and a typing test can be given to a candidate to judge his speed and accuracy in typing.

(e) Personality tests are conducted to get information about the non-intellectual nature of characteristics of a candidate which determine his personality. Personality tests provide information about the ability of the candidate to adjust himself to a certain situation, adjustment with the other persons, self-confidence, emotional set-up, ambition, co-operative nature, capacity to take initiative, self-restraint, value system, courage, sympathy for others and many more characteristics which make up the personality of an individual. For performing a job, some of these qualities are needed and the personality test helps in selecting a candidate who possesses these qualities to a greater extent as compared to other candidates.

(f) Interest tests are needed to ascertain the type of work in which the candidate is interested. Candidates have liking for certain jobs and dislike some other jobs. In order to provide job satisfaction to an employee, it is necessary to provide him the job for which he has a liking. While selecting the candidates it, therefore, becomes necessary to ascertain the amount of interest which he has for the job.

Conducting all the above mentioned tests may not be necessary for all the jobs for which selection is to be made. According to the nature of the job and the care to be taken while appointing a person for the job, the type of the tests can be decided.

4. Comprehensive Interview: Interview is an important and essential step in the selection procedure. A comprehensive interview is different than the screening or preliminary interview which is mentioned as the first step in the selection process. Comprehensive interview is conducted to decide the most suitable candidate for the job. In this interview, the candidate comes face-to-face with the employer or the senior persons in the organisation to whom the responsibility of selecting the candidate for the post is entrusted.

In the words of **Scott**, **Clothier** and **Spriegel** *"an interview is a purposeful exchange of ideas, the answering of questions and communication between two or more persons"*. An interview is a device which is used to find out maximum amount of information from the candidate on the basis of which his suitability for the job can be determined and may be conducted by one person or by the members included in the interview panel. The interview may be of structured type or unstructured type. In the structured interview, the interviewer prepares a list of questions in advance and asks those questions to the candidate to obtain information from him.

In case of an unstructured interview, the interviewer asks the questions to the candidate according to the response received from him and the questions are not pre-determined in such an interview. The purpose of this interview is to judge the candidate on the basis of his personality, behaviour, intelligence and attitude. Information about some qualities of a candidate does not become available from the written test or other selection tests and it becomes available only through the interview. Mannerism, way of speaking, neatness, outward appearance and attitude of a candidate can be understood when he is being interviewed and this information can be used to decide on the suitability of the candidate for the post for which he is interviewed.

In order to serve the purpose of interview, it is necessary that the candidate should reply the questions without tension and for this it becomes the responsibility of the interviewers to put the candidates at ease. The interviewers should ask some simple and elementary questions in the beginning which may be based upon the information provided by the candidate in his application blank. When the candidate answers these questions he gains confidence and the tension in him is reduced and he becomes relaxed. Then, gradually other questions should be asked to him from which his intelligence, grasping power, analytical ability and other information related to the requirements of the job can be understood.

An interview can be used for giving information about the job and the organisation to the candidate so that he can decide whether or not he should accept the job. An interview should be conducted by senior and experienced persons who possess the skill of interviewing. Sufficient time should be allowed for each candidate and the time should be used for obtaining maximum information about the candidate. Generally, candidates for semi-skilled and skilled jobs are interviewed for 20 to 25 minutes each while candidates for managerial posts may be interviewed for 45 to 50 minutes.

While conducting the interview, on the basis of the replies given by the candidate, the interviewers do the marking and when the interviews of all the candidates are over, they prepare a merit list of the candidates on the basis of marks allotted to them. The candidate who is most suitable for the job is thus identified as a result of the interview.

5. Medical Examination: Medical or physiological examination is conducted to find out whether the candidate is physically fit or not to perform the job for which he is to be selected. Certain jobs require certain physical qualities like good eye-sight, keen hearing capacity, stamina for physical exertion etc., Medical examination of the candidates enables the organisation to know whether or not they possess the required level of such physical qualities. Medical examination may point out that a candidate suffers from a certain disease or illness due to which he becomes unsuitable for the particular job; e.g. a person suffering from epilepsy is not a suitable person for working on a machine or for driving a vehicle. For certain jobs, physical measurements like height, weight, chest etc., are specified for the candidates to be eligible for doing the jobs. In such case, medical examination is conducted to see whether the candidates fulfil the standards set.

Medical examination may be conducted by medical practitioners appointed by the organisation or the candidates may be sent to the civil hospital for undergoing medical examination. After completing the medical examination, the reports are sent to the organisation and after considering these reports, a decision is taken about the candidate to be selected for the post.

6. Checking of References: Candidate provides references in the application blank. After the comprehensive interview and the medical examination of the candidate is over, the next step in the selection procedure is checking of the references provided by the candidate. The personnel department of the organisation writes letters to the persons whose names and addresses are given by the candidate as references. These persons may be the teachers of the candidate or the previous employers of the candidate or some respectable persons who know the candidate. When references are checked, the referees are requested to provide information about qualifications, abilities, character and special qualities possessed by the candidate. If the referee is the previous employer of the candidate, he is requested to provide information about the work-experience of the candidate, performance at the job, capacity shown to shoulder responsibility, pay drawn and the reason due to which he has left the job. Information provided by the referees in response to enquiries made about the candidate helps in judging the character and ability of the candidate and also for taking a decision about offering the job to the candidate.

7. Final Employment Decision: The final decision about employment is taken by the line manager of the department where the job is available. By considering the information available from the various steps as mentioned above, the line manager has to decide whether or not the candidate should be appointed for the job. The line manager is familiar with the nature of the job and the requirements needed on the part of the person to be able to perform it in a satisfactory way. He compares this information with the qualifications, abilities, experience possessed by the various candidates and decides who is the most suitable candidate. When the line manager communicates his final employment decision to the personnel department, it makes the arrangement for sending the offer or appointment letter to the candidate selected for the post.

8. Placement: When the candidate accepts the offer made to him by the personnel department and reports for the work in the organisation, he is placed on the job for which he is selected. Such an employee is kept on probation for a certain duration and during the probation period he is kept under observation. This is done to find out whether the employee can work satisfactorily and fulfil the expectations made from him. If there are any deficiencies which are noticed during the probation period, efforts are made to remove the deficiencies by giving proper training to the employee. On completion of the probation period, if the employee's work is found satisfactory, he is taken up in the organisation as a permanent employee and a letter to that effect is given to the employee. On the other hand, if the employee is found as unsuitable for the job, his services are terminated by giving him necessary notice and the selection process is started again to fill up the vacancy in the organisation.

2.4.5 Barriers and Limitations of Selection Process

Selection process adopted by different organisations cannot be same and also, there is diversity of selection tools such as tests, interviews etc. There is no perfect way to select the most desirable candidates perfectly. Many times, it is experienced that even carefully selected candidates have failed to perform their duties as expected of them at the time of selection. In other words, even though the candidates do reasonably well at the time of interviews, tests. etc., it does not guarantee that their performance on the jobs assigned to them will also be good. Further, even if they prove themselves efficient and qualified at the time of their selection, but if they get a better opportunity, they may leave their jobs. This implies that selection process suffers from certain barriers and limitations. The important barriers and limitations of a selection process are mentioned below.

(a) **Time-consuming, lengthy and expensive:**

Selection process is a time-consuming and lengthy one, besides being expensive. A good amount of time and money is required to be spent in the selection process. More amount is spent on advertisements, conducting the tests and interviews, fees of management consultants etc.

(b) **Problems relating to tests:**

Testing has many limitations. It is especially in respect of psychological tests. Many times, the tests are poorly designed. A test that has been validated can differentiate between employees who can perform well and those who will not. It only increases the possibility of success. Tests may not prove to be helpful for all the times.

(c) **Possibility of changes in employee's attitudes:**

A distinction should be made between what a man can do and what he will do when asked to work on job. His aptitudes, attitudes may change as time changes. Hence, the candidate may or may not perform well as was expected of him at the time of interview.

(d) **Problem of adjustment:**

Many times, newly appointed employees find it difficult to adjust to the environment of the organisation. The existing staff do not co-operate with the newly selected employees and hence, they get frustrated and leave the organisation. This leads to labour turnover.

(e) **Problems relating to interviewers:**

Interviewers must be experts and versatile in conducting interviews, tests etc. If they don't have sufficient experience and maturity, suitable candidates may not be selected.

(f) **Selection bias:**

Fairness in selection requires that no candidate should be discriminated on the basis of religion, caste, region, gender etc. If there is any selection bias on the part of selectors, suitable candidates may not be selected. Selectors may select those candidates with whom they may have some personal relations or biases.

(g) **Pressures on selectors:**

Many times, selectors are pressurised by the vested interests to select a specific candidate who may no be suitable for the job. But then selection has to be done to achieve certain business goals.

Points to Remember

- A **job** can be defined as a collection or aggregate of tasks, positions, duties and responsibilities which as a whole are regarded as a regular assignment to individual employees.
- **Job analysis** is the process or procedure of gathering the information systematically in order to determine the duties, responsibilities, abilities, skill requirements of a job and also the kind of person who should be employed for it.
- **Job description** is a broad statement of the purpose, scope, duties and responsibilities of a particular job
- **Components of Job Description**
    1. Job Identification
    2. Job Summary
    3. Job Duties and Responsibilities
    4. Relation to other jobs
    5. Supervision
    6. Information about machines, tools and equipments, materials
    7. Working conditions
    8. Hazards
- A **job specification** is a list of human qualities or requirements required to perform a job.
- A **job design** is the division of the total task to be performed into the manageable and efficient units.
- **Job evaluation** is a systematic and orderly process of determining the worth of a job in relation to other jobs.
- The five core model proposed by Hackman and Oldam are:
    1. Skill
    2. Task identity
    3. Task significance
    4. Autonomy
    5. Feedback
- **Human Resource Planning** is the process by which an organisation ensures that it has the right number and kind of people, at the right place, at the right time, capable of effectively and efficiently completing those tasks that will help the organisation to achieve its overall objectives.

- **Manpower planning** involves two stages. The first stage is concerned with the detailed planning of manpower requirements for all types and levels of employees throughout the period of the plan and the second stage is concerned with Planning of manpower supplies to provide the organisation with the right types of people from all the sources to meet the planned requirements.

- **For forecasting the demand for the manpower, the following techniques are used:**
    1. Managerial judgement
    2. Ratio-trend analysis
    3. Work study techniques
    4. Delphi techniques
    5. Statistical techniques

- **Recruitment** is the process of searching for prospective employees and stimulating to apply for jobs in the organisation.

- Internal and external factors affect recruitment.

- **Methods of Recruitment**
    1. Direct method
    2. Indirect method
    3. Third party methods

    The following are the three important stages of a recruitment process:
    (1) Planning
    (2) Implementation
    (3) Evaluation

- **The following process of selection can be mentioned as a scientific and widely used selection process:**
    1. Initial screening interview
    2. Application blank or application form
    3. Written test and other selection tests
    4. Comprehensive interview
    5. Medical examination
    6. Checking of references
    7. Final employment decision
    8. Placement.

- **Induction** is the formal introduction of a new employee to a new job with the information that employee needs to function comfortably, properly and effectively in the organisation.
- There are two ways of taking orientation and they are:
  (a) A formal and comprehensive way of orienting new employees, and
  (b) Following informal and gradual process of learning about the organisation over a period of time

Questions for Discussion

1. State and explain the definition and meaning of Human Resource Planning and explain its nature.
2. What is Human Resource Planning'? Explain the objectives of Human Resource Planning.
3. Distinguish between:
   (a) Internal sources and external sources of recruitment.
   (b) Recruitment and selection
4. What are the objectives, advantages and limitations of Human Resource Planning?
5. "Manpower Planning is the process of estimating the requirement of manpower". Explain this statement by explaining the process of manpower planning.
6. Explain the concept of Global Labour Market.
7. What are the different internal sources of recruitment? Explain advantages and disadvantages of internal sources of recruitments.
8. Explain in detail the process selection of the employees.
9. Explain the significance of the following in the selection process:
   (a) Application Bank, (b) Tests, and (c) Interviews
10. Write short notes on the following:
    (a) Main sources of recruitment
    (b) E-recruiting methods
    (c) Process of Human Resource Planning
    (d) Geographic labour markets
    (e) Manpower Estimation
    (f) Job Analysis and Job Description
    (g) Job Specification and Job Evaluation.
    (h) Employment advertising
    (i) Importance of selection

Multiple Choice Questions (MCQs)

1. Recruitment is widely viewed as a .... process.
   (a) Positive
   (b) Negative
   (c) Both positive and negative
   (d) None of the above

2. Recruitment policy usually highlights the need for establishing
   (a) Job specification
   (b) Job analysis
   (c) Job description
   (d) None of the above

3. The process of developing an applicants' pool for job openings in an organisation is called ....
   (a) Hiring
   (b) Recruitment
   (c) Selection
   (d) retention

4. Which best describes the function of Human Resources Planning?
   (a) An integrated set of processes, programmes and systems in an organisation that focuses on maximising employee contribution in order to achieve organisational success
   (b) The process of ensuring that people required to run the company are being used as effectively as possible--especially in fulfilling developmental needs--in order to accomplish the organisation's goals
   (c) The formal process of familiarizing new employees with the organisation, new job, work units and culture values, beliefs and accepted behaviour
   (d) The process of effectively and efficiently managing your assets.

5. Which of the following is the area from which applicants can be recruited?
   (a) Job agencies
   (b) Labour markets
   (c) Employment lines
   (d) Labour unions

Human Resource Management   HR Procurement

6. Which is the process of choosing individuals who have relevant qualifications to fill existing or projected job openings?

    (a) Selection process

    (b) Screening process

    (c) Interview process

    (d) Prescreening process

7. Which best identifies the second step of the Recruitment process?

    (a) Gathering of job information

    (b) Determining best recruitment method

    (c) Identifying job openings

    (d) Planning for staff needs

ANSWERS

| 1. (a) | 2. (a) | 3. (d) | 4. (b) | 5. (b) | 6. (a) | 7. (c) |

Questions From Previous Pune University Exams

1. Define Manpower Planning. What are its Objectives and Benefits?

   M.B.A. December 2005

Ans. Refer Articles 2.2, 2.2.1 and 2.2.2 of this Chapter.

2. Describe Recruitment and Selection Process and Point Out Various Sources of Recruitment. **M.B.A. April 2006**

Ans. Refer Article 2.3, 2.4 and 2.3.8 of this Chapter.

3. Write Short Notes: **M.B.A. April 2009, 2010**

   (A) Job Description. **M.B.A. April 2009, December 2005, December 2012**

Ans. Refer Article 2.1.7 of this Chapter.

4. Discuss in detail the process of Recruitment and Selection of Employees.

   M.B.A. April 2009

Ans. Refer Article 2.4.4 of this Chapter.

5. Define HRP. Why is Planning needed in the exercise of HRM?

M.B.A. December 2010

Ans. Refer Articles 2.2 and 2.2.1 of this Chapter.

6. Define Human Resource Planning and Explain the Various Sources of Recruitment.

M.B.A. April 2011

Ans. Refer Articles 2.2 and 2.3.8 of this Chapter.

7. Define Manpower Planning. Explain various steps involved in Manpower Planning.

M.B.A. April 2012

Ans. Refer Articles 2.2 and 2.2.4 of this Chapter.

✳✳✳

Chapter 3...

Training and Development

Contents ...

3.1 Introduction
3.2 Meaning and Definitions of 'Training'
3.3 Employee Training and Development
3.4 Nature of Training
3.5 Training Process
3.6 Training Need Assessment
3.7 Training Evaluation
3.8 Training Design
3.9 Implementing Training Programmes (Training Methods)
3.10 Methods of Training
3.11 Implementing Management Development Programmes
- Points to Remember
- Questions for Discussion
- Questions from Previous Pune University Examinations

Learning Objectives:
- To understand the Meaning and Definitions of Training
- To be aware of Training Needs and Identification of Training Needs
- To be able to discuss the Meaning of Training Policy and Reasons for Formulation of a Training Policy
- To gain knowledge of the Objectives of Training and Importance of Training
- To learn about the Meaning of Training Process and steps involved in the Training Process
- To be aware of the Meaning, Types of Training Programmes, Classification of Methods of Training, Types of Training Methods, Tools and Aids of Training
- To understand the Meaning of Training Evaluation and the Training Evaluation System Process

3.1 Introduction

Training makes a very important contribution to the development of the human resources of an organisation and ultimately helps to achieve its goals and objectives. Hence, training needs are to be effectively identified and effectively managed so that the right type of training can be given to the right people at the right time and in the right manner and form.

In the recent past, especially in the last few years of the 20th century and in the first decade of the present i.e. 21st century, we find fundamental changes in approaches, attitudes, philosophy, outlook, and practices in the personnel area in the form of human resource management strategy. Because of which, it has become very essential for almost all organisations to develop skills, potentialities, capabilities, talents, attitudes etc. of the people working with them to meet the challenges of the changing period.

Therefore, many organisations have evolved and adopted suitable human resource development policies and strategies which help to bring forth necessary changes in skills, capabilities, attitudes and so on for people who are expected to cope with the emerging trends and changes. Thus, human resource development has now become an integral and important part of human resource management. Nowadays, various suitable organisational development programmes are being evolved and effectively integrated with the human resource development programmes.

Training and development programmes are part and parcel of organisational development and hence they are the most decisive aspects of human resource development too. HRD efforts are described in terms of the Training and Development programmes conducted for the development of the people working in the organisation which ultimately result in the development of the organisation itself. In this chapter, some important aspects relating to training and development so far as human resource management is concerned will be studied.

3.2 Meaning and Definitions of Training

The word 'Training' consists of eight letters. To each of these eight letters, if we attribute some significant meanings in the following way, the concept of training and its objectives can be understood more properly.

(1) The letter 'T' implies talent, tenacity, tactful and technique. Training should help to enhance talent, tenacity, tactfulness and technique.

(2) 'R' stands for reinforcement, rationality and renewal.

(3) 'A' for action, awareness, alertness. Training is expected to create awareness, alertness in the trainees and make them action oriented. They are essential qualities for improving the capacity, abilities, efficiency of the employees.

(4) 'I' implies idea or idealism, imagination and innovation.

(5) The letter 'N' in the word 'Training' suggests 'Novelty'. There should be strong desire in the trainees to learn new things to acquire new skills, abilities, talents, etc.

(6) The last I: 'I' in the word training can be taken to mean Interest, 'Intensity', 'Innate' desire to learn.

(7) 'N': This other 'N" in the word training implies 'Nurturing' of talents, skills etc.

(8) 'G' is the last letter in the word 'Training' and it stands for 'gaiety', 'gaining'. Because of training, a trainee gains knowledge and skills.

Thus, training helps the trainees to acquire the above mentioned qualities which are very useful for trainees themselves and for their management also.

Training *is a process in which all sided efforts are made to improve skills, aptitudes, abilities etc. of individuals.* They may be employees, candidates, apprentices and so on. Training definitely helps the trainees in updating their talents and skills and developing new ones. It helps to increase the efficiency and productivity of the trainees. For qualitative development of all employees, training is absolutely essential and organisations will do well to take interest and give importance to training activities.

When candidates are recruited from outside or selected or promoted from inside, it is expected that they must perform their jobs with maximum efficiency and competence. Therefore, after selecting the candidates, the next logical step is to train them for better performance. Training is required to be imparted to the employees to keep them updated, effective and efficient.

At present, it is observed that all organisations, of whatever types they may be, need to have well trained, experienced and skilled people to perform various activities which have to be done or performed. If the jobs are of a complex nature, training becomes inevitable. Employee training is, therefore, not only a desirable activity but it is an activity which an organisation must commit resources to if it is to maintain a visible, efficient and knowledgeable work force.

The term or concept of 'Training' has been defined by many experts in the field of management taking into consideration different aspects. Some of the definitions of training are given below to help understand its meaning and nature.

1. **According to Elmer H. Burack and Robert D. Smith**, *"Training is a planned, organised and controlled activity designed to express some aspect or aspects of present job performance. Training is skill oriented and it is usually intended for the short run welfare of the economy (i.e. organisation). Training is also a key ingredient in the motivation of individuals. An untrained, unskilled employee feels very insecure, lacking the self-confidence necessary for comfortable group relations".*

2. **Prof. Milkovich and Prof. Boudreau stated the definition of training as follows:**

   "Training is a systematic process of changing the behaviour, knowledge, and/or motivation of present employees to improve the match between employee characteristics and employment requirements".

3. **According to Prof. Arun Monappa and Prof. Mirza Saiyadain**, *"Training refers to the teaching and learning activities carried on for the primary purpose of helping members of an organisation to acquire and apply the knowledge, skills, abilities and attitudes needed by the organisation".* They further opined that *"broadly speaking, training is the act of increasing the knowledge and skill of an employee for doing a particular job".*

4. **According to Prof. A. M. Sharma** *"Training may be defined as any organisationally planned effort to change the behaviour or attitudes of employees so that they can perform jobs on acceptable standards. Training provides knowledge and skills required to perform the job".*

5. **Prof. C. B. Mamoria** defined the concept of training as *"A process of learning a sequence of programmed behaviour. It is an application of knowledge".* He further made it clear that training gives people an awareness of the rules and procedures to guide their behaviour and attempts to improve their performance on the current job or prepare them for an intended job.

3.3 Employee Training and Development

Once the training needs are identified, the next step in the process is obviously to specify the objectives of training. If the objectives of training are to be given to employees to whom the training is to be given, the objectives are required to be well defined and clear. On the basis of the training needs and objectives, the contents of training programme are fixed. The success of any training programme depends to a great extent on the objectives fixed for the training.

Moreover, objectives also give the trainees a clear cut idea and understanding of what exactly they will have to do after training program. Therefore, it becomes very essential to lay down various objectives of a training programme.

The objectives of training can vary according to the requirements but in general, they must be helpful to the trainees to learn or acquire required skills and abilities, to get necessary knowledge and information, to create positive attitudes essential for effective work performance.

Common Objectives of Training are as follows:

1. The fundamental objective of training is obviously to induce necessary positive change in the concerned employee. Training is an important strategy for organisational development and a significant management tool in bringing about desired changes.

2. Another important objective of training is to assist employees to acquire skills, knowledge, attitudes etc. necessary for collective work performance. It not only helps to acquire these qualities, but also enhances existing knowledge, skills and performance capabilities of employees.

3. According to some experts, the main objective of training should not be merely to teach or to learn technical skills, to gain knowledge etc. but it should help employees to attain the strategic goals and objectives of their organisation. This implies that the training has to make sense in terms of the organisation's strategic goals. A strategy to improve customer service and satisfaction implies the need for customer service training.

4. Yet another important objective of training is to bring skills, capabilities of employee's upto a standard for present and future job assignments. Training helps to keep abreast of development in technical and management fields.

5. One of the objectives of training to increase efficiency and competence of employees and to improve job performance, ensure adaptation to change and to increase productivity. *Baum*, *Bernard* and *others* have rightly remarked that instructions can help employees to increase their level of performance on their present assignment. Increased human performance often directly leads to increased operational productivity and profit of the company. Further, increased performance and productivity because of training, are most evident on the part of new employees who are not yet fully aware of the most efficient and effective ways of performing their jobs.

6. According to *Bookcock* well trained workers are less likely to make operational mistakes therefore, leading to increase in quality, may be in relation to products or services of an organisation or with reference to intangible organisational employment atmosphere. Thus, training aims to improve the quality and quantity of output, to lower the wastages and thereby the cost of waste, equipment maintenance, and accidents.

Besides the above mentioned important objectives of training, the following are some other objectives of training.

(a) To inculcate a true sense of appreciation for other functional areas and to understand the linkages of their activities with various other areas.

(b) To identify and to develop value systems and thereby to learn proper behavioural practices, commitment to excellence in all efforts, endeavours in the organisation.

(c) To develop capabilities and competence to assume higher responsibilities and promote various supervisory, inter-personal and team building skills.

(d) If proper training is given, it helps to prevent industrial accidents and a safe work-environment becomes possible. It leads to more stable mental attitude on the part of the employees of the organisation. As a result, managerial mental attitudes and capacity also improves, as supervisors know they can do their work in a better way because of the training given to the employees through well designed and organised training and development programmes.

(e) Training programmes bring about the initiative and creativity of employees and thus help to prevent manpower obsolescence. Such manpower obsolescence may be due to many reasons such as age, fatigue, temperament, lack of proper motivation, inability of employees to cope up with changing technology etc. That is why the prevention of obsolescence of manpower is also considered as one of the objectives of training. Moreover, training programmes also give the participants a wider awareness, and understanding thus leading to personal development also.

Training and Motivation

The true objectives of training can only be achieved if all the parties involved are motivated and possess the ability and desire to participate in the training process wholeheartedly. Hence, trainees are required to be motivated for training. The employers can take certain steps to increase the motivation of trainees to learn. The trainees, employees can be persuaded to be interested in training programmes in one of the following ways:

(i) Trainees, employees should be convinced of the advantages of training, learning for increasing their job performance. They will definitely respond to various programmes involving changed behaviour if they believe that the resulting modification in the behaviour, abilities, skills etc. is in their own interest and they will get the benefits as a result of their training and new behaviour.

(ii) Training should be more meaningful and help the transfer of skills so that trainees may take keen interest in training and learning. If confidence is created that the trainees will be definitely benefited, obviously they will participate in the training programmes with keen interest.

(iii) A trainee can be motivated to take training if his superior or others make clear the importance of undergoing training. If a trainee comes to know that his actual performance is not upto the mark, he can be motivated to join a training programme.

(iv) Trainees can change their behaviour and attitude if they become aware of better ways of performing their jobs and gain more experience in the new pattern of behaviour after training.

Training Period

Training can range from very highly specified instruction in the procedures to be adopted while performing a particular job to a general instruction, knowledge relating to different aspects of the economy, society etc. Hence the objectives of training are required to be fixed carefully. Duration of a training programme varies with the needs, objectives and types of training, the skills to be acquired, the complexity of the subject, aptitudes, abilities etc. of trainees and also the training media used.

It is generally accepted that a training period should not be unduly long. If it is long, trainees may feel bored, uninterested also. The sessions' should also not be lengthy. An ideal session should not go beyond three hours at a stretch. There should a break between two sessions. The training period can be from one week to 6 months or even more depending upon the requirements. Nowadays, it is also found that two days' training programmes are organised at regular short intervals. It should be noted that besides the training period, physical location of the training programme is also important. The physical location of the program should be convenient and in pleasant surroundings away from the noise and tension of the work place.

3.4 Nature of Training

From the different definitions of training given in this chapter, you may understand that training is a systematic learning process which helps to increase the knowledge and improve the skills of people performing various parts of the overall tasks of the organisation.

It involves the acquisition of skills, concepts, rules, procedures, attitudes etc. to increase the performance of employees. It is an organised function which helps the employees to acquire knowledge and skills for a definite purpose.

Training gives appropriate shape to the behaviour of employees to achieve the predetermined goals. Training is something which is very essential for everyone and is the cornerstone of sound human resource management/administration.

Training makes employees more effective, efficient and productive. It also helps to mould the attitudes of employees in order to achieve better co-operation within the organisation and a greater loyalty to it. Moreover, training heightens, in a way, the morale of employees as it helps in reducing dissatisfaction and as a result it reduces the rate of absenteeism and turnover. If proper and adequate training is given to the employees, they can make a better and economic use of materials and equipment and thus because of training, wastages and spoilage can be kept to the minimum level, also the need for constant, continuous supervision can be reduced.

Training involves planned and systematic procedures for transferring technical know-how to the employees so as to increase their knowledge and skills for performing specific jobs, tasks, etc. with proficiency and efficiency. Thus, trainees can acquire technical knowledge, certain skills and problem solving ability by undergoing training programmes.

There are some people who think that unplanned learning through job experience is sufficient enough to acquire and develop required skills, abilities and efficiency to perform various jobs. To some extent, it is true that training cannot entirely substitute experience. However, many organisations have experienced that it is always advantageous to plan systematic training programmes considering the needs as a regular part of the personnel development programme. Such programmes help the personnel to learn correct job methods in order to achieve a satisfactory level of efficiency and job performance.

Relationship between 'Education', 'Training' and 'Development'

Education, training and development are correlated terms or concepts. Education is the process of acquiring background and basic knowledge of a subject and it is person-oriented rather than job-oriented. Education is common to all employees. Training is concerned with the acquisition of knowledge as well as skills that can be applied to perform work of a particular type. It is process of imparting specific skills. While development is a course of action designed to gain knowledge and to create attitudes amongst the employees to realise their potential for growth in their organisation. Development is related to future, more senior jobs or positions rather than present ones. Training an employee or an individual for a higher, bigger and more responsible job means engaging him in 'development'.

Difference between 'Training' and 'Development'

Though training and development include training of employees to perform their jobs efficiently and effectively, there is some difference between training and development.

Training is any organisational planned effort to affect or change the behaviour, attitudes etc. of employees so that they can perform their jobs efficiently on acceptable standards. It provides knowledge, skills etc. required to perform the job. It can be said that training is a process by means of which the aptitudes, skills, capabilities, efficiency etc. of the employees to perform their jobs are increased.

Development is also viewed similarly but with more stress on communicating organisational norms, values for the given roles. Development is also a process which helps employees to attain overall improvement in ability and competence and it helps to progress towards maturity and actualisation of personality. Thus, it can be said that training is meant for learning technical operations which provides specific job related information, while development makes clear theoretical conceptual ideas and provides general knowledge and helps an individual to enhance level of understanding various aspects.

Training is a short-term process in which generally non-managerial personnel learn technical aspects, skills and get technical knowledge for definite purposes utilising a systematic and organised procedure. Development is a long-term educational process in which managerial personnel especially learn conceptual and theoretical knowledge useful for management and organisation utilising a systematic, well-planned and organised procedure. Moreover, in developing human resources, the training and development functions are combined properly for developing various skills, abilities and basic attitudes and aptitudes, which lead to personal development and growth. It is considered that for many jobs, proper training is very essential to keep abreast of current developments and to raise the performance abilities of human resources even beyond acceptable levels. Therefore, now-a-days, it is accepted that training and development programmes play a major role in organisational development by changing attitudes and behaviour of the personnel.

Segments of Training

Nowadays, training programmes are gaining importance because they help to solve various problems which arise out of the introduction of new lines of production, severe competition, changes in design and technique of production, changes in the volume of business etc.

Training programmes enhance overall organisational efficiency and effectiveness. Training has become a very significant management tool for bringing about the desired changes in order to solve organisational problems and also to achieve organisational goals. Therefore to be very effective, the training function is required to be organised properly and systematically. Broadly, training function is divided into the following main segments.

(a) Identification of training needs.

(b) Deciding the objectives of training to be given.

(c) Designing and administering training programmes.

(d) Selection of training methods and tools.

(e) Training evaluation.

3.5 Training Process

Training refers to various methods used to give new or present employees the information or knowledge, the skills and their proper application needed to perform their jobs, tasks etc. efficiently, properly and effectively, while process means a series of actions and motions to achieve particular goals or objectives.

When we consider "training process" as a topic, we have to consider various actions, steps required to be taken for imparting training to the concerned individuals, candidates or employees. Generally, it is found that the following steps are important in a training process.

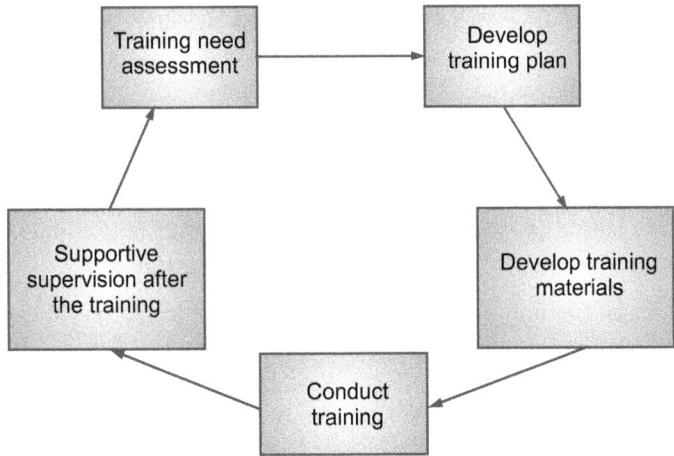

Fig. 3.1: Training Process

(1) Identification of training needs.

(2) Deciding the objectives of training to be given.

(3) Designing of the training programme or programmes.

(4) Selection of trainees and trainers.

(5) Selection of training methods and tools.

(6) Administration and implementation of training programmes.

(7) Evaluation of training.

It may be noted that all the above mentioned steps in the process of training are inter-related. Certain stages can be started simultaneously. But the ultimate object should be to give proper and necessary training to the present and new employees by following a suitable training process so that they can perform their jobs effectively and efficiently and help their organisation to achieve its objectives or goals.

3.6 Training Need Assessment

Training is a process of learning a sequence of programmed behaviour. It is application of knowledge. It gives employees an awareness of the rules, regulations and procedures to guide their behaviour and to improve their performance on the current jobs or to prepare them for the intended jobs.

The training and development function is one of the major activities of an organisation. The continued effectiveness, efficiency, growth and development of an organisation, to a great extent, besides other factors, depend on the ability of its employees to produce at high levels of efficiency, and to keep abreast with their changing job role demands. It can be achieved through proper training of employees which helps to develop specific and useful knowledge, skills, abilities, and techniques. No doubt, training is a task-oriented activity which helps to improve the performance of employees in current and future jobs. Now, let us consider various needs for training the employees.

Training needs assessment can be as simple as asking an employee what he would require to be able to do better, to as complex as developing an individualised training plan for every employee. The organisation has to adopt appropriate training needs assessment approaches and identify tools that address different areas of training.

The various areas of training are:
- Technical Training
- Training for total quality management (TQM)
- Training for Trainers
- Training for Team Management
- Training for Leadership
- Training for Creativity
- Training for Problem Solving
- Training for Cultural diversity
- Training for a New Economy
- Training for Change.

All these are specialised areas of training, with specific advantages and also techniques or models. Ultimately, they contribute to overall growth of the individual employees and the organisation. Based on this, decisions will have to be taken about the type of training, training content and the method for implementing and evaluating the training programmes.

Needs or Objectives or Importance of Employee Training

Training is given to the employees in order –

(i) To enhance the existing knowledge, skills and abilities, performance capabilities of the employees and to acquire new skills, abilities, knowledge for improving their qualities.

(ii) To increase efficiency and productivity of the employees.

(iii) To help an organisation to fulfil its future personnel needs.

(iv) To improve health and safety of employees.

(v) To prevent wastages, wear and tear obsolescence etc.

(vi) To improve organisational climate.

(vii) To help employees achieve personal growth and development.

(viii) To improve morale of employees.

(ix) To keep abreast of (i.e. up to date with) developments in technical and management fields and also to inculcate a sense of appreciation for other functional areas and an understanding of the linkage of their activities with other areas.

(x) To induct new employees into the organisation.

(xi) To minimise the resistance to change.

Identification of 'Training Needs'

Training activity is not an isolated exercise but is an integral part of the total management development activities of an organisation. Therefore, considering the goals and requirements of an organisation, identification of training needs is required to be done.

Identification of training needs is a continuous process which involves identification of areas, where employees lack skills, knowledge, abilities etc. in effectively performing their jobs and also identifying organisational constraints, problems which create roadblocks in the performance.

Many a time, the need to train personnel is felt when a gap between the present performance of employees and the desired performance is considerably widened.

Prof. Price rightly pointed out that training needs exist when there is a gap between the present performance of an employee or a group of employees and the desired performance. This gap can be ascertained by doing skill-analysis. Skill-analysis includes the following aspects:

(a) Determination and analysis of various requirements required to perform specific jobs.

(b) Finding out the activities and tasks required to be accomplished for meeting job requirements.

(c) Understanding the procedures and processes needed to accomplish each of the job requirements.

(d) Understanding and analysis of the knowledge, skills, abilities required to accomplish the procedures and processes.

(e) Identification of special problems, if any, in relation to the job and proper analysis of any specific skill, ability required to solve problems.

Training helps organisations in many ways. Because of proper training given to employees, their skills, abilities, aptitudes and attitudes, efficiency and productivity etc. increase. Besides that, various problems relating to production, workers relations can also be solved by analysing the problems and identifying the training needs.

Training needs can be assessed by observation of job performance, surveys, tests, interviews, organisation analysis, performance appraisal etc. There are various techniques which are used to determine training needs.

The *Research Committee of the American Society of Training* has suggested certain techniques for determining training needs which are as follows:

(a) Observations
(b) Interviews
(c) Group conferences
(d) Management requests
(e) Questionnaire surveys
(f) Examination and tests
(g) Performance ratings
(h) Personnel records
(i) Business and production reports
(j) Long-range organisational planning
(k) Job analysis

McGhee and *Thayel* have proposed a model of training needs identification which has the following three components:

   (i) **Organisational Analysis:** Organisational analysis involves a comprehensive study and analysis of organisational structure, goals, procedure, process of decision-making etc. If it is done properly, deficiencies can be identified and mechanisms which would be needed to make adjustments in the areas of those deficiencies can be introduced. While doing the analysis, it is studied whether an organisation possesses adequate number of people to accomplish its objectives, goals etc. and whether the persons working with an organisation possess required skills, abilities, knowledge etc. Based on the findings, training needs can be identified properly.

  (ii) **Task Analysis:** In identifying training needs, task analysis is considered as an important aspect. Task analysis involves systematic and detailed analysis of various components of jobs which indicates whether the nature of the jobs is changed over a period of time and whether the employees have adequate skills and abilities to perform the jobs.

 (iii) **Man Analysis:** Man analysis is more complicated than the two components i.e. organisational analysis and task analysis because of the uncertainty in the behaviour of human beings. While undertaking man analysis, more importance is given to the skills, abilities, aptitude, attitudes, knowledge etc. of the employees and personal records relating to behaviour, absenteeism, production done, regularity etc. are also used.

3.7 Training Evaluation

Evaluation of training is the last but very important stage of any training programme. Training evaluation is very essential because of the following reasons.

(i) The organisation giving training to its employees can come to know what returns it is getting for efforts and expenditure it has committed to training. It can also find out whether the training efforts are in the correct direction or not.

(ii) The training evaluation can justify the expenditure incurred in giving training and help the organisation to determine to what extent, objectives have been achieved.

(iii) Evaluation of training effectiveness does not only help to assess the quality of training imparted but also suggests what changes in training plans should be made to make them more effective. Weaknesses within the established training programmes can be identified and accordingly training programmes can be modified and improved. Less effective programmes can be withdrawn in order to save time, money and efforts.

Definitions and Meaning of Training Evaluation

The concept of 'training evaluation' has been defined and made clear by various experts keeping before them certain views. A few of them are considered below in order to understand the meaning of the concept of training evaluation.

- **According to Prof. Warr**, *"Training evaluation is nothing but the systematic collection and assessment of information for how best to utilise training resources in order to achieve organisational goals"*.

- While **Hasseling** puts it as *"the main task of the trainer as evaluator is to test training effectiveness or to validate his professional claim that the selected training methods have brought about the desired results"*.

- **Hamblin** rightly states that *"evaluation of training is any attempt to obtain information (feedback) on the effects of a training program and to assess the value of the training in the light of that information"*.

As there are various objectives and methods of training, it is not only difficult but impossible to evaluate the training programmes correctly. Training objectives, methods and evaluation are inseparably connected. However, the appropriateness of the objectives and the methods of training can only be known through training evaluation.

Training Evaluation Systems Process

Training evaluation consists of an evaluation of various aspects of training immediately after the training is over and the assessment of its utility in terms of the achievement of the goals of the organisation. An evaluation of various aspects of training immediately after the training is over is comparatively easier than assessing its utility to achieve the goals or objectives of the organisation. The effect of training on performance to achieve various organisational goals or objectives is very difficult to isolate as performance is a function of various complex forces and motives. Besides this, evaluation has its own problems, difficulties and pitfalls. *Tracey* points out some of the pitfalls of evaluation as poor planning, lack of objectivity, evaluation errors etc. Though there are many difficulties and pitfalls in evaluating training programmes, many experts in the field have suggested various methods, means of evaluation of training. Some of the important views presented by the experts on the training evaluation process are as mentioned below.

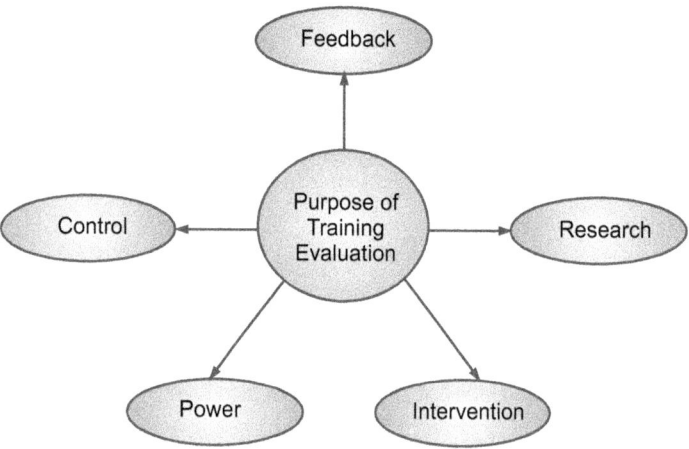

Fig. 3.2: Purpose of Training Evaluation

(A) Kirkpatric's View

Kirkpatric suggested certain procedures and techniques of evaluating training programmes. According to him, there are four training effects which can be evaluated.

(1) Reaction, (2) Learning, (3) Behaviour, (4) Results.

1. **Reaction:** Kirkpatric states that, "evaluating in terms of reaction is the same as measuring the feelings of the conferees (trainees). It does not include a measurement of any learning that takes place". This implies that measuring of reactions is concerned more with the feelings than with learning and therefore, it should be considered whether the trainees like the programme and whether they think it worthwhile. If the trainees are favourably disposed towards the programme, they are in a better position to assimilate the training provided.

2. **Learning:** This is the second step in evaluation which deals with measuring the intake of learning in various forms such as learning of skills, techniques, concepts, principles, methods etc. If the trainees learn any of these and acquire certain skills, the training imparted can be considered of great value.

3. **Behaviour:** Training should bring about positive changes in the behaviour of the trainees. Therefore, a visible positive change in trainee's behaviour in his day to day activities after training programme can be considered for evaluation of effectiveness of the training imparted.

4. **Results:** 'Results' are important outcome of any training program. Results of the training imparted can be in the form of increased efficiency, reduction in the costs and improved productivity and morale.

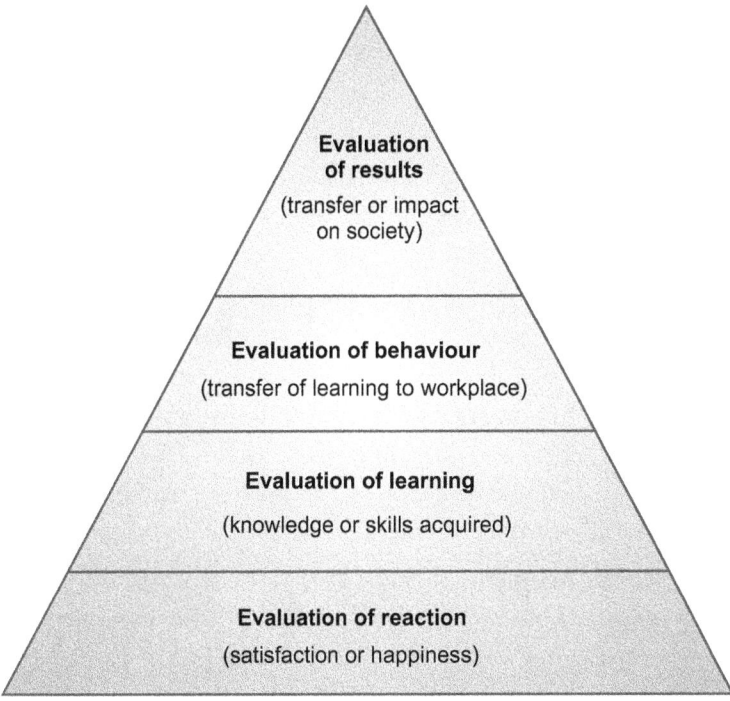

Fig. 3.3: Kirkpatrick's Model

Though the above mentioned four-way approach simplifies the complicated procedure of evaluation of training, proper methods must be developed on scientific lines and should be tested constantly if they are to improve the usefulness and effectiveness of training programmes.

(B) Tracey's View

The evaluation process of training begins with the identification of the areas of training to be evaluated and thereafter, the strategies and methods to be used in collecting the relevant information, tabulating, analysing and interpreting it to reach appropriate decision on effectiveness of training. The interpretation indicates the areas which require improvement and modification. From this point of view, the evaluation of training is considered very important.

According to Tracey, observation, ratings, trainee surveys and interviews are the most useful means of training evaluation. In the observation method, the behaviour of the trainees in a certain situation is observed. However, it must be systematic and specific. Observers must be well trained and they should have specific ideas about what they are looking for. Observation method is a direct method of evaluating or assessing the quality of formal training and of identifying defects and deficiencies.

'Ratings' is another method of evaluation outlined by *Tracey*. She states that, "various elements of the training system should be rated independently by several qualified raters. These elements include trainees, instructors, equipments, materials, training aids and facilities". However, the use of rating scales requires expertise and supervised practice to avoid errors.

A trainee survey is the third method suggested by Tracey. In this method, opinions of trainees are used for training evaluation. But these opinions cannot be used independently as they may not be objective.

Tracey suggested a fourth method i.e. trainee interviews. The views and ideas of the trainees which cannot be put down on paper can be determined by asking them skillful questions. The information thus obtained by interviewing the trainees helps to prevent ambiguity, especially in interpretation. Besides this, information relating to the training can be obtained by interviewing the instructors or trainers. These interviews with instructors help to bring about certain points onto the surface which trainees may find difficult to put down on paper. This helps to evaluate the usefulness of training imparted properly.

Thus, Tracey suggested various methods that could serve as a guide in collecting necessary data. Once the information, data has been collected, it is then tabulated, summarised and interpreted. This interpretation of data is nothing but evaluation of training.

(C) Hamblin's View

Hamblin provided a detailed structure for the evaluation and control of training while underlining the problems and practical difficulties which evaluation activities generate. He identified various important objectives in evaluating training and classified them as follows:

(a) Reaction objectives which are intended to stimulate a high level of involvement and interest.

(b) Learning objectives which are concerned with acquiring knowledge, skills, abilities, attitudes etc.

(c) Job behaviour objectives which are related to learning for bringing about desired changes in job behaviour.

(d) Organisational objectives intended to promote overall results.

Considering these objectives, Hamblin described five levels and strategies for obtaining evaluation.

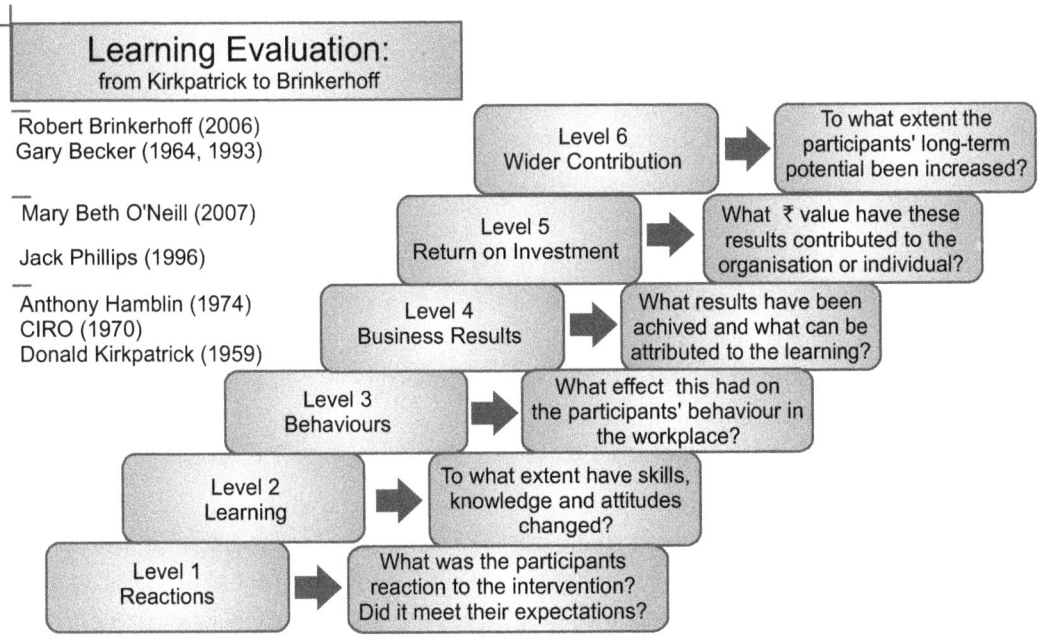

Fig. 3.4: Hamlin's Model

1. Level 1: Reaction of trainees during training towards the trainer, other trainees or participants and external factors are considered in this level. Reaction evaluation is generally determined through questionnaires administered at the end of the training programme. Reactions of trainees can be checked immediately following the training and a few weeks later on. However, only reaction evaluation is not useful for evaluating training because enthusiasm of trainees should not be taken as the only evidence of improved abilities and performance.

2. Level 2: Learning by trainees during the training programme is also important for evaluating training. What principles, concepts, facts, skills etc. were learned during the training period? Whether the ideas, principles etc. were intellectually digested by the trainees or not?

3. Level 3: Behaviour of trainees is another factor which must be considered while evaluating the training programmes. Behaviour evaluation measures how the training has influenced the employees' or trainees' behaviour on the job. The behaviour at the beginning or before training is compared with the bahaviour at the end of training. For example, it is seen whether production has increased or whether trainees acquired certain new skills, because of training. The effects of training are clearly noticed.

4. **Level 4:** The overall results are then considered, e.g. results of the training programme in terms of factors such as reduction in costs or reduction in turnover, absenteeism etc. Results evaluation attempts to measure changes in variables like accident rates, absenteeism, tardiness, productivity turnover, quality etc.

5. **Level 5:** At the end, ultimate values referring to survival, growth, profits, welfare of inferred parties, social and political welfare etc. are considered for obtaining proper evaluation.

From the various views presented by experts, it is evident that training evaluation is a difficult process which cannot be done accurately. The whole business of evaluation can be made easier if the training objectives are set clearly and costs are analysed accurately. Adequate resources for evaluation must be made available. Evaluation of training is very essential for the efficient and effective control of whole system. Unfortunately, it is found in some cases that training programmes have no definite objectives and 'training for the sake of training' appears to be the target.

Sometimes the picture has another side also. The training is imparted but further follow-up action is not taken. As a result, there remains no scope for finding out whether the training imparted has resulted in achieving the objectives for which the training programme was formulated. In such cases, it becomes very difficult to assess the results of training.

The process of examining a training program is called training evaluation. Training evaluation checks whether training has had the desired effect. Training evaluation ensures that whether candidates are able to implement their learning in their respective workplaces, or to the regular work routines.

Purposes of Training Evaluation

The five main purposes of training evaluation are:

1. **Feedback:** It helps in giving feedback to the candidates by defining the objectives and linking it to learning outcomes.

2. **Research:** It helps in ascertaining the relationship between acquired knowledge, transfer of knowledge at the work place, and training.

3. **Control:** It helps in controlling the training programme because if the training is not effective, then it can be dealt with accordingly.

4. **Power games:** At times, the top management (higher authoritative employee) uses the evaluative data to manipulate it for their own benefits.

5. **Intervention:** It helps in determining that whether the actual outcomes are aligned with the expected outcomes.

Process of Training Evaluation

Before Training: The learner's skills and knowledge are assessed before the training programme. During the start of training, candidates generally perceive it as a waste of resources because at most of the times candidates are unaware of the objectives and learning outcomes of the programme. Once aware, they are asked to give their opinions on the methods used and whether those methods confirm to the candidates preferences and learning style.

During Training: It is the phase at which instruction is started. This phase usually consists of short tests at regular intervals.

After Training: It is the phase when learner's skills and knowledge are assessed again to measure the effectiveness of the training. This phase is designed to determine whether training has had the desired effect at individual department and organisational levels. There are various evaluation techniques for this phase.

Techniques of Evaluation

The various techniques of training evaluation are:

Questionnaires: Comprehensive questionnaires could be used to obtain opinion reactions, views of trainees.

Tests: Standard tests could be used to find out whether trainees have learnt anything during and after the training.

Interviews: Interviews could be conducted to find the usefulness of training offered to operatives.

Studies: Comprehensive studies could be carried out eliciting the opinions and judgments of trainers, superiors and peer groups about the training.

Human resource factors: Training can also be evaluated on the basis of employee satisfaction, which in turn can be examined on the basis of decrease in employee turnover, absenteeism, accidents, grievances, discharges, dismissals, etc.

Cost benefit analysis: The costs of training (cost of hiring trainers, tools to learn training centre, wastage, production stoppage, opportunity cost of trainers and trainees) could be compared with its value (in terms of reduced learning time improved learning, superior performance) in order to evaluate a training programme.

Feedback: After the evaluation, the situation should be examined to identify the probable causes for gaps in performance. The training evaluation information.(about costs, time spent, outcomes, etc.) should be provided to the instructors' trainees and other parties concerned for control, correction and improvement of trainees' activities. The training evaluator should follow it up sincerely so as to ensure effective implementation of the feedback report at every stage.

Types/Methods of Evaluation

Evaluation methods can be either qualitative (e.g., interviews, case studies, focus groups) or quantitative (e.g., surveys, experiments).

Training evaluation usually includes a combination of these methods and reframes our thinking about evaluation in that measurements are aimed at different levels of a system.

Evaluating the Training (which includes monitoring) addresses how one determines whether the goals or objectives were met and what impact the training had on actual performance on the job.

Generally there are four kinds of standard training evaluation:

Formative Evaluation: Formative evaluation provides ongoing feedback to the curriculum designers and developers to ensure that what is being created really meets the needs of the intended audience.

- Formative Evaluation may be defined as "any combination of measurements obtained and judgments made before or during the implementation of materials, methods, or programmes to control, assure or improve the quality of program performance or delivery."

- It answers such questions as, "Are the goals and objectives suitable for the intended audience?" "Are the methods and materials appropriate to the event?" "Can the event be easily replicated?"

- Formative evaluation furnishes information for programme developers and implementers.

- It helps determine program planning and implementation activities in terms of (1) target population, (2) programme organisation, and (3) programme location and timing.

- It provides "short-loop" feedback about the quality and implementation of program activities and thus becomes critical to establishing, stabilizing, and upgrading programmes.

- **Process Evaluation:** Process evaluation provides information about what occurs during training. This includes giving and receiving verbal feedback.

- Process Evaluation answers the question, "What did you do?" It focuses on procedures and actions being used to produce results.

- It monitors the quality of an event or project by various means. Traditionally, working as an "onlooker," the evaluator describes this process and measures the results in oral and written reports.

- Process evaluation is the most common type of training evaluation. It takes place during training delivery and at the end of the event.

Outcome Evaluation: Outcome evaluation determines whether or not the desired results (e.g., what participants are doing) of applying new skills were achieved in the short-term.

Outcome Evaluation answers the question, "What happened to the knowledge, attitudes, and behaviours of the intended population?"

This project would produce both "outcomes" and "impacts."

Outcome evaluation is a long-term undertaking.

Outcome evaluation answers the question, "What did the participants do?"

Because outcomes refer to changes in behaviour, outcome evaluation data is intended to measure what training participants were able to do at the end of training and what they actually did back on the job as a result of the training.

Impact Evaluation: Impact determines how the results of the training affect the strategic goal. Impact Evaluation takes even longer than outcome evaluation and you may never know for sure that your project helped bring about the change.

Impacts occur through an accumulation of "outcomes."

3.8 Training Design

Training design *pertains to the planning of the entire training programme*. A **training programme** can be defined as *"a programme that involves an interpretation of the training specification in terms of units of instructions or learning set out in chronological sequence showing the time allowed for each unit"*.

Training design starts with the identification of the goals and objectives that should be achieved. The design of the training programme can be undertaken only when a clear training objective has been stated.

The training objective clearly states what goal has to be achieved by the end of training program i.e. what the trainees are expected to be able to do at the end of their training. Training objectives assist trainers to design the training programme.

The topics or contents to be covered and the appropriate methodologies for the training programme are then determined. The corresponding visual aids and learning materials are also specified.

The training design is usually made by the training staff of the organisation and sometimes by outside consultants.

Designing of the 'Training Program' is one of the steps in the training process. While designing the training program, following important issues are generally considered.

(a) Who are the participants in the training programme? Who are the trainers and trainees?

(b) What methods, techniques, materials etc. are to be used for training?

(c) What should be the level of training?

(d) How and where is the training programme to be conducted?

From these important issues, one comes to know the purpose, method and format, the three important aspects of any training programme. Hence, learning goals and objectives, designing training activities, selection of trainers and trainees, sequence of training activities, selection of methods, materials, place etc. of training, evaluation of training programme and other certain aspects are considered while designing any training program.

A typical training design usually consists of the following:
- Training Title
- Venue
- Date
- Goal
- Specific Objectives
- Sequence of Topics
- Time Allocation per Topic
- Methodology
- Resources Needed
- Evaluation

The training objectives of the training design are a critical element that should be written properly to be able to decide on the contents, methodology and the duration of the training programme.

Important Considerations in Designing Training Programmes

In order to meet training and development needs of an organisation, various training programmes are designed from time to time. It is a continuous process. Many organisations organise their own training programmes with the help of training professionals and experts. But arrangements are also made for the employees to attend the training programmes organised by outside professional organisations. However, there are some important considerations which are taken into consideration while designing the training programmes. Important considerations are:

(1) Area of training contents
(2) Characteristics of trainees
(3) Key learning principles
(4) Cost of training.

Each of these considerations are discussed below in brief:

1. **Areas of Training content:** Information, acquisition of skills and abilities, decision-making skills and problem solving skills are important basic areas of training program content and generally, training programmes include more than one of these contents. The success of any training programme depends upon the identification of proper areas of training content.

2. **Characteristics of Trainees:** Characteristics of trainees is another important area of consideration which affect the choice of a training programme. While organising training programmes, number of trainees, their abilities, skills, attitudes, needs and other such factors are required to be taken into consideration. If an organisation decides to bring about major changes in its objectives, policies then it is obvious that every employee is required to be given training.

3. **Key Learning Principles:** Training is an organised procedure through which people acquire knowledge and various skills. It is rooted in the process of learning by which skills, knowledge, habits, attitudes etc. are acquired and utilised by the learners in such a way so that their behaviour is modified. Training endeavours to induce learning for bringing about a relatively permanent change in knowledge, skills, behaviour etc. Studies of human learning imply several principles which offer valuable guidance for designing training programmes. Some of the important learning principles are conditions of practice, knowledge of results, relevance of material and transfer of knowledge to the job. Training programmes are expected to motivate trainees to learn these principles and therefore, training methods selected should incorporate important key learning principles depending upon the area of training content.

4. **Cost of Training:** Cost of training is yet another consideration in designing a training programme. Budget size of a training programme depends upon the number of trainees, methods adopted for completing a training programme etc. Cost benefit analysis is done while dividing the budget of a training programme.

Thus, when training programmes are designed along with different aspects, objectives also need to be considered properly to make the programme effective.

3.9 Implementing Training Programmes (Training Methods)

To put a training programme into effect according to a definite plan or procedure is called training implementation. Training implementation is the hardest part of the system because one wrong step can lead to the failure of whole training programme. Even the best training program will fail due to one wrong action.

Training implementation can be segregated into:

- Practical administrative arrangements
- Carrying out of the training
- Implementing Training.

Once the staff, course, content, equipment, topics are ready, the training is implemented. Completing training design does not mean that the work is done because the implementation phase requires continual adjusting, redesigning, and refining. Preparation is the most important factor to taste the success. Therefore, following are the factors that are kept in mind while implementing training programme.

The Trainer: The trainer needs to be prepared mentally before the delivery of content. Trainer prepares materials and activities well in advance. The trainer also set grounds before meeting with participants by making sure that he is comfortable with course content and is flexible in his approach.

Physical set-up: Good physical set up is pre requisite for effective and successful training program because it makes the first impression on participants. Classrooms should not be very small or big but as nearly square as possible. This will bring people together both physically and psychologically. Also, right amount of space should be allocated to every participant.

Establishing rapport with participants: There are various ways by which a trainer can establish good rapport with trainees by:

- Greeting participants simple way to ease those initial tense moments
- Encouraging informal conversation
- Remembering their first name
- Pairing up the learners and have them familiarised with one another
- Listening carefully to trainees' comments and opinions
- Telling the learners by what name the trainer wants to be addressed
- Getting to class before the arrival of learners
- Starting the class promptly at the scheduled time
- Using familiar examples
- Varying his instructional techniques
- Using the alternate approach if one seems to bog down.

The trainer must tell the participants the goal of the programme, what is expected out of trainers to do at the end of the programme, and how the programme will run. The following information needs to be included:

- Kinds of training activities
- Schedule
- Setting group norms
- Housekeeping arrangements
- Flow of the programme
- Handling problematic situations

The success of training depends upon the selection of method or methods and ability and efficiency of the training officer to work closely with the management in constructing a training programme which is relevant to the needs of the employees and aims of the organisation. Therefore, a training programme is required to be formulated both in terms of needs and future possibilities.

Steps in a Training Programme

In order to make any training programme effective, it is very essential to understand fully the nature, needs and relevance of different jobs in the context of overall activities of an organisation. If the training is need-based, it can generate sufficient interest among the trainee-employees. As training programmes are a costly affair and a time consuming process, they are required to be drafted neatly and very carefully. Generally, while organising training programmes, the following steps are considered necessary:

(a) To set overall training objectives by identifying the training needs.

(b) Selection of trainees and trainers.

(c) To decide training methods, relevant training material etc.

(d) To decide the level of training to be given.

(e) To assess training timings and construction of time table in respect of the training programme.

(f) To decide the place for training to be given. To communicate the schedule to 'Trainees' well in advance to ensure attendance.

(g) To brief the trainers about the presentation of operations and knowledge and the trainees, the objectives, methods of training etc.

(h) To monitor, follow-up and evaluate the training programme.

Types of Training Programmes

A well organised training programme gives the management an opportunity to explain its policies, rules, procedures, regulation, objectives to the employees. These employees include unskilled, semi-skilled and skilled workers, salesmen, supervisors, etc.

Unskilled workers are given training to acquaint them with various methods of handling machines, materials, way of doing work in order to reduce the cost of production and waste and to perform their jobs in the most efficient way. Semi-skilled workers require training for coping with the requirements of an organisation arising out of adoption of rationalisation. Even skilled workers are given training to heighten their level of skills, abilities and capacities.

Besides the above mentioned types of employees, typists, clerks, computer operators, salesmen etc. also need training in their fields to improve their performances. As supervisory staff forms an important link in the chain of administration, they need training. The training imparted to supervisory staff helps them to cope with increasing demand of their organisation and to develop amongst them team spirit. Generally, the training programmes for supervisors are tailormade to suit the needs of their organisation. Some of the important aims of such programmes are as follows.

(a) To help the supervisors to improve their performance by gaining appropriate knowledge and acquiring necessary skills and abilities.

(b) To assist them to prepare for the greater responsibilities in their organisation at the higher level of management.

(c) To ensure their technical competence to enable them to know and properly understand the various processes and operations in which the employees participate.

(d) To build up the status of supervisors.

(e) To train the supervisors in those areas which are closely related to their day-to-day jobs.

Considering the needs of the employees training, different types of training programmes can be organised. Some of such types of training programmes are as follows:

(a) **Induction Training:** It is the initial training provided to employees on their admission to an organisation. The basic objective of such training is to introduce employees to the organisation in order for them to understand conditions of service, rules, nature of jobs or work to be done .etc. Such type of training is generally given during the probation period and under study schemes.

(b) **Job Training:** Job training programmes help the newly recruited employees to know and learn various technical aspects of their jobs. Such programmes help the employees to get an idea about handling of material equipment necessary for performing their jobs. Because of such programmes, they can work properly and chances of meeting accidents can be avoided or at least can be reduced to minimum.

(c) **Training for Promotions:** Such type of training programmes are obviously organised for the purpose of promotions of the employees. Many times, some vacancies are filled in through promotions. When the employees are to be promoted to occupy superior positions in the organisation, it becomes necessary to provide them some sort of training so that they are well prepared to shoulder their new responsibilities.

(d) **Supervisory Training:** As supervisors form a very important link in the chain of administration, the training to supervisors is considered very important and the areas of their training are generally as follows.

(i) Planning, allocation and control of work and employees

(ii) Control of production, materials handling and maintenance at the departmental level

(iii) Company's policies and practices

(iv) Personnel policies, procedures and programmes

(v) Communication, effective instructions, report writing

(vi) Grievance handling

(vii) Techniques of disciplinary procedures

(viii) Training of subordinates

(ix) Appraisal of employees, their rating

(x) Dealing with various problems such as absenteeism, tardiness, insubordination etc.

(xi) Leadership qualities

(xii) Industrial legislation and principles and practice of administration, management etc.

(xiii) Creativity and positive thinking.

This list is not complete. But training relating to supervisors jobs and responsibilities is given in training programmes organised for them and such programmes include supply of books, holding of staff meetings, visits to various other industrial organisations, job rotation in order to give them a wide inplant experience, lectures, role-playing, conferences, case studies etc. Institutes like the National Productivity Council (NPC), the Central Labour Institute at Bombay, Delhi etc. have done a great deal of work in this area.

(e) Management Development Training: This type of training proves to be very useful for people at different management levels. Such training helps to improve decision-making skills and bring about favourable changes in the attitudes of the people in management. Various institutions have been established to conduct short-run training courses. Various aspects of training programmes considering the area, subject, objects etc. are determined and training facilities are provided accordingly.

3.10 Methods of Training

Training methods are useful for attaining desired objectives in a learning situation. A variety of training methods are available and used by various organisations and training agencies. Many new training methodologies and techniques have been developed in recent past in order to meet certain specific needs. Every method has certain structured procedures for the conduct which offer definite advantages in developing qualities of trainees. However, at the same time they have certain limitations too. Therefore, while adopting a particular method, one has to take into consideration its strengths, weaknesses, objectives etc. under given circumstances and analyse its relevance, usefulness etc. As a matter of fact, the forms, types etc. of various training methods are inter-related. It is very difficult to say which of the method or their combination is more useful than the other. The best method under one situation and for a particular class of trainees may not be the best under another situation and for all classes of trainees. Therefore, it is considered that the choice of a method or combination of methods is a function of various considerations.

Some of the important considerations are as follow:

1. One of the most important consideration in the choice of methodology is the purpose of training. Training methods have a number of overlapping purposes or objectives. Demonstration value, development of interest amongst the trainees, motivation, gaining of knowledge and skills are important objectives of training methods. Knowledge can be provided by arranging lectures, organising seminars and by other such traditional methods, while skills, attitudes etc. can be developed by experiential methods of training such as T-group; on-job training methods.

2. The level of trainees in the hierarchy of the organisation is another consideration. To a great extent, this consideration determines the nature of the method of training. Techniques like in-basket exercise or management games are considered for management levels, as they are not very effective at worker's level.

3. The nature of training to be given or its contents also determine the nature of training methodology. Various concepts, theoretical aspects can be clarified through class-room lectures while various mechanical operations can be learned by adopting vestibule training or job instruction training method.

4. Every organisation has to give attention to the cost factor of training while selecting training method. But it is required to be seen that the cost consideration does not override the quality consideration.

Classification of Training Methods

Training methods can be classified in the following manner considering various objectives and needs of the training.

(a) Knowledge-based methods

(b) On the job oriented training methods

(c) Simulation methods

(d) Experimental methods.

(a) Knowledge-based training methods: Class-room lectures, educational training programmes, seminars, firms, group discussion and other such methods are included in this category of knowledge-based training methods. These methods are especially useful when employees are to be exposed to concepts, theories, basic principles etc. in a particular subject. They create awareness of knowledge of fundamentals amongst the employees who are to be trained.

(b) On the job oriented training methods: In the category of job oriented training methods, training methods such as on-the-job training, guidance and counselling, brainstorming sessions etc. are included. The main objectives of providing training through these methods centre around the job or jobs. It is expected that such methods should help to acquire skills, abilities and develop trainees through performance on the jobs.

(c) Simulation methods: Simulation technique plays an important role in the field of training. This technique duplicates as far as possible real life situations or conditions encountered on jobs. In other words, real-life situations are simulated or imitated for imparting training. Role play method, vestibule training method, in-basket exercise method, business game or management game method are some examples of business simulations. In the aeronautical industry, such types of methods are commonly used.

As the operations, actions etc. of trainees closely duplicate real job situations, motivation and interest of trainees are at a high level in simulation exercises. Such type of training is very much required where on the job-work might cause serious injuries to the employees or costly errors resulting in the destruction of valuable materials.

(d) Experiential methods: The experiential methods provide an atmosphere of self-learning through group interaction and dynamics. Obviously, the purpose is to increase the sensitivity of trainee participants to their own functions and also the functions of others in the group. T-group method also known as sensitivity training, transactional analysis, achievement motivation workshop and other such methods are included in this category of experiential methods. The basic objective of these methods is to integrate knowledge, principles and theories with experience and practice. Such knowledge and understanding of principles and theories help the trainees to understand the problems of human relationships in a work situation. More attention is paid to things such as listening ability and communicating properly with others, learning to give and receive feedback, understanding of complexities of group dynamics etc. Sensitivity training is a powerful tool in bringing about attitudinal changes.

Classification of 'Training Methods' on the basis of 'On-The-Job Training' and 'Off-The-Job Training'

There are various on-the-job training methods as well as off-the-job training methods.

On-the-job training is also known as job instruction training. A trainee is placed on a regular job and is taught certain required skills necessary to perform the job in the on-the-job training methods. He learns necessary skills and acquires them under the supervision and guidance of a qualified, experienced worker, instructor or supervisor. In on-the-job training methods, the trainees get first hand knowledge and experience under the actual working conditions. As the trainees learn how to perform their jobs under actual working conditions, the problem of their transfers is also solved. This is the great advantage of on-the-job training methods. These methods include job rotation, job instruction, coaching, committee assignment etc.

Under off-the-job training methods, trainees are separated from job situations. Attention is focused upon learning and knowledge required for performing the future jobs. As trainees are not distracted by job requirements, they can concentrate on learning and gaining knowledge relating to jobs rather than spending their time in performing the jobs entrusted to them.

Further, they also get the opportunities to discuss and express their opinions while learning. Off-the-job training methods include various methods such as Role Playing Method, Vestibule Training Method, Conference Method, Programmed Instruction Method, Lecture Method etc. all the above mentioned methods of training are also explained below:

Types of Training Methods

There are various types of training methods and aids used for imparting knowledge, training etc. Some important types of training methods and aids are as follows:

1. **Lectures:** Lecture method of training is one of the 'Off-the-Job-training' methods and is the oldest and traditional method of training. Off-the-Job-training implies that training is not a part of every day or routine job activity, but training is given in the class-room. Actual location of training given may be in the class-rooms of the company or colleges or universities or at such other places. Besides lectures, conferences, group discussions, role-playing, case studies etc. are examples of 'Off-the-Job training' methods.

Fig. 3.5: Lecture Method

Lectures are considered as the simplest ways of imparting necessary knowledge to trainees. In the lecture method, a trainer verbally presents necessary information to a group of trainees and makes clear concepts, principles, theories etc.

The lecture method is very useful when a large group of trainees is to be trained within a short period of time. Visual aids such as black-boards, power point slides, films etc. are used in conjunction with lectures. Audio-visual aids enhance the value of the lecture method.

The important merit of the lecture method is that it is very simple, efficient and effective and through this method, more knowledge can be imparted within a given time. Besides this, other merits of the lecture method are as follows –

(a) It provides a basic theoretical knowledge, introduces the subject properly and presents an overview of its scope which is very essential for the conduct of participative training sessions.

(b) By using the lecture method, large number of employees can be instructed at a time and thus the cost of training is reduced and time can also be saved.

(c) It is a direct method of training in which principles, theories, concepts etc. can be taught in a shorter period as compared to other methods of training. It also provides a common background for various other subsequent activities.

Limitations of Lecture Method

However, there are certain important limitations of the lecture method which are as follows:

(i) The learning method does not follow the principle of learning by doing. Except for questions from trainees, there is the one-way communication in the lecture method. For the most part during lectures, the trainees sit passively listening to the trainers or lecturers or take notes with little feedback. Thus, the trainees remain passive instead of being active participants.

(ii) Even though a lecturer or a trainer is an expert and possesses various skills who can adapt his material to the specific group of trainees; many times, he finds it very difficult to adjust with the group for individual differences within that group.

(iii) If the lecturer or trainer is not well trained and experienced, he may either ramble or give too much information in his lectures. Such lectures often become boring to the trainees and the presentation of material cannot be geared properly to a common level of knowledge.

(iv) If the group interest is not motivated and is not adapted to its needs, the trainees do not pay proper attention to the lectures and do not take part in discussions following the lectures. Moreover, the lecture method gives more importance to accumulation and memorisation of facts, figures, theories etc. and does not lay more stress on the application of knowledge gained. In addition to this point, it should be remembered that the attention span of listeners may range from 20 minutes to 30 minutes in the course of an hour and if any lecture continues beyond that, the attention of listeners' drifts.

Though there are many limitations of the lecture method, it has not lost its importance because of low cost per trainee and certain other advantages or merits.

2. Programed Instruction Method: This method is also known as 'Teaching by Machine Method'. In this method, information or knowledge is imparted either in a book form or through a teaching machine by way of programmed instructions. Programmed instructions are mainly based on behavioural laws particularly relating to principles of reinforcement. Here reinforcement implies reward for a correct response and punishment for a wrong response. In this method, instructions are designed in such a way that all future learning depends to a great extent on acquisition and retention of previous learning.

Program instructions involve breaking of information into various meaningful units and then arranging them in a proper way to form a sequential learning program. Thus, after studying each unit, a trainee understands related basic lessons. Subsequently, a trainee attempts the questions based on the basic learning. If the response is correct, he can go to the next stage. Otherwise, he has to go back and start again. Thus, feedback in the form of correct answers is provided after each response. Today, there are a number of programmed books available in various fields such as science, statistics and computers etc.

Some of the important advantages of this method are as follows:

(a) The trainees adjust their learning at a pace and rate suitable to them.

(b) As the course material is broken down into small units and well structured, trainees get opportunity for practice without the help of instructors. In this method, the role of instructors is minimised as they do not play a key role in learning.

(c) Programed instructions provide a high degree of reinforcement and knowledge of results and thereby motivate the trainees to learn the basic concepts, principles, theories etc. properly. This is achieved by focusing during training, on such aspects as ability to listen to others, to communicate, ability to diagnose the problem correctly and properly, understand complexities of group dynamics etc.

(d) Active learner participation takes place in this method at each stage in the programme wherein immediate feedback is available.

(e) As learning material is pre-arranged and organised, training can be imparted even at odd times and in odd places.

(f) A number of trainees can be given training at different times and in different locations.

However, there are certain demerits of this method which are as follows:

(i) Since learning situation is unlike the job situation, transfer of learning properly becomes a problem. Philosophical and attitudinal concepts, motor skills cannot be taught by this method.

(ii) Development costs of creating such programmes are high.

(iii) Only factual subject matters can be programed and an advanced study does not become possible until preliminary information is acquired and programmed appropriately.

3. Conference Method: This is also known as 'Discussion Method'. This method can be used more effectively for managerial training. In this method, participants confer to discuss various points of common interest to one another. The conference method is a directed discussion on a particular topic conducted for a relatively small group of trainees. Though this method is used for a variety of objectives, it is particularly suitable for acquiring and understanding conceptual data and also for the development or modification of attitudes. In a sense, it is a formal meeting conducted with an organised plan wherein the leader tries to develop knowledge and understanding of trainees by motivating them in a planned and structured way. Trainees get an opportunity of verbal interaction with the leader as well as with one another and therefore, this method is proven to be very useful for learning and exploring conceptual material and also for changing attitudes and opinions. Moreover, it provides an opportunity for feedback, reinforcement, motivation etc. due to active participation of trainees.

Though the conference method is very useful for analysing problems and examining trainees from different viewpoints, developing the conceptual knowledge, for reducing dogmatism and modifying their attitude, it suffers from the following important limitations.

(a) It is an expensive method as only a small group upto 20 trainees (whereas 16 is considered ideal size for the group) can be accommodated in this method more effectively. If large groups are formed, the active participation of all the trainees is not possible.

(b) In this method, generally all those willing to speak in the conference are generally allowed to present their views. Consequently irrelevant issues easily creep in and many times, fruitful discussion does not take place so that the main purpose of the conference is not served. Lot of diversion from the topic happens thus wasting time at the cost of planned inputs.

If the conference method is to be made more effective, the following points must be remembered.

(i) Selection of good and stimulating trainers or leaders should be done carefully so that they can summarise the material at appropriate times and think properly alongwith the participants to analyse and reach decisions during discussions. They should be able to control the more verbose participants, bringing out more reserved participants or conferees, develop their sensitivity to the thoughts and feelings and to ensure a general consensus on points without forcing agreement or side-stepping disagreement.

(ii) The group of trainees should be of small size limited upto twenty conferees so that each conferee may get an opportunity to participate and become personally involved in the deliberations.

(iii) Such conferees should be selected for participation in conference who have some basic knowledge of the subject to be discussed.

(iv) The topics, subject-matter or issues selected for discussion in the conference should be interesting to the conferees, so that they can participate properly in the conference and their difficulties, problems can be solved satisfactorily.

4. Case Method: This method is also known as "Learning by doing method" and is one of the popular methods of learning. It is based on the principle that managerial competence can best be attained through study, contemplation or proper thinking and discussion of certain cases pertaining to the business of the organisation. Each case is a set of data which can be real or fictional, written or an oral miniature description and summary of such data. Such information or data brings out certain issues, problems calling for solutions or actions on the part the trainees. Analysis of any case plays an important role and it requires problem identification, analysis of the situation and its causes. After analysing the cases, trainees are asked to recommend tentative alternative solutions.

The basic objective of the case study method is to help the trainees to learn to analyse the data and information, generate alternative decisions and also to evaluate the alternatives. Moreover, this method provides feedback and reinforcement due to thorough analysis of cases either through oral discussion in the class-room or written comments from the instructor. Trainees can learn to transfer necessary principles to examples of the problems. Another important aspect of this method is that often teams of trainees are made to come in a conclusion. Thus, trainees learn to appreciate need for consensus.

The case method or learning by doing method of training was first developed by *Christopher Langdell* of the *Harvard Law School* in the 1880s in order to help the students to learn by thinking independently various principles and their applicability. This method is primarily used as a training technique for supervisors for learning decision-making skills and for broadening their perspective. This is one of the least expensive methods of learning decision-making and problem-solving skills.

5. Role-Play: The credit of developing this method goes to a great Venetian psychiatrist, *Dr. Morano* who coined the terms 'role-playing' or 'role-reversal'.

In this method, the situation is described in a case format on the basis of a written script or an oral description of a particular situation, so that each trainee gets the same information. Two or more trainees are assigned certain roles to play before the rest of the trainees. Typical role playing situations are a manager conducting an interview, salesman making presentation of goods to purchasing agents, supervisors conducting an appraisal interview with an employee or discussing a grievance with an employee etc.

This method is widely used for human relations and leadership training. Role play teaches interpersonal skills by making two or more trainees interact within the context of a realistic situation. Because the trainees are required to place themselves in a simulated situation and play the roles assigned to them, it is really a method of human interaction which involves realistic behaviour in imaginary situation. *Norman Major* rightly pointed out that, "a role-playing experience demonstrates the gap between thinking and doing. The idea of role playing involves action, doing and practice."

In this method, more emphasis is laid on learning by doing wherein human sensitivity and interactions are stressed. This method is very useful to project living conditions between learning in a class-room and working on a job and creating a lively business situation in the classroom. It helps to develop skills and ability to apply knowledge already gained and brings about desired changes in the behaviour and attitudes of the trainees. However, the success of this method largely depends upon the skill, experience and abilities of the trainer. If not handled properly, it could turn into a childish exercise and instead of focusing on the problem or problems to be understood, the situation might get over-dramatised. Moreover, the cost of this method is also high because a large number of participants cannot be involved at one time.

6. T-group Training Method: The T-group method is also known as sensitivity training. Here 'T' stands for training. Generally, it is a small group exercise and around 10 to 15 participants can be accommodated, at a time, with one or two trainers. Participants meet the trainers and gain insight into their own and other's behaviour by discussing various points, aspects freely. As far as possible "structural relationship i.e. boss-subordinate relationship is purposely avoided in order to create an environment where participants can freely question the assumptions, concepts, values and understand them appropriately". In effect, it becomes 'a group dynamics laboratory in human relationship'. Therefore, many times, T-group or sensitivity training is also called the laboratory method of training where, the group experiments on itself.

The important objectives of T-group or sensitivity training generally include (1) better insight into one's own behaviour and the way one appears to others, (2) better understanding of group processes, and (3) development of various skills in diagnosing and intervening in group processes.

The T-group is the core element of sensitivity training and has the following important characteristics.

(i) No one has formal authority over the group and no one is given any special status in a group.

(ii) The training begins without any special established agenda. Participants are provided with professional journals, audio-visual aids etc. Records, tapes, films etc. are generally used in conjunction with other conventional methods of training such as lectures, group discussion etc.

(iii) No particular direction is given for problem solving and T-groups are highly involving and give trainees or participants certain opportunities to practice new behaviour.

7. **Job-instruction Training:** Job-instruction training is one of the older methods of on-the-job training. Every employee is expected to get some on-the-job training when he joins the organisation. On-the-job training methods such as job instruction training, coaching, vestibule training, job rotation etc. are commonly accepted and most widely used for providing training to employees for acquiring certain skills and abilities for job performance. In on-the-job training methods, trainees/employees learn, in one way or the other, their jobs and acquire certain skills, abilities etc. under the watchful eyes of master mechanics or craftsmen. Trainees/employees are coached, instructed and trained by skilled co-workers, supervisors or by special training instructors. Trainees learn their jobs by personal observations, practice and occasionally handling of equipment and machines. It is really learning by doing and proves to be very useful for those jobs which are either very difficult to stimulate or which can be learned easily and quickly by watching and doing.

Job instruction training method is also referred to as "Tell, show, do and review" or "training through step-by-step learning method" because of its various steps. This method involves listing various necessary steps required to perform the job and these steps are arranged in a proper sequence which show what is to be done at various levels. Generally, the actual training follows the following steps:

(a) The preparation of the trainees for instructions. The trainees are given proper instructions necessary to perform their job duties and responsibilities.

(b) The trainees are shown how to work and perform their duties. This includes positioning the trainees at the work site, telling and showing them each step or process involved in the job. This helps the trainees to understand why and how each step is carried out.

(c) Thus, the trainees are allowed to gain work experience and if there are any errors, they are corrected.

(d) The trainers are given opportunities to get their difficulties solved by encouraging the trainees to ask questions and allowing them to work alongwith trainers.

The job instruction training method provides quick feedback on results, immediate correction of errors besides provision of extra practice whenever required. However, it demands skilled, experienced and able trainers. If on-the-job training is well planned and structured, this method can be very effective. This is considered as an excellent method, though somewhat costly in terms of trainers time, since it requires trainees to be monitored closely.

8. **Coaching:** Coaching or understudy method, which is also known as **'internship'** and **'apprenticeship'** method, is also a on-the-job training method. Under this method, a trainer or a coach works with one or a few trainees. He assigns tasks to trainees, monitors their behaviour and also provides reinforcement and feedback. Coaching can be used for all kinds of trainees, from unskilled to managerial. However, **internship** is usually applied to managerial personnel while apprenticeship is generally used to impart skills requiring long period of practice usually required in trade, crafts and technical fields.

The effectiveness of the coaching method is mainly dependent upon the abilities, skills and quality of the trainer or coach. This method is time consuming and expensive if only one trainer or coach has to serve as a full-time coach for only one or a few trainees.

9. **Vestibule Training:** The dictionary meaning of Vestibule is 'entrance hall or porch' and as such the term 'vestibule training' implies the initial training which is generally given in a classroom in the form of lectures, conferences, case studies, role-playing, discussion etc. to especially semi-skilled personnel, clerks etc. when many employees have to be trained for the same kind of work at the same time.

Vestibule training is very much like job instruction training except that it occurs off-the-job in a class-room which is away from the production area. In vestibule training, procedures, equipment etc. similar to those used for the actual job are set up in a special working area called a vestibule and trainees are taught how to perform their jobs by the trainers. Thus, the trainees learn their jobs without the pressures of production schedule. The main aim is learning new skills rather than performing actual jobs and therefore the emphasis is not given on production. Thus, using this method, trainees are typically taught how to use the machinery, tools etc. while on-the-job. This method is often used to train clerks, semi-skilled workers, bank tellers, machine operators, typists, testers etc. and it proves to be very effective especially when philosophical concepts, theories, attitudes, problem solving techniques and abilities are to be taught.

Merits of Vestibule Training

Some of the important advantages or merits of the vestibule training are as follows:

(a) As this method attempts to duplicate on-the-job situation in a class-room or at other suitable places and training is often imparted with the help of equipment and machines which are identical with those used at the work place, the trainees can concentrate on learning and give more emphasis on practice.

(b) There is no fear of loss even if mistakes are committed by the trainees.

(c) As training is imparted in a separate room, distractions are minimised, so training becomes more effective. Trainees can develop necessary skills and abilities in a pressure-free environment.

(d) At a time, more employees can be provided training under this method, thus keeping the cost of training to the minimum.

Though learning principles are followed in vestibule training, there are certain problems with the transfer of learning unless machinery, tools and other equipments are identical to those actually used on-the-job. Besides this limitation the important disadvantages or demerits of this method are as given below.

Demerits of Vestibule Training

(i) This method is expensive because additional investment in training equipment is required to be done.

(ii) This method is of limited value for the jobs which utilise machinery and equipment which cannot be duplicated.

(iii) The training situation created is somewhat artificial and therefore, trainees have to face certain difficulties to adjust with the actual production work.

10. Job Rotation: Job rotation is one of the methods of on-the-job-oriented training. Job rotation is a frequently used training method. In job rotation, management trainees are made to move from job to job at certain intervals. The jobs vary in content.

The main purpose of job rotation is to broaden the knowledge and exposure of the trainees. When the trainees are rotated periodically from one job to another job, they gather more experiences concerning skills and knowledge.

The trainees may rotate through (a) non-supervisory work, (b) various managerial training positions, (c) middle-level assistant positions, (d) there is even unspecified rotation to various managerial positions in different departments such as production, finance, purchase, sales etc.

If job rotation is well planned, it provides a general background to the trainees and demonstrates the nature and significance of management principles. Moreover, training takes place in practical situations and competition can be stimulated among the trainees. A more co-operative attitude by exposing trainees to their colleagues problems and view points can be created. Though, the idea of job rotation is good, there are certain difficulties. As the term indicates, in some job rotation programmes, participants do not actually have managerial authority. They merely observe or assist the managers without any responsibility. Even in rotations to managerial positions, the participants in the training programme may not remain in each position for a long time to prove their future effectiveness as managers. Moreover, when the rotation programme is over, there may not be suitable positions available for the newly trained managers. Inspite of these difficulties or drawbacks, if the inherent difficulties, problems or drawbacks are properly understood by both managers and trainees, job rotation method of training has certain positive aspects and hence it benefits the trainees.

11. Business or Management Games: In this method of training, real-life situations are simulated for imparting training. Business or management games are classroom simulation exercises wherein teams of trainees are formed, which compete against one another or against an environment in order to achieve given objectives. Business or management games technique requires trainees to make sequential decisions. These games are more dynamic than case studies since decisions made early in the games affect the alternatives available later in the games and their outcome.

The games are built around the models of business situations and trainees are divided into teams representing the management of competing companies. Under these, an atmosphere is created in which the trainees play a dynamic role and enrich their skills through involvement and simulated experience. Thus, they simulate the real-life process of taking decisions.

When games are expressed in the form of a mathematical model, controlled and manipulated by a computer, decisions are analysed by a computer and a series of implications of these decisions are feedback. Thus, quicker, feed-back is available, clerical work is avoided and time is controlled. Some games are interacting type of games, while others are non-interacting types. The games are played in several rounds to take the time dimensions into account.

Usually, games consist of several teams and each team consists of 2 to 7 members. Trainees-work by themselves or in teams in which each trainee takes the role of the manager of a functional area such as personnel, finance, marketing and so on. Teams take various decisions regarding production, prices, expenditure, marketing etc. and attempt to maximise hypothetical profits or benefits in the simulated environment. Each game continues for 6 to 12 periods as required and at the end of that period, final results are worked out by each team which are compared with those of other teams.

Trainees usually regard these games as highly involving and motivating since a score is kept and trainees compete each other. These games are intended to teach trainees how to take various managerial decisions in an integrated manner. They learn by analysing problems to take proper decisions. These games also illustrate various group processes such as communication, the emergence of leadership, resolution of conflicts, development of ties of friendship etc.

Though these games are relatively expensive to develop and practise, properly developed and well-run games definitely provide an unique method of teaching trainees how to analyse information, make decisions and work within the context of the decisions. It is a good technique to develop problem solving and leadership skills.

12. In-Basket Exercise Method: This is one of the simulation type training method designed around the incoming mail of a manager. In this method, trainees are provided with a file of correspondence relating to a functional area of management. Each trainee has to study the file and to make his own recommendations on the situation. If required, necessary information is supplied. A variety of situations is presented which would usually be dealt with by an executive in his working day. His reactions, observations, responses etc. noted and then analysed. They are then put down in the form of a report. For this purpose, the incident method, the syndicate method, conference method or other such methods are used.

The feedback on a trainee's decisions forces him to reconsider his administrative actions as well as his behavioural style. In-basket technique can be developed for any type of job involving managerial or professional decision-making. It has very good motivational properties and also provides opportunities for growth. The value of this method as a training technique depends to a large extent upon the amount of feed-back and reinforcement.

13. Behavioural Modelling: It is comparatively a newer technique for training and teaching interpersonal skills and attitudinal change. By presenting the best model of behaviour to be learned and by allowing the trainees to follow the modelled behaviour, behaviour modelling helps to teach specific supervisory skills. However, this technique requires that specific behavioural models be developed with the help of films, audio-visual videotapes.

This technique of training is flexible enough to make available sufficient time and opportunities to slower learners placing trainees at different levels in various groups.

This method is a relatively expensive training method because of two important reasons i.e. (1) in this method, videotapes, film etc. are to be developed and used which is a costly affair and (2) at a time, only 9 to 12 trainees can be included in a group for imparting training.

14. Brainstorming Sessions: Brainstorming sessions are very helpful in determining training needs specially of a particular group. This technique consists of involving professionals from different backgrounds and assigning them a particular task. Time limit is fixed for completing the task entrusted. After the sessions are over, the ideas generated are closely analysed, scruitinised and conclusions drawn. The variety of backgrounds in various brainstorming sessions is of immense use and significance as it facilitates different views. Moreover, these sessions also reveal what type of training is required for performing various tasks. One of the most important aspect of these sessions is that all the ideas are noted and no on the spot judgements are passed.

15. Multiple-Management Method: This method is also known as 'Participation in deliberations of the junior board and committees'. It is a method in which advisory Board or committees are established to study the actual problems of the organisation. Junior managers or employees get an opportunity to participate in this method. Once the problems have been discussed, different alternative solutions for solving the problems are suggested after which proper decisions are taken. This method is relatively inexpensive and helps to identify the members who have the skills, abilities, capabilities of an effective manager. This method is suitable for middle and senior level managers.

16. Incident Method: *Paul* and *Faith Pigors* developed this method of training which aims to develop employees in the areas of intellectual ability, practical judgement and social awareness. These qualities are essential for self-development. Under this method, each trainee participates in group process. Incidents are prepared on the basis of actual situations which have happened in different organisations. Every trainee in the group is asked to study the incident and to make decisions in the role of an executive or a manager who has to cope with the incident in the actual situation. In this method, the trainees in the group study and discuss the incident for taking certain decisions relating to the incident. There is group interaction for taking decisions. Efforts are made to find out about the what, when, where and how of the situation in which the incident developed. This helps the trainees to learn properly and every one in the group gets a chance to participate. This method is similar to a combination of case method and in-basket method.

17. Managerial Grid or Grid Training Method: This method was developed by *Robert R. Blake* and *Jane S. Moutan* for upgrading, managerial skills and improving group relations. It is a five or six phase programme lasting from three to five years. The grid represents many possible leadership styles and each style has a combination of two basic orientations i.e. (1) Concern for people, and (2) Concern for production. The phases include conference, discussion, outlining of procedures for accomplishing the organisation's development targets, evaluation and beginning of discussion on other or new problems.

18. Committee Assignment Method: Under this method, a group of trainees is given a certain assignment involving an actual organisational problem and asked to find out the solution for the same. The trainees make the efforts to solve the problem jointly and learn the skills of problem solving though this exercise. This method helps to develop team-work and understand group dynamics.

3.11 Implementing Management Development Programmes

Executives and Managers need to constantly innovate and evolve practical ideas about critical management issues. In the ICE-age (Information, Communication, Entertainment), it is mandatory for all to think beyond the confines of one's discipline and administrative responsibilities. These ideas can be evolved through carefully structured developmental initiatives. In this context, Management Development Programmes (MDPs) provide a chance to; complement natural skills with new knowledge, identify opportunities for growth and build individual strengths. The idea is to incorporate broader strategic considerations into management decisions.

The manager is the person responsible for planning and directing the work of a group of individuals, monitoring their work and taking corrective actions whenever necessary. Managers may direct the workers directly or they may direct several supervisors who direct the workers. The manager must be familiar with the work of all the groups he/she supervises, but does not need to be the best in any or all of the areas. It is more important for the manager to know how to manage the workers than to know how to do their work.

Management Development is a systematic process of management training and growth by which individuals gain and apply knowledge, skills, insights and attitudes to manage the departmental activities effectively. Training is the process of skill formation and skill improvement and development is the growth process of the person as a whole. Through Management Development Programmes, managers can be made competent and capable of decision making and meeting all the exigencies that arise.

Training managers to undertake their responsibilities in general includes the following aspects:

- Enabling learning.
- Facilitating meaningful personal development.
- Helping them to identify and achieve their own personal potential.

Development is not restricted to training. It is anything that helps a person to grow in abilities, skills, confidence, tolerance, commitment, initiative, inter-personal skills, understanding, self-control, motivation etc.

The main attribute which makes people really effective as managers is their attitude. This is true whether they are leaders, managers, operators or technicians. Skills, knowledge and the processes available to people provide very limited advantage. What makes people effective and valuable for an organisation is their attitude.

Attitude includes qualities that require different training and learning methods. Attitude stems from a person's mind-set, belief system, emotional maturity, self-confidence and experience. These are the greatest training and development challenges faced and there are better ways of achieving this sort of change and development than putting them in a classroom or delivering different types of conventional business or skills training which people see as a chore.

Hence, training and learning must extend far beyond the conventional classroom training courses. If a person is creative, innovative and open-minded, he/she will discover learning in virtually every new experience, whether it concerns him/her, the team or the organisation. If a person wants to make a difference, he/she has to think about what really helps people change. The models used for management development programmes are discussed at the end of this chapter.

A manager's title reflects what he/she is responsible for. An Accounts Manager supervises the accounting function. An Operations Manager is responsible for the operations within the company. The Manager of Design Engineering supervises engineers and their support staff. As there are many management functions in an organisation, there are many managerial titles. Regardless of the title, the manager is responsible for planning, directing, monitoring and controlling the people and their work. His job is to improve performance. To do this, he has to ensure that each employee is in the right role and is able to contribute to the performance of the department.

Managers need to be multidimensional personalities, as they have to manage various situations and people with different backgrounds and capabilities. To be effective, they have to develop a number of skills such as:

- Leadership
- Team management
- Decision making
- Problem solving
- Project planning and management
- Information and analytical capabilities
- Communication
- Memory
- Stress management.

These are the soft skills or people skills which would help the manager to plan the departmental activities, lead the people, guide them and motivate them, resolve conflicts and rise to the occasion when problems arise. He/she should have excellent written and spoken skills to communicate the goals of the organisation and the expectations from the employees. He/she should be able to meet the stress and pressures with a positive approach.

Like all other skills, managerial skills also need to be updated from time to time as the business environment and the challenges the organisation faces change. Therefore, managers must accept the need for continuous education, training and development to improve their abilities. Management or executive development has been the most prominent area of personnel or human resource management. It is also called Management Revolution.

As the business environment is becoming highly competitive, management development is assuming greater importance. Managers have to undergo relevant training skills to stay ahead. It is in their interest that they attend these programmes and grow in the organisational hierarchy.

There are two ways to provide development opportunities for the managers:
1. Active and intelligent participation in management training programmes.
2. Learning the technique of management through actual job experiences in the work environment itself.

No person can be developed without his/her own interest, thus, self-development is an important component of any management development program.

Principles of Management Development

A Management Development Programme should be based on the following principles:
1. All developments pertaining to managers essentially are self-development.
2. Development programmes should recognise individual differences.
3. Development is a long-term process and a manager cannot produce results overnight after a training programme.

Objectives/Aims of Planned Management Development Programmes

1. To ensure that the organisation is staffed both, now and in the future, with a sufficient number of managers with the necessary skills, experience and abilities to secure continued growth and profitability.
2. To check that the human resources in the organisation are being properly and fully utilised or in other words, to ensure optimum utilisation of the human capital.
3. To provide an opportunity for the staff within a company to prepare themselves for higher assignments and to reach their maximum capabilities.

In addition, there are many other objectives such as prevention of managerial obsolescence, preparation for new businesses and expansion, to replace old executives with younger talent and to promote high morale and a good organisational climate to promote productivity, profit etc.

Areas contributing to Management Development

There are three areas in which management development training can contribute to build the capabilities of managers:
- Knowledge
- Skills
- Attitudes

The content of the management development programmes would depend on the difference between the level they are performing on and the level they are expected to perform on. At the lower levels, managers need considerable technical skills, whereas at higher levels they need considerable administrative skills. To impart this knowledge, various methods can be used.

Models for Management Development Programmes

All supervisors and managers should be provided training and opportunities for development. The top management should ensure that this training develops people, improves their performance and raises their morale. It should be seen that it raises the level of their emotional maturity. Training and developing people and enabling them to learn increases health and effectiveness of the organisation and the productivity of the business. It helps in improving the quality, customer satisfaction, productivity, morale, management succession, business development and profitability. The focus is on developing the person and not the skills.

The ethics, values and behaviour of the leaders set the standard for their subordinates and the effect of any training and development program is seen in how they apply it. Training can be effective only if there is motivation to apply it effectively.

The leaders have to see things from the subordinate's point of view and provide learning opportunities and experiences that they would like for their own personal interest, development and fulfilment. Performance and capabilities are ultimately dependent on the people's attitude and their emotional maturity. If they are helped to develop themselves according to what they want to achieve on a personal level, this provides a platform for trust, emotional contracting or bonding with the organisation and for the subsequent development of required skills, processes and knowledge etc.

Participative workshops work well in initiating this type of attitudinal development. A questionnaire could be developed to understand what they want with examples of 'alternative' learning opportunities. When people develop confidence, integrity and emotional maturity, they automatically become more proactive, solutions focused and responsive, which would have a cumulative effect on the team.

Model 1: Johari's Model

Very often, in organisations, the people at work function without questioning anything. This conformity or risk aversion is often because they feel insecure, lack confidence to do what they think is right or are nervous about being bold. This stops their creativity and initiative to take greater responsibility. Boldness cannot be taught, but through development activities they can be motivated to take risks. This motivation is not just seen in financial returns, but as an opportunity to grow in the organisation, extra responsibility, recognition and involvement in new and interesting projects.

Human Resource Management — Training and Development

The Johari Window model was developed by American psychologists **Joseph Luft** and **Harry Ingham** in the 1950s while researching group dynamics. Luft and Ingham gave the name 'Johari' to this model after combining their first names, Joe and Harry. The Johari Window soon became a widely used model for understanding and training self-awareness, personal development, improving communications, interpersonal relationships, group dynamics, team development and inter-group relationships.

This model is a simple and useful tool for illustrating and improving self-awareness and mutual understanding between individuals within a group. It can also be used to assess and improve a group's relationship with other groups. Today, the Johari Window is especially relevant due to the recognition of the importance of training in 'soft' skills, behaviour, empathy, cooperation, inter-group development and interpersonal development.

The Johari Window is also referred to as a 'disclosure/feedback model of self-awareness' and by some people as the 'information processing' tool, as it actually represents information such as feelings, experiences, views, attitudes, skills, intentions, motivation etc., within or about a person in relation to their group and also for a group in relation to another.

Regions or Areas or Quadrants in a Johari Window

Johari's model is based on a four square grid which represents:

1. What is known to the person about himself/herself and is also known to others - open area, open self, free area, free self or 'the arena'.

2. What is unknown to the person about himself/herself but which others know - blind area, blind self or 'blind spot'.

3. What the person knows about himself/herself that others do not know - hidden area, hidden self, avoided area, avoided self or 'facade'.

4. What is unknown to the person about himself/herself and is also unknown to others - unknown area or unknown self.

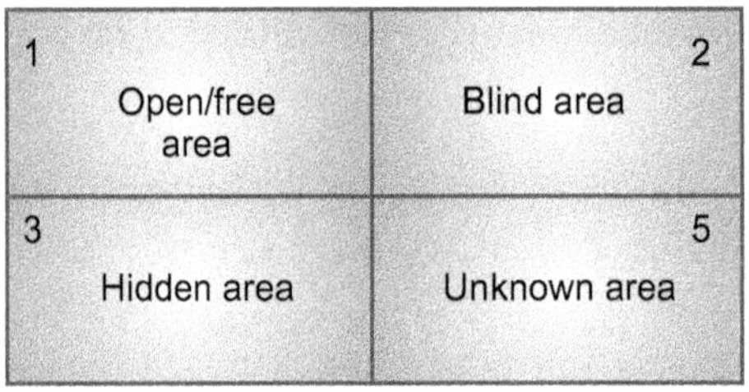

1 Open/free area	2 Blind area
3 Hidden area	5 Unknown area

Fig. 3.6: Quadrants of a Johari Window

The figure shown above is the standard representation of the Johari Window model, showing each quadrant having the same size. The size of the quadrants can be altered depending on the relevant proportions of each type of knowledge. As the team member becomes better established and known, the size of his/her open/free area quadrant increases. By analysing the information in each 'area', development programmes can be designed to suit the individual or group.

Model 2: Emotional Intelligence (EQ)

The Emotional Intelligence Theory, as a behavioural model, was originally developed during the 1970's and 80's by the work and writings of psychologists **Howard Gardner** (Harvard), **Peter Salovey** (Yale) and **John Mayer** (New Hampshire). Emotional Intelligence is increasingly relevant to organisational development and developing people, because these principles provide a new way to understand and assess people's behaviours, management styles, attitudes, interpersonal skills and potential. Emotional Intelligence is an important consideration in human resources planning, job profiling, recruitment interviewing and selection, management development, customer relations, customer service etc. This theory gained prominence with **Daniel Goleman's** 1995 book called 'Emotional Intelligence'.

Emotional Intelligence strongly links the concepts of love and spirituality, bringing compassion and humanity to work and also to multiple intelligence theory, which illustrates and measures the range of capabilities people possess and the fact that everybody has a value.

According to the EQ concept, IQ or the conventional intelligence quotient is too narrow as it ignores essential behavioural and character elements and that there are wider areas of emotional intelligence that dictate and enable how successful one is. It does not follow that academically brilliant people will always succeed. If they are socially and inter-personally inept, all that intelligence would be of no avail.

The essential premise of EQ is that, to be successful one has to have effective awareness, control and management of one's own emotions and those of other people. EQ covers two aspects of intelligence:

- Understanding yourself, your goals, intentions, responses, behaviour etc.
- Understanding others and their feelings.

The five 'domains' of EQ identified by Goleman are:

1. Knowing your emotions.
2. Managing your own emotions.
3. Motivating yourself.
4. Recognising and understanding other people's emotions.
5. Managing relationships, i.e., managing the emotions of others.

Emotional Intelligence encloses and draws from numerous other branches of behavioural, emotional and communication theories, such as NLP (Neuro-Linguistic Programming), Transactional Analysis and empathy. A person can become more productive and successful and can help others to be more productive and successful too by developing his/her Emotional Intelligence in these areas and the five EQ domains. The process and outcomes of Emotional Intelligence development also contain many elements known to reduce stress for individuals and organisations by decreasing conflict, improving harmonious relationships and understanding, increasing stability and continuity.

Model 3: Transactional Analysis and Leadership

Transactional Analysis (TA) is a very useful and fascinating framework for analysing the behaviour of both individuals and other people who come into contact with them. It offers some very useful insights into the impact of different behavioural styles on relationships between people.

It was defined and evolved by **Dr. Eric Berne**, who argued that in everyone there existed three quite clearly distinguishable sets of attitudes and behaviours. He called these **ego states**, i.e., configurations of states or frames of mind. These are readily recognisable by the things that people say, the ways in which they say them and the ways in which they use body language to support their statements. The ego states are, 'parent', 'adult' and 'child'.

TA involves using knowledge and skills to recognise the frames of mind. This knowledge helps a person to choose the frame of mind that he/she would like to adopt, which in turn, determines whether the transaction, i.e., the communication, is to be effective, ineffective, business-like or a crossed transaction leading to a misunderstanding.

Transactional Analysis is a wide ranging set of theories and techniques that can be used by individuals and groups to enable and help themselves and also others to grow and develop to their full potential.

The underlying philosophy is one of self-respect and mutual respect and caring. It is a very useful and fascinating framework for analysing the behaviour of both oneself and other people. It allows one to see how ones behaviour is interpreted by others.

Briefly, transactional analysis shows us that people relate to each other in one of 3 ways:
- Parent to child - telling others what to do, talking down to them.
- Child to parent - being submissive, throwing temper tantrums and flaunting authority.
- Adult to adult - relating as equals, reason dominating emotion.

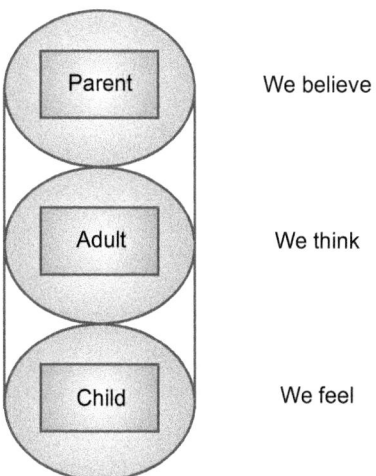

Fig. 3.7: Transactional Analysis: Ways of Relating

The understanding of what TA refers to as frame of mind indicates that an adult can display any of the above relationships in his/her communications or transactions leading to any of the following positions:

- An adult is not as 'grown-up' as he/she thinks. Sometimes his/her emotions can get the better of him/her, making him/her revert to either the parent or child mode.
- Any time a person loses his/her temper and shouts revenge, he/she is operating in either parent or child mode or a bit of both.
- Paternalistic nurturing, coaching and sympathising with people is also a form of parent-child way of relating to people.
- In some ways, the emotional intelligence approach is an attempt to make people behave more in an adult way as far as possible.
- An adult-adult relationship helps to reduce emotional distortions in communications. However, in a traditional superior-subordinate top-down relationship, the authoritative position of the superior fosters a parent-child mode of relationship. Any attempt to bring it to an adult-adult mode will not sustain because of the reality of the power differential. Hence, a conception of leadership which is not based on power of a higher position can promote an adult-adult mode of relationships.
- This indicates that leadership qualities can be developed. However, true leadership is harder for managers to display simply because there is a thin line which demarcates genuine influence and authority. The question may rise in the minds of the subordinates whether the superior is genuinely trying to give some new direction or he/she is politely giving an instruction.

It should be noted that none of the frames of mind (ego states) is intrinsically "better" than the others, but each is appropriate in different situations and will have a different effect on those with whom one communicates.

An understanding of these positions or mindsets would help the managers to make positive changes in their approach towards their subordinates. This will promote better understanding, reduce conflicts and promote more harmonious relationships in the organisation.

There are many ways in which TA can be applied to enhance people skills.
Conflict often begins when a person approaches with an ulterior motive or it may be that sometimes people infer an ulterior motive when none was intended. Either way, the result would be a conflict. However, knowledge about the internal ego states would give an opportunity for the person to modify his/her behaviour or understand the other person better. Either way, conflict is avoided. The options are:

- Natural child would let them know that one is hurt by the criticism. They may not have realised that they have said something unkind.
- An adopted child could accept the criticism as justified and ask how they want one to be different. Adult could be employed to question the basis of the criticism and discuss what one might decide to change.
- Controlling Parent could tell them firmly that they are criticising unjustly or unhelpfully.
- Nurturing Parent could reassure them that the action will not cause a problem for them.

This model highlights that a successful communicator is flexible and chooses an appropriate parent, adult or child state to understand people, meet their needs and get the desired results. He/she is an active listener, thinks more broadly and is more effective as he/she has heard different points of view. He/she has fewer on-the-job problems. With his/her superior understanding of the situation, he/she is better equipped to face the challenges that change brings about.

Points to Remember

- *Training is a planned, organised and controlled activity designed to express some aspect or aspects of present job performance. Training is skill oriented and it is usually intended for the short run welfare of the economy (i.e. organisation). Training is also a key ingredient in the motivation of individuals. An untrained, unskilled employee feels very insecure, lacking the self-condifence necessary for comfortable group relations*

- **Training Process**
    (1) Identification of training needs.
    (2) Deciding the objectives of training to be given.
    (3) Designing of the training program or programmes.
    (4) Selection of trainees and trainers.
    (5) Selection of training methods and tools.
    (6) Administration and implementation of training programmes.
    (7) Evaluation of training.
- **Training is given to the employees in order –**
    (i) to enhance the existing knowledge, skills and abilities, performance capabilities of the employees and to acquire new skills, abilities, knowledge for improving their qualities.
    (ii) to increase efficiency and productivity of the employees.
    (iii) to help an organisation to fulfil its future personnel needs.
    (iv) to improve health and safety of employees.
    (v) to prevent wastages, wear and tear, obsolescence etc.
    (vi) to improve organisational climate.
    (vii) to help employees achieve personal growth and development.
    (viii) to improve morale of employees.
    (ix) to keep abreast of (i.e. up to date with) developments in technical and management fields and also to inculcate a sense of appreciation for other functional areas and an understanding of the linkage of their activities with other areas.
    (x) to induct new employees into the organisation.
- The success of training depends upon the selection of method or methods and ability and efficiency of the training officer to work closely with the management in constructing a training programme which is relevant to the needs of the employees and aims of the organisation. Therefore, a training program is required to be formulated both in terms of needs and future possibilities.
- **Steps in a Training Programme**
    (a) To set overall training objectives by identifying the training needs.
    (b) Selection of trainees and trainers.

(c) To decide training methods, relevant training material etc.

(d) To decide the level of training to be given.

(e) To assess training timings and construction of time table in respect of the training program.

(f) To decide the place for training to be given. To communicate the schedule to 'Trainees' well in advance to ensure attendance.

(g) To brief the trainers about the presentation of operations and knowledge and the trainees, the objectives, methods of training etc.

(h) To monitor, follow-up and evaluate the training programme.

- **Types of Training Programmes**
    1. Induction Training
    2. Job training
    3. Training for promotions
    4. Supervisory training
    5. Management development training

Classification of Training Methods

(a) Knowledge-based methods

(b) On the job oriented training methods

(c) Simulation methods

(d) Experimental methods

Types of Training Methods

1. Lectures
2. Program Instruction Method
3. Conference Method
4. Case Method
5. Role - Play
6. T-Group Training Method
7. Job Instruction Training
8. Coaching
9. Vestibule Training
10. Job Rotation

    11. Business or Management Games
    12. In Basket Exercise Method
    13. Behavioural Modelling
    14. Brainstorming Sessions
    15. Multiple Management Method
    16. Incident Method
    17. Managerial Grid
    18. Committee Assignement Method
- ***Training evaluation*** *is nothing but the systematic collection and assessment of information for how best to utilise training resources in order to achieve organisational goals.*
- ***Training Evaluation Systems Process***
    1. Kirkpatrick's View
    2. Tracey's view
    3. Hamblin's view

Questions For Discussion

1. What is training? Explain training needs and objectives.
2. Define training and explain its importance in human resource development.
3. What are the segments of training? Explain various techniques for determining training needs.
4. How should one go about identifying training needs in an organisation?
5. Why is the formulation of training policy considered essential? Explain the various objectives of training.
6. What is 'training programme'? Describe the various types of training programmes.
7. Define a training programme and discuss important considerations in deciding training programmes.
8. What is training? Explain the different methods of training.
9. Explain the various types of training methods and aids.
10. Define training evaluation and explain training evaluation systems.
11. Explain the importance of training in management development.
12. Discuss the various reasons for the growing demand for development programmes for managers and executives.
13. Explain important considerations in evaluating training effectiveness.
14. Discuss various factors in evaluating training effectiveness.
15. Which of the methods of training are most suited for managerial training and why?
16. How would you identify the training needs of a supervisor?

17. What criteria would you use to evaluate a training programme? Give reasons.
18. Give a brief account of methods of 'on the job' and 'off the job training'. Explain the advantages of training.
19. Write short notes on the following:
    (a) Meaning of training
    (b) Identification of training needs
    (c) Objectives of training
    (d) Importance of training
    (e) Training programmes
    (f) Methods of training
    (g) Evaluation of training programmes
    (h) Training Process
    (i) Tools and Aids of Training
    (j) On-the-job training methods
    (k) Off-the-job training methods

Multiple Choice Questions (MCQ)s

1. Career counseling is included in which of the functions of HRM?
   (a) Compensation and benefits
   (b) Planning and selections
   (c) Training and Development
   (d) Maintaining HRIS

2. The process by which people acquire skills and abilities required to perform jobs at hand, is known as ....
   (a) Learning
   (b) Training
   (c) Development
   (d) Need analysis

3. Organisation, where employees are provided with the opportunity to learn on continous basis is known as ....
   (a) Formal
   (b) Informal
   (c) Bureaucratic
   (d) Learning

4. Socialisation process of newly hired employees is usually conducted by ....
   (a) Marketing department
   (b) HR department
   (c) Accounts department.
   (d) All the above

ANSWERS

| 1. (c) | 2. (b) | 3. (d) | 4. (b) |

QUESTIONS FROM PREVIOUS PUNE UNIVERSITY EXAMINATIONS

1. Why Training to Employees has become essential in Industries in Recent Decades? Why Training Need Evaluation? **M.B.A. December 2005**

Ans. Refer Articles 3.6 and 3.7 of this chapter.

2. Explain the Need and Objectives of Training. **M.B.A. April 2006**

Ans. Refer Article 3.6 of this chapter.

3. What is the Need and Objectives of Training in the Organisation? Why Training Programmes should be Evaluated? **M.B.A. April 2007**

Ans. Refer Articles 3.6 and 3.7 of this chapter.

4. Explain the importance of Training and Development and further describe the need for evaluation of training programmes. **M.B.A. April 2009**

Ans. Refer Article 3.6 of this chapter.

5. Discuss in detail the objectives and Need of Training in any Organisation. **M.B.A. December 2009**

Ans. Refer Article 3.6 of this chapter.

6. What is Training and Development? Explain various Methods of Training in detail. **M.B.A. April 2010**

Ans. Refer Articles 3.3 and 3.10 of this chapter.

7. Explain various Methods of Training. **M.B.A. April 2011**

Ans. Refer Article 3.10 of this chapter.

8. Write Short Note:
   (A) Evaluation of Training Programme. **M.B.A. December 2009**

Ans. Refer Article 3.7 of this chapter.

***

Chapter 4...

Employee Appraisal and Compensation

Contents ...
4.1 Performance
    4.1.1 Why Measure or Appraise Performance
        4.1.1.1 Employee or Performance Appraisal
        4.1.1.2 Need for Employee Appraisal
    4.1.2 Use of Performance Appraisal Data
    4.1.3 Measurement Process
    4.1.4 Performance Feedback
4.2 Concept of Compensation
    4.2.1 Traditional Approach to Compensation
    4.2.2 Current Trends in Compensation
    4.2.3 Advantages of Linking Compensation with Performance
    4.2.4 Problems of Linking Compensation with Performance
    4.2.5 Team Based Incentives
- Points to Remember
- Questions for Discussion
- Questions from Previous Pune University Examinations

Learning Objectives:
- To state the Definition of Employee Appraisal
- To understand the Need for Employee Appraisal and how the Data Collected is put to use
- To list the Process Employed for Appraisal and know the Importance of its Feedback
- To understand the Meaning of Compensation
- To understand and List Traditional Approaches of Compensation
- To recognise and Recount Current Trends in Compensation
- To understand the Advantages of Linking Compensation to Performance
- To list the Problems associated with Linking Compensation with Performance
- To recount what Team-Based Incentives Mean
- To list the Advantages and Disadvantages of Team-Based Incentives

Introduction

The technique of performance appraisal or employee appraisal is not a new one. Formal appraisal of an individual's performance began in the Wei dynasty [A. D. 221-265] in China, where, an Imperial Rater appraised the performance of members of the official family.

In 1883, the New York City Civil Service in U.S.A. introduced a formal appraisal programme shortly before World War I. The U.S. Army adopted the "man-to-man" rating system for evaluating military personnel during the World War I. During 1920-30, rational wage structures for hourly paid workers were adopted in industrial units on the basis of merits of the workers. At that time, the appraisal plans were called "Merit rating programmes".

Up to the mid-fifties, most of the employee appraisal programmes were based on the rating scales, giving more emphasis on personal traits. Thereafter, attention was devoted to the performance appraisal of technical, professional and managerial employees separately.

Performance management is an integrated process which sets various objectives, appraises employees, formulates the objectives into results, and determines wages and salaries of the employees. In a way, it helps the organisations to achieve their goals and objectives. Performance management is considered as an important tool for employees as it facilitates performance improvement, training and career development. Performance management involves thinking through different facets of performance, identifying different dimensions of performance, planning, developing and enhancing employee performance. Infact, it is an ongoing communication process which involves the managerial staff and the employees.

To become successful, besides other things, an organisation should set specific, measurable, achievable, relevant and time-bound objectives which give opportunity to measure properly the performance targets. Further, it should do all efforts to find out the loopholes in setting the targets and efficiently map the future strategies aligning the employees with their organisation. This helps the organisations to appraise their employees and as a result, performance appraisal becomes more effective.

The success of an organisation basically depends upon the quality and performance of its human resources i.e. employees working in it. An organisation is always interested in utilising various available resources effectively and the human resource is a very important and valuable resource among these resources. After an employee is selected and trained to do a job and after he has worked on the job for some time, it is necessary to evaluate his performance to ensure optimum productivity. Performance is measured in terms of results which mean the degree of the tasks assigned to an employee by way of job contents. Performance reflects how well an employee is fulfilling the job requirements. To appraise means to fix the value. In performance appraisal, the work performance of the employees working in an organisation is evaluated by the management in a systematic and orderly manner. It is a continuous process and a key managerial activity. Performance appraisal helps to reveal the strengths and weaknesses of the employees and also to improve their future performance. In simple words, 'performance appraisal' is a process of judging the performance of an employee.

At present, the term 'Performance Appraisal' is used as a method of measuring quantitative as well as qualitative aspects of an employee's work performance. It is a technique of evaluating the employees. If carried out effectively and systematically, it helps to reinforce the strengths, identify the weaknesses of the employees in service and improve their future performance in the organisation.

In modern organisations, performance appraisal systems have undergone major changes. Today's system requires a co-ordinated effort between the managers responsible for conducting performance appraisals and the human resource department of their organisation.

The success of an organisation depends upon the quality and performance of its human resources i.e. employees working in it. An organisation is always interested in utilising various available resources effectively and the human resource is a very important and valuable resource for them.

After an employee is selected and trained to do a job and after he has worked on the job for some time, it is necessary that his performance be evaluated to ensure optimum productivity. Performance is measured in terms of results and points to the number of the tasks assigned to an employee by way of the job content. Performance appraisal reflects how well an employee is fulfilling the job requirements.

If it is carried on effectively and systematically, it helps to reinforce the strengths, identify the weaknesses of the employees in the service and improve their future performance. In modern organisations, performance appraisal systems have undergone major changes. Today's system requires a co-ordinated effort between the managers responsible for conducting performance appraisals and the human resource department of their organisation.

4.1 Performance

Business Dictionary defines Performance as *"the accomplishment of a given task measured against preset known standards of accuracy, completeness, cost, and speed"*.

Performance is simply the production of **valid results.**

The success of an organisation basically depends upon the quality and performance of its human resources i.e. employees working in it. An organisation is always interested in utilising various available resources effectively and the human resource is a very important and valuable resource among these resources.

After an employee is selected and trained to do a job and after he has worked on the job for some time, it is necessary to evaluate his performance to ensure optimum productivity. Performance is measured in terms of results which mean the degree of the tasks assigned to an employee by way of the job contents.

Performance reflects how well an employee is fulfilling the job requirements. To appraise means to fix the value. In performance appraisal, the work performance of the employees working in an organisation is evaluated by the management in a systematic and orderly manner. It is a continuous process and a key managerial activity.

Performance of human resources results from skills, abilities, attitudes and aptitudes, physiological and mental capacities of human resources. Performance is translated into productivity and leads to efficiency. The level of performance of an employee is a function of his skills, abilities and aptitudes, motivation, efficiency, etc. It determines what he can do, how he can do. Where there is effective performance, the output produced by an employee increases with quality. The important task of management is to arrange the organisational conditions and methods of operations in such a way so that its employees put in their best efforts, skills etc. and increase their performance, by putting in all their efforts for attaining the goals and objectives of their organisation.

A performance or employee appraisal is a review and discussion of an employee's performance of assigned duties and responsibilities. The appraisal is based on results obtained by the employee in his/her job, and not on the employee's personality characteristics. The appraisal measures skills and accomplishments, with reasonable accuracy and uniformity. It provides a way to help identify areas for performance enhancement and to help promote professional growth. It should not, however, be considered the supervisor's only communication tool. Open lines of communication throughout the year help to make effective working relationships.

4.1.1 Why Measure or Appraise Performance?

Periodic appraisals help the HR department or supervisors gain a better understanding of each employee's abilities. The goal of performance appraisal is to recognise achievement, to evaluate job progress, and then to design training for the further development of skills and strengths.

Performance appraisal is done in order to attain certain objectives. Of course, these objectives are many and they may vary from organisation to organisation and also in the same organisation, from time to time depending upon the needs. It is found that almost all organisations practice performance appraisal in one form or the other keeping before them certain objectives in mind.

Performance appraisal is necessary for the administration comprising such actions as determining job assignments, promotions and terminations, getting feedback and identifying coaching and training needs.

According to **Lochar** and **Teel**, the primary reasons or objectives for implementing performance appraisal system in an organisation are as follows:

(a) Feedback; (b) Documentation; (c) Performance Improvement; (d) Compensation; (e) Training; (f) Promotions; (g) Transfers; (h) Discharge; (i) Lay-off; (j) Personnel Research; (k) Manpower or Human Resource Planning.

According to **M. W. Cumming**, *"The overall objective of performance appraisal is to improve the efficiency of an enterprise by attempting to mobilise the best possible efforts from individuals employed in it. Such appraisals achieve four objectives viz., salary reviews, the training and development of individuals, i.e., employees, planning job rotation and also promotions"*.

According to **Levinson**, the following are the three functions or objectives of performance appraisal.

(a) To provide an adequate feedback to each employee for his or her own performance.
(b) To serve as a basis for improving or changing behaviour towards more effective working habits; and
(c) To provide data to managers so that they can judge future job assignments.

Objectives revealed by the studies and surveys conducted by the experts, organisations, etc., show that many objectives of the performance appraisal are similar in respect of private organisations and organisations belonging to the government. But the following are some of the unique objectives kept before by the government organisations:

(1) To decide whether the employees should be allowed to cross the efficiency bar.
(2) To identify employees for deputation.
(3) To decide whether to confirm an employee or not.
(4) To help in taking decisions or premature retirements, or to give extension in service.
(5) To determine the quantum of punishment in case of disciplinary action.

Objectives of Performance Appraisal:

The various objectives of performance appraisal are as follows:

(1) To identify strengths and weaknesses of employees in their job knowledge, skills and capabilities.
(2) To estimate the overall effectiveness of employees in performing their tasks, jobs.
(3) To help the employees to overcome their weaknesses and to improve themselves so that they can perform their jobs more effectively and efficiently as per the expectation of their management.
(4) To generate adequate feedback of the work performance of the employees from their intermediate superiors to the employers as well as to the management.

(5) To make necessary information regarding the work performance of the employees in order to identify employees for the purposes of proper, suitable training and development programmes.

(6) To provide necessary inputs to the systems of rewards, salary administration, retirement, termination, retrenchment, etc.

(7) To suggest the measures to improve the performance of employees when they are not found to be up to the mark during the review period.

(8) To plan career development, human resources planning based on the work performance of employees.

(9) To provide some controlling regulatory measures on the basis of performance appraisals.

(10) To suggest measures to prevent grievances.

(11) To help increase the analytical abilities of the supervisors.

(12) To help the supervisors to have proper understanding about the employees working under them.

(13) To generate significant and valid information about employees.

(14) To help in creating the desirable culture and tradition in the organisation.

Thus, in general, the objectives of performance appraisal can broadly be classified as:

(1) The evaluation objectives,

(2) The development objectives, and

(3) Controlling objectives.

Whatever may be the objectives, the performance appraisal should provide answers to the important questions and guide to the employee as well as the management or the organisation.

(1) How well is an employee doing?

(2) What he is expected to do?

(3) What are the opportunities offered to an employee to fulfil the expectations?

(4) How well are the employees doing individually and collectively?

(5) What can the management or the organisation do in order to help its employees to do better for their organisation and themselves?

(6) What is the reward given in accordance with the performance?

(7) Is any training possible for effective job performance?

By making effective use of performance appraisal, an organisation can:

(a) improve productivity,

(b) get performance feedback,

(c) promote internal control through timely detection of the weaknesses of the employees,
(d) create a positive work environment,
(e) provide necessary training for employee development,
(f) stimulate, recognise and reward achievements,
(g) provide necessary objective measures for improvement of work/job performance,
(h) furnish information for other human resource sub-systems,
(i) provide necessary data for human resource planning,
(j) distinguish effective and ineffective performers,
(k) maintain good management-employee relations,
(l) ensure organisational effectiveness through correcting employees for standard and improved performance,
(m) bring about better operational, business results.

There is no doubt that performance appraisal is an important tool and technique. Performance appraisal system can be put to a very wide range of utility covering the entire spectrum of human resource functions in an organisation. It facilitates in many ways the accomplishment of objectives of employees as well as of the organisation wherein they work.

4.1.1.1 Employee or Performance Appraisal

In performance appraisal, the work performance of the employees working in an organisation is evaluated by the management in a systematic and orderly manner. It is a continuous process and a key managerial activity.

Employee appraisal is a methodical evaluation of the employee's performance at work. It is done by the superiors or other experts in the organisation. It is seen as a process of obtaining, analysing and recording information about the relative worth of an employee and aims to measure what an employee does. The appraisal process focuses on measuring and improving the actual performance of the employee as well as the future potential of the employee.

According to **Prof. Gary Dessler**, *"Performance Management is a process that consolidates goal setting, performance appraisal, and development into a single, common system, the aim of which is to ensure that the employee's performance is supporting the company's (i.e. organisation's) strategic aims"*.

Yet another definition of an employees' appraisal is given by **Sir Wayne Cascio**. He defines it as *"Performance appraisal is the systematic description of an employee's job, relevant strengths and weaknesses."*

Hayel observes, *"It is the process of evaluating the performance and qualifications of the employees in terms of the requirements of the job for which he is employed, for purposes of administration including placement, selection for promotions providing financial rewards and* *other actions which require differential treatment among the members of a group as distinguished from actions affecting all members equally".*

Heyel's observation throws light on the meaning of performance appraisal and purposes for which the performance appraisal can be done. Performance appraisal is also very important in planning for the employee's development.

The following views of experts in the field of management make the meaning of 'Performance Appraisal' clearer:

(1) W. D. Scott, R. C. Clothier, and W. R. Spriegel:

These experts express their views so far as the performance appraisal is concerned in their book, "Personnel Management: Principles, practices and points of view" that, *"A performance appraisal is a process of evaluation of an employee's performance of a job in terms of its requirements".*

(2) Alford and Beatty:

"A performance appraisal is the evaluation or appraisal of the relative worth to the company of man's services on his job".

(3) Wayne Cascio:

"Performance appraisal is the systematic description of an employee's job relevant strengths and weaknesses".

(4) Michael Crino:

"Performance appraisal is the process of assessing quantitative and qualitative aspects of an employee's job performance".

(5) Sexton Adams:

"Performance appraisal is a method for management to make fair and impartial analysis of the value of employees to the organisation".

(6) Prof. Dale Yoder:

"Performance appraisal includes all formal procedures used to evaluate personalities and contributions and potentials of group members in a working organisation.

It is a continuous process to secure information necessary for making correct and objective decisions on employees".

(7) Prof. E. B. Flippo:

"Performance appraisal is a systematic, periodic and so far as humanly possible, an impartial rating of an employee's excellence in matters pertaining to his present job and to his potentials for a better job".

(8) Prof. Mirza. S. Saiyadain:

According to Prof. Mirza S. Saiyadain, *"Performance appraisal could be seen as an objective method of judging the relative worth or ability of an individual employee in performing his tasks. If objectively done, the appraisal can help to identify a better worker from poor one".*

In this view of Prof. M. S. Saiyadain, the following are the two important aspects relating to performance appraisal.

(a) It is an objective method of judging the relative worth or ability of an employee in performing his tasks.

(b) A performance appraisal, can make clear the relative strengths and weaknesses of an employee, if done objectively, helps to identify a better worker from the poor one. This is important from the viewpoint of the management to identify better workers/employees for placing more responsibilities on the better ones.

(9) Prof. Arun Monappa and Prof. Mirza Saiyadain:

Prof. Arun Monappa and Prof. Saiyadain have expressed their views on a performance appraisal more comprehensively. Characteristics, traits and performance of others are appraised and judged. On the basis of these judgements, value of others can be assessed and what is good and what is bad also can be identified.

In the industrial field, according to them, *performance appraisal is a systematic evaluation of employees/personnel done by their superiors or supervisors of their performance. Such appraisals can be used for making various administrative decisions relating to selection, training, promotion, transfer, wage and salary administration, etc.*

(10) Dale S. Beach:

Dale S. Beach has stated the definition of performance appraisal in very simple words. According to him, *"Performance Appraisal is the systematic evaluation of the individual with regard to his or her performance on the job and potential for development"*.

It is a powerful tool to calibrate, refine and reward the performance of the employee. It helps to analyse the employees' achievements and evaluate his contribution towards the achievements of the overall goals of the organisation.

Performance appraisal helps to reveal the strengths and weaknesses of the employees and also to improve their future performance. In simple words, 'performance appraisal' is a process of judging the performance of an employee.

4.1.1.2 Need for Employee Appraisal

Performance management is a system composed of various related activities including goal setting, tracking changes, training and coaching, motivation, employee appraisal and employee development. Performance management provides guidelines on how an employee is expected to achieve an objective and how he will be monitored while performing with a set of given resources within a specified time frame.

Performance appraisal is considered as a most significant and indispensable tool for an organisation. It provides highly useful information in making various decisions regarding various aspects such as promotions, training and development, retirements, transfers, salary administration, etc. It also provides basis for judging the effectiveness of the employees.

Accurate information collected through performance appraisal plays a vital role in an organisation as a whole. Hence, performance appraisal should be done accurately following an objective method of judging the relative worth or abilities or performance of an individual employee in performing the tasks entrusted to him. The effectiveness of performance appraisal, to a large extent, depends upon how well the organisation has prepared itself for doing it.

An employee appraisal programme is important to the employees' professional development, to meeting the organisation's goals or objectives and, ultimately, to contributing to the growth of the organisation. No employer, whether a small CPA firm, a Big Four firm, a non-profit organisation, a government institution or a private or public company, should be exempt from having such a formal programme. Other benefits that could be derived from having an employee appraisal programme include:

- better communications,
- an opportunity to effectively address performance problems,
- improved employee morale.

From an employer's perspective, however, it is good to take the time to consider whether or not they are achieving the goals that have been set, preferably through discussion with their managers. The management may need to discuss new goals that need to be addressed during the coming period of time that may arise due to the changing circumstances, alterations in how the business is run, the staff changes that bring different responsibilities and many other possibilities.

Managements of organisations can use the results of the employee appraisals to:

- Assess performances.
- Analyse the effectiveness of existing goals.
- Set modified goals that cater to changing scenarios.
- Set up appropriate training programmes for the employees.

Employee appraisal has a very important role to play in managing individual and group performances in an organisation. There is a considerable amount of agreement among managers and researches about the positive impacts of personnel rating and evaluation of the performance. Performance appraisals can prove to be very helpful and successful if they focus primarily on the improvement of organisational performance as a whole, and especially if its attributes are in line with those of the organisational aims and goals

A performance appraisal is done in order to attain certain objectives. Of course, these objectives are many and they may vary from organisation to organisation and also in the same organisation, from time to time depending upon the needs. It is found that almost all organisations practice performance appraisal in one form or the other keeping before them certain objectives.

According to **M. W. Cumming**, *"The overall objective of performance appraisal is to improve the efficiency of an enterprise by attempting to mobilise the best possible efforts from individuals employed in it. Such appraisals achieve four objectives viz., salary reviews, the training and development of employees, planning job rotation and also promotions".*

According to Levinson, the following are the three functions or objectives of performance appraisal.

(a) To provide an adequate feedback to each employee for his or her own performance.

(b) To serve as a basis for improving or changing behaviour towards more effective working habits.

(c) To provide data to managers so that they can judge future job assignments.

Objectives revealed by the studies and surveys conducted by the experts, organisations, etc., show that many objectives of the performance appraisal are similar in respect of private organisations and organisations belonging to the government. But the following are some of the unique objectives kept before by the Government organisations:

(1) To decide whether the employees should be allowed to cross the efficiency bar.

(2) To identify employees for deputation.

(3) To decide whether to confirm an employee or not.

(4) To help in taking decisions or premature retirements, or to give extension in service.

(5) To determine the quantum of punishment in case of disciplinary action.

The various objectives of performance appraisal are as follows:

(1) To identify the strengths and weaknesses of employees in their job knowledge, skills and capabilities.

(2) To estimate the overall effectiveness of employees in performing their tasks, jobs.

(3) To help the employees to overcome their weaknesses and to improve themselves so that they can perform their jobs more effectively and efficiently as per the expectation of their management.

(4) To generate adequate feedback of the work performance of the employees from their intermediate superiors to the employers as well as to the management.

(5) To make necessary information regarding the work performance of the employees in order to identify employees for the purposes of proper, suitable training and development programmes.

(6) To provide necessary inputs to the systems of rewards, salary administration, retirement, termination, retrenchment, etc.

(7) To suggest the measures to improve the performance of employees when they are not found to be up to the mark during the review period.

(8) To plan career development, human resources planning based on the work performance of employees.

(9) To provide some controlling regulatory measures on the basis of performance appraisals.

(10) To suggest measures to prevent grievances.

(11) To help increase the analytical abilities of the supervisors.

(12) To help the supervisors to have proper understanding about the employees working under them.

(13) To generate significant and valid information about employees.

(14) To help in creating the desirable culture and tradition in the organisation.

Thus, in general, the objectives of performance appraisal can broadly be classified as:

(1) The evaluation objectives,
(2) The development objectives, and
(3) Controlling objectives.

Whatever may be the objectives, the performance appraisal should provide answers to important questions and a guide to the employee as well as the management or organisation.

(1) How well is an employee doing?
(2) What he is expected to do?
(3) What are the opportunities offered to an employee to fulfil the expectations?
(4) How well are the employees doing individually and collectively?
(5) What can the management or the organisation do in order to help its employees to do better for their organisation and themselves?
(6) What is the reward given in accordance with the performance?
(7) Is any training possible for effective job performance?

By making effective use of performance appraisal, an organisation can:

(a) Improve productivity,
(b) Get performance feedback,
(c) Promote internal control through timely detection of weaknesses of employees,
(d) Create a positive work environment,
(e) Provide necessary training for employee development,
(f) Stimulate, recognise and reward achievements,
(g) Provide necessary objective measures for improvement of work/job performance,
(h) Furnish information for other human resource sub-systems,

(i) Provide necessary data for human resource planning,

(j) Distinguish effective and ineffective performers,

(k) Ensure organisational effectiveness through correcting employees for standard and improved performance,

(l) Bring about better operational, business results.

There is no doubt that performance appraisal is an important tool and technique. Performance appraisal system can be put to a very wide range of utility covering the entire spectrum of human resource functions in an organisation. It facilitates in many ways the accomplishment of objectives of employees as well as of the organisation wherein they work.

4.1.2 Use of Performance Appraisal Data

As has been discussed earlier in the chapter, performance appraisal is the process of evaluating the performance, qualities, abilities, skills etc. of employees at work in terms of the requirements of the jobs for which they are employed.

Performance appraisal is useful for the purposes of administration including placement, selection for training and promotion, giving rewards and also for other suitable actions like transfer, demotion etc. There are many objectives of performance appraisal. Some of the common uses of performance appraisal are given below.

(a) Performance appraisal helps to put a sort of pressure on employees for better performance. Employees know that they are appraised or evaluated and they tend to show their performance. Performance appraisal indirectly works as an automatic control device.

(b) Performance appraisal helps to suggest the areas in which improvement in job performance is necessary. Thus, it helps to determine the training needs by identifying the areas of weaknesses of the employees.

(c) Performance appraisal is useful in determining appropriate salary increases, bonuses for the employees on performance measure.

(d) Performance appraisal is also useful in respect of promotions, transfers, demotions, considering the strengths and weaknesses of the employees.

(e) It can motivate the employees by showing them where they stand, what they should do to improve their performance. It provides feedback to the employees about their performance.

(f) It is also useful in taking decisions in respect of premature retirements or in respect of giving extension in service to the concerned employees.

(g) It helps in career development, human resource planning based on the work performance of employees. On the basis of performance appraisal, an individual employees' development needs also can be identified or ascertained.

From the discussion done so far, one comes to know that performance appraisal is useful from the viewpoint of management as well as of employees also.

Performance appraisal is considered as a most significant and indispensable tool for an organisation as it provides highly useful information in making various decisions regarding various aspects such as promotions, training and development, retirements, transfers, salary administration, etc. It also provides basis for judging the effectiveness of the employees. Accurate information collected through performance appraisal plays a vital role in an organisation as a whole. Hence, performance appraisal should be done accurately following an objective method of judging the relative worth or abilities or performance of an individual employee in performing the tasks entrusted to him. The effectiveness of performance appraisal, to a large extent, depends upon how well the organisation has prepared itself for doing it. It is a basic function of performance management. Performance management is nothing but managing the performance appraisals of the employees periodically and systematically and covers basically the following areas or steps.

(1) Setting of proper standards for the purpose of appraising the performance.

(2) Measuring actual performance of employees by adopting suitable method/ methods.

(3) Comparing it with standards.

(4) Finding out reasons for deviations from standards.

(5) Taking corrective actions to eliminate these reasons.

(6) Revising of performance stands and adopting suitable methods of performance appraisal according to the needs or changing circumstances or requirements.

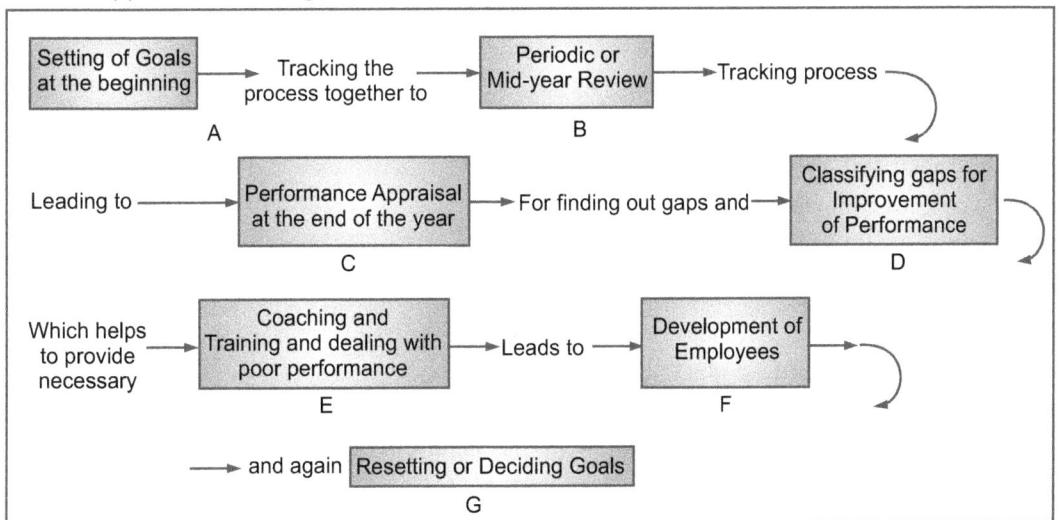

Fig. 4.1: Process of Performance Management System

There is no doubt that performance appraisal definitely provides feedback about job performance of an employee. However, getting merely the feedback is not enough. There are many other activities need to be undertaken to complete the process such as performance interview, achieving performance data, and also use of appraisal data etc. All such activities constitute the core of performance management system. Performance management integrates the performance of employees with the organisational performance.

All the above mentioned important tasks are required to be performed by the performance management. It is the important function of the performance management to lay down a well and neatly designed performance appraisal process or plan. Following points make clear the utility of such plan.

(1) It unifies the appraisal procedure:

The procedure of performance appraisal is basically dependent upon the purpose or purposes of appraisal. Once the procedure is laid down, in the same manner, the performances of all the employees should be evaluated or judged. Then, it becomes possible to compare the performances of the employees properly by finding out their weaknesses and strengths.

(2) It provides useful information:

Management has to take many decisions relating to training, transfers, promotions, increments, discharge, retirement, salary adjustments, etc. They all are related to the performance appraisals of the employees. Such decisions can be taken properly on the basis of information by the appraisal plan.

(3) It facilities creation of records:

Firstly, for the purpose of performance appraisal, necessary information is required to be collected on the basis of how the performance appraisal is done. After it is done the results of the performance appraisal are stored in the form of records. All such records can be used as evidence for different purposes e.g. while handling grievances related to the decisions based on such appraisals.

(4) It weeds out inefficiencies:

When inefficient, incapable, indisciplined, lethargical employees are identified, chances to improve them can be given to them. But, after giving them chances, if they do not improve, they can be weeded out on the basis of performance appraisals.

(5) It keeps superiors more alert:

Performance appraisals are considered as a development technique in the hands of the management. It aims at calling attention of the superiors to the subordinates' behaviour flows in order to improve their performances. It makes the superior more alert as it is their responsibility to appraise the subordinates.

Thus, performance management is important function and has a wide range of utility.

4.1.3 Measurement Process

Performance Appraisal Process

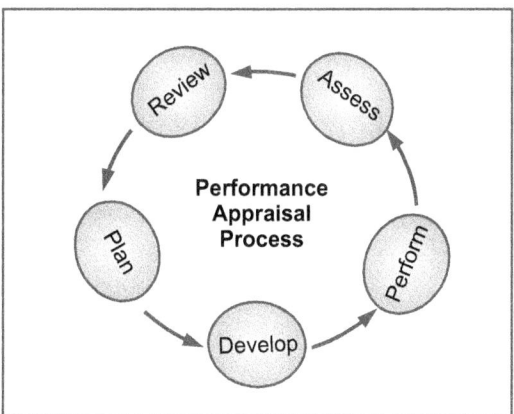

Fig. 4.2: Performance Appraisal Process

Once the objectives of performance appraisal are decided considering the policy, the performance appraisal process begins and has the following steps:
- Establishment of performance standards.
- Communication of standards.
- Measurement of actual performance.
- Comparison of actual performance with the standards.
- Discussion of the appraisal with the appraisee.
- Taking of corrective actions.

Now, let us try to know in brief the above mentioned steps used to design a performance appraisal plan.

1. Establishment of Performance Standards:

Certain standards to judge the performance of employees must be decided considering the objectives for which the performance appraisal is to be done. These standards must relate to the desired results of each job. The standards should be objectively measurable. Further, these standards should be updated from time to time considering the changes in technology, production processes, etc.

2. Communication of Standards:

This is the second step in the process of performance appraisal. Job description gives clear idea to the appraisee about what he is expected to do and other related matters. The idea about performance standards must be given to an appraisee as well as to an appraiser. If there are changes made in the standards, they must be communicated to them. Feedback is essential from the appraisees to make the communication effective. It ensures that the information communicated by the superiors to their subordinates has been received and understood properly in the way it was intended.

3. Measurement of Actual Performance:

The next step is to measure the actual performance of an employee or appraisee. In order to determine actual performance of an employee necessary information is gathered and the suitable technique or techniques are used.

4. Comparison of Actual Performance with the Standards:

The mere measurement of actual performance has no meaning in absolute sense. It must be compared with the predetermined standards to know whether it is up to the desired level or below it. If it is below the desired levels than appropriate actions are taken to help the employee improve.

5. Discussion of the Appraisal with the Appraisee:

Once the process of measurement of the actual performance and its comparison with the standards is completed, the results of it should be communicated to the appraisee concerned. It gives the idea to the appraisee about his strengths and weaknesses. Moreover, he gets a chance to discuss if he is not satisfied with the observations.

6. Taking Corrective Actions:

If the performance appraisal report reveals weaknesses and/or shortcomings, efforts should be made to remove those. This can be done through proper counselling, coaching, training, giving suitable project, etc. Long-term action is desired to eliminate the reasons permanently. Of course, if an appraisee has proven himself/herself very efficient, salary increase or promotion or both should be recommended and given. If appraisal report is negative, the appraisee concerned should be made to understand areas identified for improvement instead of putting the blame for shortcomings on him. This helps in maintaining positive relations.

Of course, the process and the details of the steps discussed about may vary from organisation to organisation according to the needs and objectives of the performance of appraisal.

4.1.4 Performance Feedback

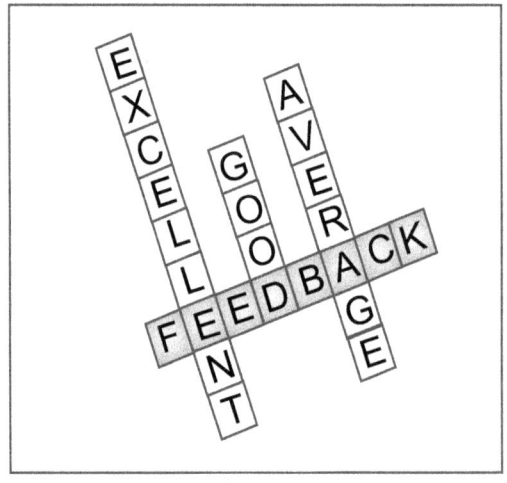

Fig. 4.3

Possibly the most challenging part of the performance appraisal meeting is giving feedback to employees on their performance. This step is necessary for the betterment of the employee as well as the organisation in which they work. For many employees, a face-to-face performance review is the most stressful work conversation they'll have all year. For managers, the discussion is just as tense. Evaluating an employee's job performance should consist of more than just an annual chat.

Performance appraisal feedback (or any performance feedback) is always easier to give (and receive) when managers follow a structured process of:

(a) Common performance objectives or standards.

(b) Monitored employee performance.

(c) Give employees ongoing performance feedback (not just at performance appraisal time).

No matter what kind of appraisal system an organisation uses, there are several strategies that help make performance review season less nerve-racking and more productive.

A few steps that might be helpful are listed here:

Dos

- Make it clear at the beginning of the year how you'll evaluate your employees with individual performance planning sessions.
- Give your employees a copy of their appraisal before the meeting so they may have their initial emotional response in private.
- Deliver a positive message to your good performers by mainly concentrating on their strengths and achievements during the conversation.

Don'ts

- Offer general feedback; be specific on the behaviours you want your employee to stop, start, and continue.
- Talk about compensation during the review; but if you must, divulge the salary information at the start of the conversation.
- Sugar-coat the review for your poor performers; use the face-to-face as an opportunity to demand improvement.

Performance Appraisal Preparation: Get the feedback ready

As in performance appraisal and people management in general preparation prevents poor performance. Here's how to prepare the performance feedback:

1. Keep standards agreed at the last meeting ready at hand.
2. Open your 'performance file' or wherever it is that you have collected samples of your employee's actual performance.
3. Look for gaps – if you do not have examples or samples of performance for an objective you need to find some!

4. For each performance objective or standard, compare actual performance so that you can:
   - Identify achievements and successes.
   - Identify any areas for improvement.
5. Think about any barriers to performance the employee might have encountered.
6. Consider any special projects undertaken / work 'above and beyond' the agreed objectives or standards.

Performance Appraisal: Before giving performance feedback, listen

Most employees, given the opportunity, are willing and able to review their own performance – with some help. Always ask the employee for their opinion first – before offering your feedback.

Performance Appraisal: Giving (and sharing) the performance feedback

1. Take each performance objective or standard and ask your employee to evaluate their actual performance against the objective or standard.

If the reviewer agrees with the employee's evaluation:
(a) Simply state the agreement.
(b) Give examples to support the agreement.
(c) Remember to congratulate the employee on meeting the objective.

If the reviewer disagrees with the employee's evaluation:
(a) Ask them to give evidence of having met the objective.

If they can give sufficient evidence or examples of meeting the objective then the reviewer simply need to re-evaluate their opinion.

If they cannot give examples they will see that they have not met the objective. If they don't see this then –
(b) Give examples to support the disagreement

Feedback should be given in a manner that will best help improve performance. Since people respond better to information presented in a positive way, feedback should be expressed in a positive manner. This does not mean that information should be sugar-coated. It must be accurate, factual, and complete.

When presented, however, feedback is more effective when it reinforces what the employee did right and then identifies what needs to be done in the future. Constant criticism eventually will fall upon deaf ears.

The ten keys for conducting an effective formal review discussion are:
1. Schedule sufficient time in a private setting.
2. Rehearse the conversation prior to the meeting.

3. Provide the employee with performance review documentation.
4. Begin with strengths and then discuss development areas.
5. Focus development areas on employee behaviours and not on personality traits.
6. Provide examples to substantiate the review.
7. Provide suggestions for performance improvement.
8. Use clear and simple words during the discussion.
9. Solicit the employee's questions or comments.
10. End on a positive note and discuss the next steps.

The Fig. 4.4 below shows the effects of positive and negative feedback:

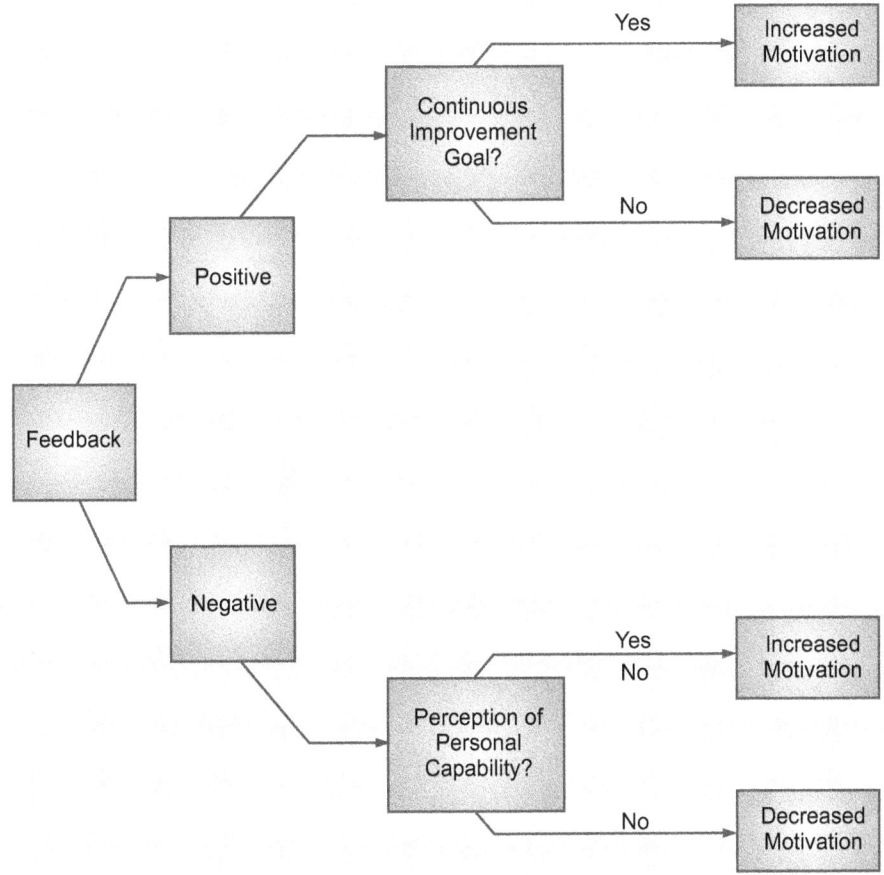

Fig. 4.4: Effects of Feedbacks

(**Source:** *Information from Avraham N. Kluger and Angelo DeNisi, "The Effects of Feedback Interventions on Performance: A Historical Review, A Meta-Analysis, and a Preliminary Feedback Intervention Theory," Psychological Bulletin 119(1996): 254–284.*)

4.2 Concept of Compensation

An organisation's goals or objectives can be achieved when its employees put in their best efforts in the right direction. Hence, they should be nurtured properly and paid well for their work, performance, services, etc. Besides wages or salaries, organisations provide different kinds of incentives, benefits and services to their employees. Money paid to employees for their work in the form of gross pay is included under direct compensation; while benefits come under indirect compensation and they may consist of life, accident and health insurance, the contribution of an organisation to retirement i.e. retirement benefits, expenses incurred for employee welfare as social security etc. All these things are nothing but the compensation the employees receive in return for their contribution to their organisation. From the viewpoint of an organisation, compensation management is a major function. Compensation Management is one of the most important topics in HRM. This is one area which needs all the attention as it can have a direct impact on all others.

Compensation Management is concerned with the compensation to employees for their work and contribution for attaining organisational goals. Obviously, it is concerned with designing and implementing total compensation package. It is also known as wage and salary administration or remuneration management.

Every organisation requires suitable human resources to achieve its objectives. To get the effective results, the employees must be paid and compensated properly even though this is not the only motivator for the employees to work. Any unjustifiable inequality or an unacceptably low level of reward definitely causes great dissatisfaction among employees.

Hence, sound wage and salary policies and programmes are very essential to attract, induct, retain and develop the employees working in the organisation in order to get the best results from them. As already mentioned above, wage and salary administration or compensation management is considered as one of the vital areas of "Human Resource Management".

Compensation Management refers to the establishment and implementation of sound policies, programmes and practices of employee compensation. It is essentially the application of a systematic and scientific approach for compensating the employees for their work in a fair, equitable and logical manner. The factors affecting the determination of fair and equitable compensation are many and are very complex. Compensation Management includes various areas such as job evaluation, surveys of wages and salary analysis of relevant organisational problem, development of suitable wage structure, framing of rules for administering wages and salaries, wage payment, incentive, control of compensation cost etc. Hence, in the era of globalisation, privatisation, liberalisation, compensation management has become very complex and depending upon the size of the organisation, it may be helpful to induct a specialist to handle this specific portfolio under HRM.

Wages and salaries mean different things to different people and organisations. From the view point of employees, white collar or blue collar, a salary or a wage is an income and a return they get for offering their services to their organisation. From the view point of an organisation or management, wages and salaries constitute a cost of production. A wage or salary is a price paid to an employee for hiring his services.

Compensation is defined as the consolidated amount, allowances received and various other kinds of benefits and services which are offered by the organisation to their employees. In other words, *compensation refers to all forms of financial returns, services and benefits received by the employees from their organisation as a part of their employment relationship.*

Such compensation may be received in the form of cash i.e. wages/salaries, bonus, overtime payments, incentives (i.e. gross payment). This is called as 'direct compensation'. While benefits that come under indirect compensation may consist of life, accidents and health insurance, pay for vacation or illness, retirement benefits and so on.

Thus, in short, compensation is direct and indirect monetary benefits and rewards received by employees on the basis of the value of the jobs, their personal contributions and overall performance. Such rewards are given to employees by their organisation according to the ability of the organisation to pay and the legal provisions.

Important components of compensation are mentioned below:

(a) Wages and Salary:

In Economics, the term 'Wages' implies the payments made for the services of labour. Such labour can be physical labour or mental labour.

Prof. Benham defines a wage as, *"a sum of money paid under the contract by an employer to a worker in exchange of services rendered"*.

- According to **T. R. Turner**, *"a wage is a price which is paid by an employer to his worker on account of labour performed"*. Thus, a wage is the reward of labour, a factor of production, for its contribution in the production.

- According to **I.L.O**, *wage is the remuneration paid by the employer for the services of his worker who is engaged by the hours, days, week or fortnight"*. It implies that the wages are the periodical payments made to the workers for their services and they are paid to the production and maintenance workers and to blue collar employees.

On the other hand, the term 'Salary' normally refers to the payments periodically made i.e. weekly, fortnightly or usually monthly at certain rates to the clerical, administrative, professional employees i.e. white collar employees. It can also be defined as the remuneration paid to the clerical, managerial employees for their services at certain rates on monthly or even on annual basis.

However, from the point of view of human resource management, there is no need to distinguish between 'wage' and 'salary'. It is simply because, human resource approach considers all employees as human resources and they are viewed at par. Hence, wage and/or salary are viewed as the direct remuneration paid to an employee as the compensation for his services to his organisation. It is also found that both these terms are used interchangeably.

Wages and Salary are the most important components of compensation and they are essential irrespective of the type and size of organisation. Generally, wages represent hourly rates of pay and salary refers to the monthly rate of pay irrespective of the number of hours put in by an employee. Normally, they are not associated with productivity of an employee at a particular time. They also differ from employee to employee and depend upon the nature of job, seniority and merit.

(b) Fringe Benefits:

Fringe benefits refer to compensation given to the employees by their organisation over and above their wages. They often are not related directly to output, performance or time worked. They represent supplemental forms of payments beyond stated wage or salary rates. They may be in the form of monetary payments or financial rights which form the part of the organisation's manpower costs. Fringe benefits increase the income of the employees and help them enhance their standard of living.

Fringe benefits include benefits such as provident fund, gratuity, pension, medical care, hospitalisation, accident relief, health and group insurance, canteens, recreation, uniforms and so on.

(c) Incentive Wage:

Incentives are the extra payments received by the employees for higher standards of performance than expected. They are related to earnings received by the employees for more productivity, efficiency etc. and include monetary payments connected to or linked with some measurement of an employee's output with the objective of motivating him for better performance.

Incentives are also called as 'Payments by results' which depend upon productivity, sales, profits or cost reduction efforts. These incentives are given on individual basis or group basis by adopting individual incentive schemes or group incentive programmes. Individual incentives are applicable to specific employee performance, where completion of task, demands group activities, and efforts of incentives are paid to the group of employees as a whole and the amount is divided among the group of employees on an equitable basis.

(d) Earnings:

Earnings are different from wages. Earnings include total amount of payment an employee receives for his work in a given period of time. From this point of view, earnings are the total of overtime payments, dearness and other allowances, incentives and so on.

Prices of various commodities and services increase due to various reasons. Hence, dearness allowance is paid to the employees in order to enable them to face the growing prices of commodities and services. Most of the organisations pay Dearness Allowance as per the Government's index of consumer points announced month to month.

(e) Perquisites:

Perquisites are normally provided to the officer, managers and executives to facilitate their job performance and also to retain them in the organisation. Perquisites include company car, free residential accommodation, club membership, paid holiday trips, stock option schemes, furnishing and refurnishing of residence, car or housing loans.

(f) Non-monetary benefits:

These benefits include challenging job responsibilities, recognition of merits, growth prospects, comfortable working conditions, flexitime i.e. system of flexible working hours, job sharing etc.

Fig. 4.1: Components of a Compensation Programme

Compensation	
Direct	**Indirect**
Base Pay • Wages • Salaries **Variable Pay** • Bonuses • Incentives • Stock options	**Benefits** • Medical/Life insurance • Paid time off • Retirement pensions • Workers' compensation • Others

The components of compensation can be summed up as given below:

1. **Financial Elements**

Table 4.2 Financial Elements

Form of Compensation	Employee Needs	Company Needs
Base Salary	- Sets standard of living - Reflects employer's evaluation	Key to pay competitiveness
Premium Payments	Extra income for special purchases	- Sometimes a legal requirement - Induce employees to work longer or under difficult circumstances
Bonuses	- Reward for achievement of goal - Opportunity for higher income	- Variable cost - Motivates short-term performance - Attract key personnel
Long-Term Income	- Reward for achievement of goal - Opportunity for higher income	- Helps retain key employees - Motivates long-term performance
Pay for Time Not Worked	Rest and recreation for employees	- Competitive need - Rejuvenated employees
Benefits	- Tax-sheltered income - Protection against economic risks	- Competitive need - Social responsibility/public relations
Extra Pay Plans (e.g. stock purchase, profit sharing, etc.)	Extra savings	Build favourable employee attitudes

2. **Non-Financial Elements**

Table 4.3: Non-Financial Elements

Element	Examples
Company Environment	Prestigious companies or companies with a good reputation for making quality products.
The Work	Employees enjoy their jobs.
Physical Conditions	Cleanliness, brightness, comfort and safety.
Work Environment	Location of the company, management style, dispute resolution, friendliness of employees
Perquisites	Company cafeteria, company products sold at a discount, service awards

At a glance direct compensation can be summed as:

Table 4.4: Compensation Type

Base Pay	The basic monetary compensation that an employee receives, usually as a wage or salary.
Wages	Payments calculated on the amount of time worked.
Salary	Consistent payments made each period regardless of the numbers of hours worked in the period.
Variable Pay	Compensation linked to individual, team or organisational performance.
Benefit	An indirect reward given to an employee or groups of employees as a part of employee membership.

4.2.1 Traditional Approach to Compensation

Companies have traditionally used a variety of approaches for managing the compensation function. Many continue to use relatively simplistic internally developed software tools, often based on generic desktop programmes. Some companies utilise broad HR and/or enterprise resource planning (ERP) software offerings, which include some compensation management capabilities but typically lack the specialised functionality to adequately address compensation management.

Newer approaches have emerged since keeping in mind the changing job profiles and organisational structures.

The traditional approach to compensation requires an in-depth analysis of the job at hand. The job is analysed on the basis of its rating and hierarchy. A market survey of similar jobs could also form a step in this direction. This analysis is then documented in detail.

The analysis is then followed by internal and external reconciliation of facts and considerations. Only after this careful consideration the pay structure is developed. This traditional approach to compensation has the following salient features:

- Compensation primarily base pay.
- Bonuses for executives only.
- Fixed benefits tied to seniority.
- Pay grade progression based on organisational promotions.
- One organisation-wide pay plan for all employees.

The obvious drawback to this system is a tendency for long-standing employees to become comfortable with their guaranteed salary and become less motivated. Additionally, there was little incentive for younger - possibly more ambitious and energetic - employees to shine since all they would receive as a reward for their effort would be a pat on the back and the satisfaction of a job well done unless they shone brightly enough to be awarded a promotion.

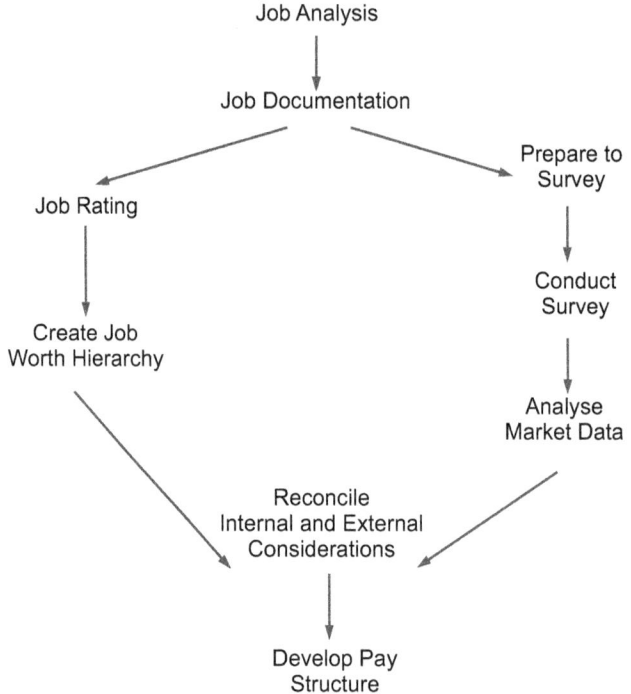

Fig. 4.5: Traditional Approach to Compensation

4.2.2 Current Trends in Compensation

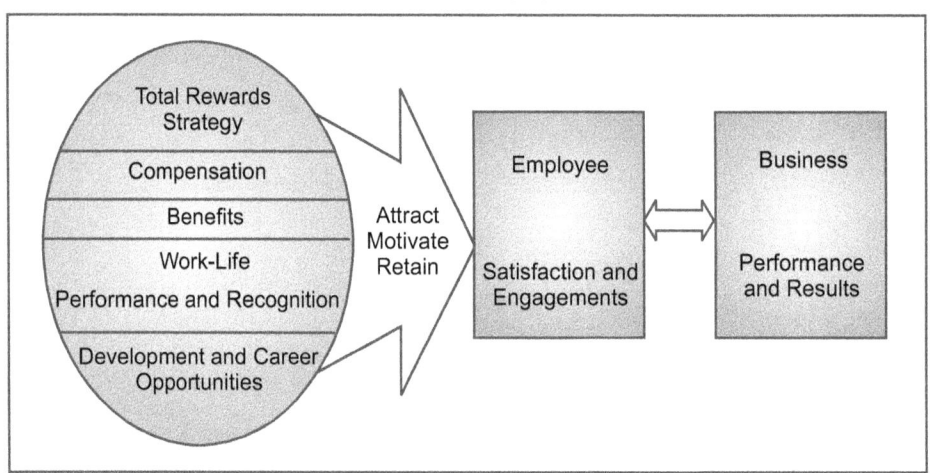

Fig. 4.6

Given the shifts occurring in attitudes and practices about salary and compensation, organisations are struggling to keep up with changes in salary and compensation thinking. Gone are the days when organisations gave equivalent increases to all organisation members. These salary increases, in the one percent to five percent range, send the wrong message to the underperformers. They left organisations with too small a budget to adequately reward their top performers. While many companies still use this as their salary criteria, forward thinking organisations are thinking about salary and compensation in a very different way.

Some of the newer trends that organisations are looking to include is the total rewards approach. Here variable pay is used with the base pay for a job type. Annual/long-term incentives are provided to all employees and not to just a select few. Employees can look forward to flexible and portable benefits offered by organisations. Knowledge-based broadbands determine pay grades and replace traditional narrow salary ranges to fewer wider bands that are most appropriate for higher level positions.

Multiple pay plans consider job, family, location, and business units when structuring the compensation plan. Team based pay and skill-based pay are two more avenues that organisations are toying with. Table 4.5 below shows as the two compensation approaches:

Table 4.5: Compensation Approaches

Traditional Compensation Approach	Total Rewards Approach
Compensation is primarily base pay.	Variable pay is added to base.
Bonuses/perks are four executives only.	Annual/long-term incentives are provided to executives, managers and employees
Fixed benefits are tied to long tenure.	Flexible and portable benefits are offered.
Pay grade progression is based on organisational promotions.	Knowledge/skill-based broad bands determine pay grades
Organisation-wide standard pay plan exists.	Multiple plans consider job, family, location, and business units.

4.2.3 Advantages of Linking Compensation with Performance

A performance-based pay system is a common method used by organisations to increase productivity. As companies try to remain competitive and control costs, performance-based pay systems are becoming increasingly popular.

Performance pay attempts to link compensation to performance. Reasons to utilise a performance-based system include:

- to retain top performers,
- to align labour costs with productivity, and
- to reinforce company objectives.

A company can base pay on individual or group output, or company-wide performance. For a plan to be successful, regardless of its implementation, employees must:

- desire more pay,
- believe they will receive more pay if they improve their performance,
- be physically able to improve their performance, and
- trust the company to administer the plan fairly.

During the time when our parents started to work, salary was generally based on seniority; every employee in a comparable position earned the same, with annual increments and cost-of-living raises. Seniority was rewarded, youthful enthusiasm perhaps not. This induced a tendency for long-standing employees to become comfortable with their guaranteed salary and become less motivated. No additional incentive for the younger employees and more enthusiastic employees left the organisation as a dissatisfied lot.

Performance-based pay would therefore seem to present a far better deal for both employers and employees. Rewarding the best performers seems only reasonable and is obviously the clear way to motivate employees.

The benefits of performance-based pay structures are self-evident. There is a positive correlation between effort and performance and employee retention is likely to be enhanced since those who perform best, being rewarded for their efforts, are more likely to stay.

Some companies have used a performance-based compensation scheme to not only reward their high achievers, but also to weed out their weakest performers.

But, does a performance based pay structure actually improve the workforce? The answer is in the affirmative. A well-constructed performance-based pay system can be seen as an interactive process that translates the overall strategic initiatives into daily actions, with quantitative and attainable rewards provided to the employees who accomplish their goals. Studies as well as our experience have consistently shown that recognition for a job well done is the top motivator of the employee performance.

Performance based programmes tap into the purest source of human potential. With performance based pay systems employees assume more responsibility for end results, as well as a clearer understanding of the overall business objectives.

Linking pay to performance should be a top priority for organisations. Management needs to change the view of compensation as the "cost of doing business" to a functional tool that supports the organisation's business plan. Compensation then becomes a financial investment applied in a manner designed to maximise its return.

4.2.4 Problems of Linking Compensation with Performance

So does all the discussion so far mean that performance based compensation is void of any drawbacks? Saying so would be ignoring the obvious. Beside the unfortunate employees who fall into the lowest category and lose their jobs, there are other drawbacks to performance-based pay structures.

Implementation of this system can be problematic and perhaps more importantly, this supposedly motivating process can actually be damaging to self-esteem, teamwork and creativity.

The Teams anxious to improve their performance may avoid working with colleagues they perceive to be less able, leading to some employees being excluded from the more rewarding projects. Keen competition for limited rewards can also create a hostile working environment where trust and cooperation are sacrificed in the interests of self-promotion. In addition to this, projects can fail due to factors that are completely beyond an employee's control, such as delays in receiving supplies or a downturn in the economy and so on.

If performance based compensation is to be successful in an organisation, there must be reasonable, achievable and measurable goals that are potentially achievable by any employee. Achievements must be quantifiable, so a comprehensive system must be put in place to monitor and assess whether or not employees have met their designated targets. Communication and transparency are essential; everyone must be aware of, and understand, the criteria. Training and education facilities should be in place to improve the performance of weaker employees and enable ambitious employees to widen their knowledge and skills and be able to hit targets.

4.2.5 Team-based Incentives

Team-based incentive plans are initiatives designed to encourage and reward exceptional levels of professional achievement. You can use incentives in your small business as motivators for staffers to work collectively to earn monetary and non-monetary rewards. It is also a way for small business owners to boost overall productivity and earnings while simultaneously rewarding employees for a job well done. The objective of team incentives is to encourage group goal-setting, collaboration and teamwork.

Group incentive plans were designed for situations in which the goals of the project are best-suited to individuals working together rather than apart, as is common in creative agencies, such as advertising or film. When the work has to be done interdependently, there is a strong reason to base earnings on the performance of a group

Group incentive plans can reward things that individual incentive plans cannot, such as teamwork and cooperation. When an organisation has many complex aspects to its business, group incentive plans are an appropriate way to structure the payment of employees. Incentive plans offer flexibility in their structuring.

Types of team based incentive plans are discussed below:

- **Profit Sharing:** Profit sharing is a team-based incentive plan in which you pay your employees a percentage of your company's overall profits. Profit sharing builds a sense of ownership among employees and encourages greater team performance levels. Staffers know that the better their performance, the better the business's financial picture, and the higher their own potential cash rewards.

- **Gain Sharing:** Similar to a profit-sharing plan, gain sharing is a team incentive in which you reward employee groups for measurable, non-financial achievements in pre-established areas. For example, teams may enjoy a bonus if customer satisfaction levels rise a certain percentage above figures from the previous year. The focus of this type of incentive is for employees to recognise the role they play in continually moving your small business forward in key areas.

- **Goal-Based Incentives:** Goal-based team incentives reward employees for reaching specific goals. For example, topping a certain rupee amount in sales, landing a specific number of contracts or hitting a membership recruitment figure. The approach encourages teamwork and gives employees a firm target to aim for. This incentive plan is good for small businesses because it promotes team work and collective effort, and you only issue the reward if the goal is met.

- **Merit-Based Incentive:** A more subjective approach to incentive programmes is the merit-based incentive approach. Following this model, you reward employee teams for effort, regardless of outcome. For example, if your marketing employees stay late every night to finish a major advertising campaign that doesn't perform as anticipated, their dedication and effort are still recognised. Because of the discretionary element of this type of incentive, it can be a challenge for employees to know what they aiming for or how they will know when their efforts or actions are viewed as "good enough" to merit reward.

- **Financial vs. Non-Financial Incentive:** It's up to you, as the business owner, to decide what type of incentive you want to offer employee teams. If cash rewards are too much for your small business budget, other incentives to extend include paid time off, free company services or merchandise, or preferred parking or office space. Ask employees what they consider to be a viable and worthwhile reward and consider if it fits your budget.

Advantages

Group incentive plans have a number of advantages over other payment structures. They encourage cooperation within a team because pay depends on achieving a result that takes a group to accomplish. They cultivate managerial skills within a team, skills that can be translated to other teams or the organisation as the whole.

Group incentive plans are useful when there are no clearly defined individual goals that may act as the basis for individual incentive plans. For example, for salespeople, individual incentive plans might fit well because their performance can be tied directly to the number of sales they make in a given period; but in an environment in which more of the employees aren't salespeople – such as a creative agency, where each employee has a specific set of skills that is hard to compare – individual incentive plans may not be appropriate.

(i) **Incentive Pay:** Incentive pay rewards employees for achieving defined goals. The company sets performance objectives at the beginning of the pay period and if these are achieved, employees receive a lump-sum payment. Incentive pay plans can be based on the performance of the individual, team, business unit or company. Company-wide incentive pay schemes include gain sharing and profit sharing. The ability of an individual to influence the outcome of the incentive pay plan declines as the group being measured grows larger. However, team-based incentive pay plans offer advantages to companies.

(ii) **Encourage Teamwork:** Companies offer team-based incentive pay to encourage team members to work together effectively. Individual incentive schemes can encourage competition between employees and may even lead to conflicting priorities. Team-based incentives encourage collaboration and cooperation to achieve shared goals. For example, a team member with planning skills will organise the work flow while team members with technical skills will focus on completing the work.

(iii) **Increase Effort:** In a 2010 study, researchers from the University of California, Santa Barbara found that team-based incentives increase the willingness of workers to put effort into their tasks because they do not want to let their teammates down. Increased effort resulting from the social effect of the team was observed even when there was a lower probability of receiving a payoff. The motivational effect of a team-based incentive was most significant on individuals who require external incentives. Internally motivated workers were less affected.

(iv) **Reduce Employee Turnover:** Attractive total rewards packages reduce employee turnover because employees who feel satisfied with their pay and conditions are less likely to be enticed by a competitor. In a 1996 study, researchers found that companies with long-term, team-based incentive pay experienced lower than average employee turnover. Members of the team become committed to the shared goal and are reluctant to leave their colleagues. Lower employee turnover benefits companies by reducing costs of recruiting and training new employees.

Disadvantages

The downside to group incentive plans can severely damage the functioning of an organisation. These disadvantages can be seen in a number of ways. For example, it can take time for members of a group to work well with each other, know their roles and have well-defined tasks. If a member of a group feels his particular role in that group isn't very important, his self-worth might suffer.

Further, peer pressure can affect group creativity. In addition, the pressure for the group to succeed could lead to think of certain members as "under-performers" and result in bickering and even harassment.

Even if a group is working well, competition between groups can be unhealthy for the organisation as a whole. Finally, successful groups can resist change. If a new member is added, the group might perceive him as a weight rather than as help. In addition, even if the market or organisational conditions require breaking up a group, the successful group might try to avoid being broken up.

Points to Remember

- Employee appraisal was first practiced in China.
- Up to the mid-fifties, most of the employee appraisal programmes were based on the rating scales.
- The term 'Performance Appraisal' is used as a method of measuring quantitative as well as qualitative aspects of an employee's work performance.
- In modern times, performance is measured in terms of results and points to the number of the tasks assigned to an employee by way of job content.
- Employee appraisal is a methodical evaluation of the employee's performance at work that is done by the superiors or other experts in the organisation.
- Performance appraisal is also very important in planning for the employee's development.
- Performance appraisal helps to reveal the strengths and weaknesses of the employees and also to improve their future performance.
- Accurate information collected through performance appraisal plays a vital role in an organisation as a whole.
- Job description gives clear idea to the appraisee about what he is expected to do and other related matters.
- Performance appraisal feedback is always easier to give when managers follow a structured process.
- Most employees, given the opportunity, are willing and able to review their own performance.
- Feedback should be given in a manner that will best help improve performance.
- A wage or salary is a price paid to an employee for hiring his services.
- Compensation is direct and indirect monetary benefits and rewards received by employees on the basis of the value of the jobs, their personal contributions and overall performance.

- The traditional approach to compensation requires an in-depth analysis of the job at hand.
- Some of the newer trends that organisations are looking to include the total rewards approach.
- A well-constructed performance-based pay system can be seen as an interactive process that translates the overall strategic initiatives into daily actions.
- Performance based programmes tap into the purest source of human potential.
- For performance based compensation to be successful in an organisation, there must be reasonable, achievable and measurable goals that are potentially achievable by any employee.
- Group incentive plans were designed for situations in which the goals of the project are best-suited to individuals working together rather than apart.
- Group incentive plans have a number of advantages over other payment structures and encourage cooperation within a team because pay depends on achieving a result that takes a group to accomplish.

Questions For Discussion

1. "Performance appraisal is not merely for appraisal but it is also for the accomplishment and improvement of performance". Discuss.
2. Describe in detail the process of performance appraisal.
3. What is 'Performance Appraisal'? Explain the process.
4. What is 'Performance Appraisal'? Explain its objectives.
5. Explain the objectives, meaning and features of performance appraisal.
6. What is meant by the term 'Compensation'?
7. What are fringe benefits? Explain the objectives, coverage and types of fringe benefits.
8. What do you understand by Performance Appraisal management system?
9. "Compensation Management plays a vital role in various aspects of HRM". Discuss.
10. Explain concept of performance management system. How does it differ from performance appraisal.
11. Write short notes on:
    (a) Employee Appraisal
    (b) Use of appraisal data
    (c) Appraisal process
    (d) Performance feedback
    (e) Compensation
    (f) Current trends in compensation
    (g) Team based incentives

Multiple Choice Questions (MCQ)s

1. Performance management is viewed as a process carried out as a(n):
   (a) Once a year task
   (b) Twice a year activity
   (c) Ongoing process or cycle
   (d) None of the above

2. Performance evaluation can be defined as a process of evaluating:
   (a) Past performance
   (b) Present performance
   (c) Future performance
   (d) Past and present performance

3. The term performance rating system stands for:
   (a) A grade or score concerning the overall performance
   (b) The information about the extent to which the work objectives are met
   (c) The past objectives of the organisation
   (d) The achievements for a period of one year

4. Rewards offered to labours involved in production are categorised as:
   (a) Salary
   (b) Fringe benefits
   (c) Wage
   (d) commission

5. Who is in the best position to observe and evaluate an employee's performance for the purpose of a performance appraisal?
   (a) Peers
   (b) Customers
   (c) Top management
   (d) Immediate supervisor

ANSWERS

| 1. (c) | 2. (d) | 3. (a) | 4. (c) | 5. (d) |

QUESTIONS FROM PREVIOUS PUNE UNIVERSITY EXAMINATIONS

1. Explain the Need and Importance of Performance Appraisal System in the Organisation. **M.B.A. April 2007**

Ans. Refer Articles 4.1.1.2 and 4.1.2 of this chapter.

2. What do you understand by Performance Appraisal Management System? **M.B.A. April 2009**

Ans. Refer Article 4.1.1.1 of this chapter.

3. Explain the importance of Performance Management System. **M.B.A. December 2009**

Ans. Refer Article 4.1.2 of this chapter.

4. Explain: Performance Appraisal. **M.B.A. April 2010, 2011**

Ans. Refer Article 4.1.1.1 of this chapter.

5. Explain concept of Performance Management System. **M.B.A. April 2012**

Ans. Refer Article 4.1.1.1 of this chapter.

✼✼✼

Chapter 5...

Managing Employee Relations

Contents ...

5.1 Concept
5.2 Importance
5.3 Organisational Entry of the Employee
5.4 Employee Status
5.5 Flexible Working Arrangement
5.6 Employee Surveys
5.7 Employee Handbooks
5.8 Violations of Policy/Discipline
5.9 Organisational Exit
    5.9.1 Termination
    5.9.2 Resignation
    5.9.3 Downsizing/Layoff
    5.9.4 Retirement
- Points to Remember
- Questions for Discussion
- Questions from Previous Pune University Examinations

Learning Objectives:

- To understand the Concept and Importance of Managing Employee Relations
- To Comprehend what an Induction Process is and why it is necessary for a New Employee
- To distinguish between the Different Types of Employee Status
- To list the Various types of Flexible Working Arrangements that an Organisation can Implement
- To understand the Importance of Employee surveys for an Organisation
- To be aware of the Meaning of an Employee Handbook and why it is needed
- To recount the Repercussions of Violating the rules of any Organisation
- To distinguish between the different Types of exits from an Organisation

Introduction

Managing employee relations in an organisation is the key towards achieving balance in the workplace. This branch of management is called "Employee relationship management" or ERM as it is referred to, and is a term that is associated with relationship development and management between employers and their employees.

This branch of management in the organisation puts to use many technologies in the management of human resources. This concept is based on client relationship management, with the employee at its center.

5.1 Concept

Managing employee relations is an important aspect of human resource management in an organisation. This branch of management focuses on the employee, their relationships in the organisation and their ability to contribute productively to the growth of the organisation.

Fig. 5.1

Management of employee relations requires dedicated effort on the part of the management and revolves around the comfort level that an employee is able to achieve in his or her workplace. Managing employees and their requirements and needs may involve implementing a dedicated information system for the management of human resources. This system makes it possible to cover all problems that are related with the relationship between a company and its employees, in particular:

- Training
- Pay
- Recruiting
- Competence and career management
- Time management
- Internal communication
- Balancing Work and Life Needs
- Other requirements/needs of the employee

5.2 Importance

Every individual at the workplace shares a certain relationship with his fellow workers. Human beings are not machines and need people to talk to, discuss ideas with and share their happiness and sorrows. An individual cannot work on his/her own. An isolated environment demotivates an individual and spreads negativity.

It is essential that people are comfortable with each other and work together as a single unit towards a common goal. It is therefore important that employees share a healthy relation with each other at the work place.

The HR department plays a critical role in this process. They are responsible for training and coaching managers and executives on how to effectively establish and nurture relationships with employees. They are also responsible for measuring and monitoring those relationships to determine whether objectives are being met.

Some of the core issues that can be controlled with effective employee relationship management are:

- **Communication:** Open communication both amongst employees and between the employees and the management team. When employees feel that they are not heard, they can become frustrated, leading to lowered employee morale. Lowered morale can result in lowered productivity and an uncomfortable, or even hostile, work environment.
- **Conflict management:** This is a fundamental aspect of employee relationship management. Sometimes those conflicts occur between employees and employers.
- **Employee growth:** Employees who feel they can become a valuable asset to the organisation based on their work, as well as their ability to provide important ideas, offer input, and perhaps pursue growth opportunities within the company are an asset to it. They create a positive atmosphere within the corporate culture.

5.3 Organisational Entry of the Employee

After the candidate is selected, he is told what his duties and responsibilities are, what is required of him and what his future prospects in the organisation are. Generally, this information is conveyed to the selected candidate at the time of the final selection interview. He is formally appointed by issuing an appointment letter or by concluding with him a service agreement. It contains the terms and conditions of the employment, pay scale and so on.

This is the way the candidate is inducted. The dictionary meaning of 'Induction' is the formal introduction to a new job.

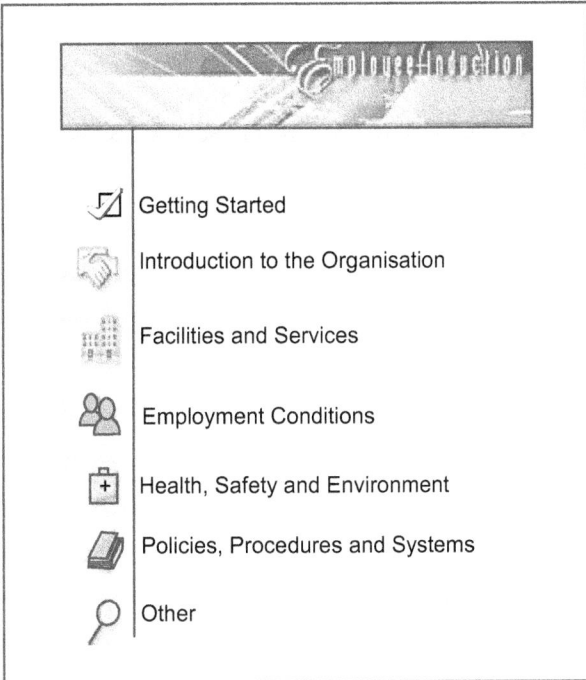

Fig. 5.2: Employee Induction

Induction is the formal introduction of a new employee to a new job with the information that employee needs to function comfortably, properly and effectively in the organisation. It is a planned introduction of newly appointed employees to their jobs, their colleagues or peers and the organisation in which they are appointed. Induction is also called as '**Orientation**'.

Michael Armstrong defines inductions as, *"The process of receiving and welcoming an employee when he first joins a company and giving him the basic information he needs to settle down quickly and happily and start work."*

Induction is the process of introducing a new employee to the organisation, and also the organisation to the employee by providing him necessary and relevant information. However, what type of information is to be provided to a new employee depends upon the organisational policies and practices. There are two ways of conducting orientation. They are:

(a) A formal and comprehensive way of orienting new employees
(b) Following informal and gradual process of learning about the organisation over a period of time.

Generally, a formal orientation is preferred as it tries to bridge the information gap of the new employees. A formal orientation may provide information about:

(1) The organisation, its mission and philosophy, goals and objectives, structure of the organisation, product lines, marketing etc.
(2) Human resource policies and practices i.e. promotion policy, pay scales, leave rules, holidays, training and development programmes, disciplinary procedure etc.
(3) Employee benefits, e.g. provident funds, gratuity benefits, insurance benefits, retirement benefits, etc.
(4) Job duties i.e. overview of job/jobs, job objectives, relationship to the jobs, office timings and breaks, information about officers, colleagues, subordinates, etc.

Some organisations prepare booklets known as "Induction Manuals" with necessary information to be conveyed to new employees. Such booklets are provided to the new employees at the time of induction/orientation. **R. P. Billimoria** says that *"Induction (Orientation) is a technique by which a new employee is rehabilitated into the changed surroundings and introduced to the practices, policies and purposes of the organisation"*.

Induction or orientation is important from the viewpoint of the management of human resources. It is in fact a welcoming process. The idea behind orientation or induction is to make a new employee feel comfortable and to generate in him a feeling that his job, may it be small,but is meaningful and has significance as a part of the total organisation wherein he is appointed.

Generally, new employees feel anxious on entering their organisation. They worry about how they will perform the tasks entrusted to them. They feel inadequate when they compare themselves with their peers or co-workers. Effective induction/orientation programmes definitely help to reduce their anxiety by providing them necessary information about their organisation, nature of work, responsibilities and so on to make them feel at home. This is the first and basic objective of induction.

Other objectives of 'Induction' are as follows:

(a) To help new employees to become acquainted and to help them to accommodate each other.
(b) To put a new employee at ease on joining work.
(c) To create an interest in their job and also in the organisation they join.

(d) To provide necessary information about working arrangements.

(e) To let them know the standards of performance and behaviour expected. It helps the newly inducted employee to know that their job is meaningful and that they are not merely a cog in the vast wheel.

(f) To give them necessary information about training facilities and development opportunities available to him in the organisation.

(g) To create the feeling of social security.

Importance of Induction:
- Settling smoothly of the new employees.
- A well developed and organised induction will form a base for future training and development.
- Can save high cost of recruitment and selection.
- Results in intefration of the new employees with the team.

Advantages of Induction

There are certain advantages of induction. The following are some of the important advantages of induction.

(i) Induction helps to minimise what might be called the reality shock which some new employees undergo. This reality shock is caused by the incompatibility between what the new employees expect in their new job and the realities they are faced with. The new employees expect opportunities for advancement, social status and prestige, opportunity to be creative etc. But when these expectations are not fulfilled, it results in a reality shock for them. Proper orientation or induction can help them overcome this problem by providing for more realistic orientations on the part of new employees and proper understanding on the part of their officers. Induction, if done properly results in less employee turnover.

(ii) New employees can adjust to their jobs or work quickly if properly inducted and this saves time.

(iii) Induction helps to reduce employee dissatisfaction and grievances.

(iv) Induction develops a sense of belongingness and makes the new employees more responsible.

Disadvantages of Induction:
- Supervisor who is entrusted with the job is not trained or is too busy
- Employee is thrown into action too soon
- Employee's mistakes can damage the company
- Employee is overwhelmed with too much information in a short time
- Employee is overloaded with forms to complete

Comparison between an effective induction and non effective induction is shown in Table 5.1 below:

Table 5.1

Effective induction	Non-Effective Induction
• Decreases the chances of attribution.	• Increase the attribution.
• Makes employees more energetic.	• Demoralizes the new entrant.
• Makes positive impact.	• Possesses negative impact.
• Reduces cost.	• Increase the cost.
• Increases team work.	• Reduces team work.

5.4 Employee Status

The category that a worker falls into depends on what they actually do, the way they do it and the terms and conditions under which they are engaged. These terms and conditions may be written, verbal or implied.

There are three types of employment status: a 'worker', an 'employee' or 'self-employed'. The employment status will help define what rights and responsibilities one has at work.

The definition of 'employee' and 'worker' differs slightly in areas of legislation, but generally if rights are applied to a 'worker' then they also apply to an 'employee'.

The majority of people in an organisation are employees. They are classed as an employee if they work under a contract of employment. A contract need not be in writing as it exists when the employee and the employer agree on terms and conditions of the employment. It can also be implied from their actions and those of the person for whom they are working.

As an employee, here are some of the benefits that one is entitled to:
- maternity, adoption and paternity leave
- the right not to be unfairly dismissed
- statutory redundancy pay
- all the rights that are given to 'workers'

The worker category is a broader one than the 'employee'. It normally does not include those who are self-employed.

A worker is any individual who works for an employer, whether under a contract of employment, or any other contract where an individual undertakes to do or perform personally, any work or service.

Workers are entitled to basic employment rights and protections. The following groups of people are likely to be workers but not employees:
- most agency workers
- short-term casual workers
- some freelancers

Most workers have rights to the following depending on their country of work:
- the National Minimum Wage
- rest breaks, paid holiday and limits on night work
- protection against unauthorised deductions from pay
- maternity, paternity and adoption pay (but not leave)
- protection against less favourable treatment because of being part-time
- statutory sick pay
- protection against less favourable treatment if they make a disclosure in the public interest (often called 'whistleblowing')
- not to be discriminated against unlawfully

5.5 Flexible Working Arrangements

Flexible work arrangements are alternate arrangements or schedules from the traditional working day and week. Employees may choose a different work schedule to meet personal or family needs or they may initiate various schedules to meet their customer needs.

Many benefits have been reported by various studies conducted for these arrangements. Some of these findings include:
- increased ability to attract, retain and motivate high-performing and experienced employees
- reduced absenteeism
- helping employees manage their responsibilities outside of work
- increased job satisfaction, energy, creativity, and ability to handle stress

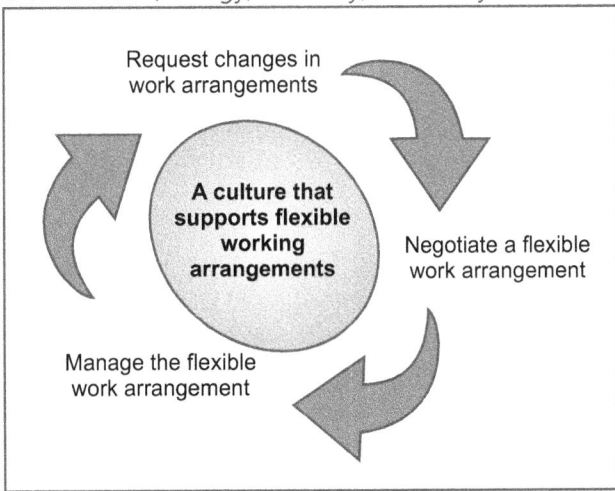

Fig. 5.3: Flexi Working Arrangements

Flexible working arrangements may include:
- changing hours of work (e.g. working less hours or changing start or finish times)
- changing patterns of work (e.g. working 'split shifts' or job sharing)
- changing the place of work (e.g. working from home).

Irrespective of which program or how many options are available, the duties, expectations, and deadlines of the arrangement should be clearly outlined by the supervisor and agreed upon by both the supervisor and as well as the employee.

Though flexible working arrangements are becoming popular, some issues if addressed appropriately ensure the success of this arrangement. Supportive organisational culture, clear communication, teamwork and reciprocal support between management and employees are a few. Other issues that should be considered include:

- Initial start-up costs and additional administrative duties/time.
- How to schedule meetings and training courses so most employees can attend.
- Workload management.
- Meeting customer demands.
- Impact the employee's absence will have on the group or the organisation.
- Impact on terms and conditions of employment

5.6 Employee Surveys

Every employee has a voice, but it's not always heard. If your staff feels unvalued, under-appreciated, or overlooked, they'll look for opportunities elsewhere.

Focusing on employee relationship management, can have profound effects on how a business operates. A lot of different issues affect employee satisfaction. This has a direct result on employee productivity and overall corporate culture. Managing employee relationship effectively can be mobilised using employee surveys to engage employees in the issues that are most important to them. From the food that is served in the cafeteria, to the benefits offered, to the leadership, the survey results from a workforce questionnaire which can give the organisation the data they need to help avoid staff turnover and create a productive and rewarding working environment.

Conducting employee surveys is a useful tool towards reaching a beneficial level of employee relationship because they provide an opportunity for candid feedback and analysis that isn't possible in everyday business communication. Surveys are of different types depending on the purpose for which they are employed and include surveys to measure employee satisfaction, survey to assess corporate culture, employee job satisfaction surveys, survey for measurement of employee productivity and so on.

Conducting an employee satisfaction survey provides the organisation an opportunity to listen to employees on levels that aren't easily made possible in normal business communication. Sometimes it's difficult for employees to speak up in situations where, for some reason, they might not feel comfortable. By providing an employee satisfaction survey to the employees, the organisation provides them the opportunity to be heard.

A corporate culture can contribute to or detract from the success of an organisation. The senior management of an organisation usually has a vision of the type of culture needed to compete successfully in a competitive landscape. However, there are certain cultural elements that will be detrimental to the success of any organisation if they exist -- disrespectful treatment of employees, lack of teamwork, and poor planning, to name a few.

A corporate culture survey is a way to measure the pulse of an organisation's culture. It is especially necessary to measure this when:
- there is a suspicion that the culture is not in sync with management's desired culture
- the management has determined that the culture must be changed to ensure the success of the enterprise
- there has been a leadership change at the top level of the organisation (or when such a change is being contemplated)

Workplace diversity is an important subject that plays a significant role in how employees feel about their workplace and how customers and clients view the organisation. It is just one of the many issues that help overall employee satisfaction. An employee job satisfaction surveys focuses on workplace diversity helps an organisation to directly engage with the employees to reach a better understanding of what their perspectives are regarding diversity in it.

Employee job satisfaction surveys act as a tool towards reaching a deeper understanding of employees and how diversity plays a role in the business.

Employee productivity can be directly related to employee satisfaction. It is in the interest of every organisation to understand what drives, and what deters, employee satisfaction. Some organisations inadvertently work against productivity improvement by failing to take steps to understand the attitudes and expectations that determine employee satisfaction.

There are a number of practices that create stumbling blocks to better employee satisfaction. Here are a few of them:
- Failing to listen to employees or, having listened, failing to act on what has been heard.
- Tolerating office politics and favouritism.
- Persisting with recognition programs that have outlived their relevance to employees.
- Ignoring the importance of career development to employee satisfaction.

Employee satisfaction surveys provide one way to "listen" to employees, and to understand their views on these and other issues. Some of the points to be kept in mind to get a great response from the survey is:
- Keep it casual: don't use language that's stuffy or overly technical. Keep the employee survey questions conversational.
- Provide incentives. Offer small gifts or prizes for completing the employee survey, or create contests among departments for the highest response rate.
- Make it anonymous. Be sure the employees know their employee survey answers are 100% anonymous. In order to gain the most insight, the organization should communicate to the employee their feedback is completely safe.
- **Let them know they've been heard.** If the employees feel like their feedback is going into a black hole, they'll be less likely to participate again. The organization should offer an employee survey presentation to show what knowledge has been gained, and what's being done with the survey results.

- Ask about things your employees care about. Employee survey questions about commutes, food, benefits, and working environment can help get the conversation started.

Here is a sample employee survey:

Table 5.2: Employee Satisfaction Survey

ABC Small Business Employee Satisfaction Survey

Please circle the number that corresponds with your level of agreement.
Strongly Disagree = 1, Disagree = 5, Strongly Agree = 10

#	Statement	1	2	3	4	5	6	7	8	9	10
1.	Overall, I am satisfied as an employee of ABC small business.	1	2	3	4	5	6	7	8	9	10
2.	My pay is competitive with other places I could wok.	1	2	3	4	5	6	7	8	9	10
3.	ABC Small Business cares about its employees.	1	2	3	4	5	6	7	8	9	10
4.	ABC Small Business cares about its customers.	1	2	3	4	5	6	7	8	9	10
5.	I receive the information I need regarding the issues that affect me.	1	2	3	4	5	6	7	8	9	10
6.	My superior shows appreciation for the work that I do.	1	2	3	4	5	6	7	8	9	10
7.	My job description accurately reflects what I am asked to do.	1	2	3	4	5	6	7	8	9	10
8.	I have received the training I need to perform my job duties.	1	2	3	4	5	6	7	8	9	10
9.	I feel I am part of a team helping to fulfil the mission of ABC Small Business.	1	2	3	4	5	6	7	8	9	10
10.	Managers confront employees who are weak in customer service.	1	2	3	4	5	6	7	8	9	10
11.	I have the ability to meet or exceed the needs of my customers.	1	2	3	4	5	6	7	8	9	10
12.	I feel secure my job at ABC Small Business as long as I perform well.	1	2	3	4	5	6	7	8	9	10
13.	I believe our mission and vision drive the decisions that are made.	1	2	3	4	5	6	7	8	9	10
14.	I am provided opportunities for job growth and development.	1	2	3	4	5	6	7	8	9	10
15.	My superior helps me understand the strategic goals for ABC Small Business.	1	2	3	4	5	6	7	8	9	10
16.	I intend to continue my employment at ABC Small Business	1	2	3	4	5	6	7	8	9	10

Comments:
_____
_____
_____

Please check one box in both sections:
   = hourly employee   = salaried employee   = full-time   = part-time

(**Source:** thethrivingsmallbusiness.com)

5.7 Employee Handbooks

An employee handbook, sometimes also known as an employee manual or staff handbook, is a book given to employees and contains information about company policies and procedures.

The employee handbook is an excellent medium to list out employment and job-related information which employees need to know. These include holiday arrangements, company rules and disciplinary and grievance procedures. It can also be provided as a useful source of information to new staff as part of the induction process.

A written employee handbook gives clear advice to employees and creates a culture where issues are dealt with fairly and consistently.

It is recommended that organisations make employee handbooks right at the onset.

The handbook could vary from business to business depending upon the focus of the organisation. Here is a list of specific pointers that an employee handbook may include:

- A **welcome statement**, which may also briefly describe the company's history, reasons for its success and how the employee can contribute to future successes. It may also include a mission statement, or a statement about a business' goals and objectives.
- Orientation procedures. This usually involves providing a human resources manager or other designated employee completed income tax withholding forms, providing proof of identity and eligibility for employment and other required forms.
- Definitions of full- and part-time employment, and benefits each classification receives. In addition, this area also describes timekeeping procedures (such as defining a "work week"). This area may also include information about daily breaks (for lunch and rest).
- Information about employee pay and benefits (such as vacation and insurance).
- Expectations about conduct and discipline policies. These sections include conduct policies for such areas as sexual harassment, alcohol and drug use, and attendance; plus, grounds for dismissal (i.e., getting fired) and due process.
- Guidelines for employee performance reviews (such as how and when they are conducted).
- Policies for promotion or demotion to a certain position.
- Rules concerning mail; use of the telephone, company equipment, Internet and e-mail; and employee use of motor vehicles for job assignments.
- Procedures on handling on-the-job accidents, such as those that result in injury. Describe the organisation's policy for creating a safe and secure workplace, including compliance with the Occupational Safety and Health Administration's laws that

require employees to report all accidents, injuries, potential safety hazards, safety suggestions and health and safety related issues to management. Safety policies should also include the organisation's policy regarding bad weather and hazardous community conditions. Add the organisation's commitment to creating a secure work environment, and the organisation's responsibility for abiding by all physical and information security policies, such as locking file cabinets or computers when not in use. The Workplace Safety & Health guide provides information on the organisation's requirements as an employer.

- How an employee may voluntarily terminate his/her job (through retirement or resignation), and exit interviews.
- A requirement that employees keep certain business information confidential. This area usually includes information about releasing employee records and information, as well as who may retrieve and inspect the information.
- **Non-Disclosure Agreements (NDAs) and Conflict of Interest Statements:** Although NDAs are not legally required, having employees sign NDAs and conflict of interest statements helps to protect your trade secrets and company proprietary information.
- **Anti-Discrimination Policies:** As a business owner, you must comply with the equal employment opportunity laws prohibiting discrimination and harassment. Employee handbooks should include a section about these laws, and how your employees are expected to comply.
- **Computers and Technology:** Outline policies for appropriate computer and software use, and steps employees should take to secure electronic information, especially any personal identifiable information they collect from the customers.

Below is a screenshot of the employee handbook:

Employee Handbook Screenshot:

STANDARD EMPLOYMENT PRACTICES
At Will Employment
Company X does not offer tenured or guaranteed employment. Except as Company X has otherwise expressly agreed in writing, your employment is at will and may be terminated or by Company X at anytime.
Equal Employment Opportunity
Company X is committed to provide equal employment opportunities to all individuals without regard to race, color, religion, sex, national origin, age, disability, marital status, sexual orientation, or any other characteristic protected by law.

Company X will make reasonable accommodations for qualified individuals with known disabilities unless doing so would result in an undue hardship. An employee with a disability for which reasonable accommodation is needed should contact a human resources representative to discuss possible accommodations.

Employees with questions or concerns about any type of discrimination in the work place are encouraged to bring these issues to the attention of a human resources representative. Employees can raise legitimate concerns and make good faith reports without fear of reprisal. Anyone found to be engaging in any type of unlawful discrimination will be subject to disciplinary action, up to and including discharge.

Sexual and Other Unlawful Harassment

Company X will endeavour to maintain a work environment that nourishes respect for the dignity of each individual. This is adopted in furtherance of that tradition.

It is against the policies of Company X for an employee to harass another person because of the person's sex, race, colour, religion, national origin, age, disability, sexual orientation, marital status, or other characteristic protected by law. Actions, words, jokes, or comments based on such characteristics will not be tolerated.

Consequently, it is against the policies of Company X for an employee to sexually harass another person. Unwelcome sexual advances, requests for sexual favours, and other verbal or physical conduct of a sexual nature constitute sexual harassment when: (1) submission to such conduct is made either explicitly or implicitly a term or condition of an individual's employment; submission to or rejection of such conduct by an individual is used as the basis for employment decisions affecting such individual; or such conduct has the purpose or effect of unreasonably interfering with an individual's work performance or environment.

Any employee who believes that he or she is being unlawfully harassed should immediately contact their supervisor or a human resources representative.

5.8 Violations of Policy/Discipline

Discipline in the workplace is the means by which supervisory personnel correct behavioural deficiencies and ensure adherence to established company rules. The purpose of discipline is correct behaviour. It is not designed to punish or embarrass an employee. Often, a positive approach may solve the problem without having to discipline. However, if unacceptable behaviour is a persistent problem or if the employee is involved in a misconduct that cannot be tolerated, management may use discipline to correct the behaviour.

In general, discipline should be restricted to the issuing of letters of warning, letters of suspensions, or actual termination. Employers should refrain from "disciplining" employees by such methods as altering work schedules, assigning an employee to do unpleasant work, or denying vacation requests.

Most organisations take a breach of policies and lapses in discipline very seriously. When such a breach or lapse comes to light the employee is warned or reprimanded depending on how severe the lapse is. Following which the employee may be allowed a period of time to show improvement in behaviour. A failure to comply with the said requirement may lead to the employee being terminated from employment with the organisation.

In the case of performance-based termination, employees are usually given a 90 day notice to improve their performance. But unlike performance-based termination, severely violating the rules of an organisation can lead to immediate dismissal.

Before the management fires an employee for a rules violation, they need to ensure that expectations were obvious to all employees from the start. All company policies should have been posted and conveyed through training and/or a handbook. A necessary step prior to the dismissal is to document all the details of the violation and the termination.

Here is a checklist of some things to note about rules violations.

- **Consistency:** Make sure your decision is consistent with other cases you've handled.
- **Clear expectations:** Rules should be documented and clearly conveyed. It can be as simple as a single-page document that everyone signs, but postings, training seminars and handbooks are also helpful.
- **Document:** Even if it is a rules issue – the employee is caught stealing or lying to a customer – the management still needs to document the incident, even if the firing is immediate.
- **Fire without notice:** In the case of a rules violation, depending on the severity, like embezzlement, the management will want to suspend them during the investigation. If it's serious enough, they may want to fire the employees without notice.
- **Protect information:** If the management lets someone go immediately, they need to cut off their access to sensitive information right away.

Examples of misconduct which could result indiscipline:

1. Excessive tardiness
2. Failure to notify of an absence
3. Insubordination
4. Rude or abusive language in the workplace
5. Failure to follow "Departmental Rules or Policies ", i.e., not wearing safety equipment, not following correct cash handling procedures
6. Dishonesty
7. Theft.

Of course, discipline may be required for a number of other misconducts. The question that needs to be asked is if the Employer has "just cause" to impose a form of discipline.

In reviewing whether or not management was correct in its choice to discipline, arbitrators have looked at a number of factors. These factors must be taken into account by management when deciding to use discipline:

1. Did the employee clearly understand the rule or policy that was violated?

For example, were the work rules or policy provided to the employee prior to the violation. It is management responsibility to prove that the employee knew the rule or policy.

2. Was the rule or policy consistently and fairly enforced by management?

For example, did management have a history of ignoring the departmental policy on wearing safety equipment, but singled out an employee for discipline anyway.

3. Did the employee know that violating the rule or policy could lead to discipline?

4. The seriousness of the offense in terms of violating company rules of conduct or company obligations.

For example, being a few minutes late for a shift would not be viewed as being as serious an offense as striking another employee or stealing company property.

5. The long service of the employee.

6. The previous good (or bad) work record of the employee.

7. Provocation.

Was the employee pushed into acting rudely or violently as a result of management or a customer's actions? This is a very common defense for employees involved in insubordination.

8. Did the employee admit to the misconduct and apologise for their behaviour?

Arbitrators will often rule harshly against employees who are deceptive during an investigation and who show no remorse for their actions.

The following sequence of events summarises the typical steps taken once a misconduct occurs at the workplace.

1. A misconduct occurs in the workplace.
2. Management investigates the misconduct, interviews witnesses and gathers evidence.
3. Management interviews with the employee suspected in the misconduct.
4. Management reviews all the evidence and consults with H.R. on the appropriate discipline.
5. Issuing the letter of reprimand, letter of suspension, or termination.

5.9 Organisational Exit

Losing employees is a natural part of running an organisation but losing key people at the wrong time can cause major setbacks for it. Exit Interviews can highlight why employees leave. Understanding why people leave is critical to managing staff turnover. When a valued employee departs, recruitment costs go up, organisational productivity goes down and some valuable intellectual property may be lost.

An Exit Interview also helps the management look into the departing employees' concerns. Some of the reasons for employees leaving an organisation can be understood with the help of the chart given here.

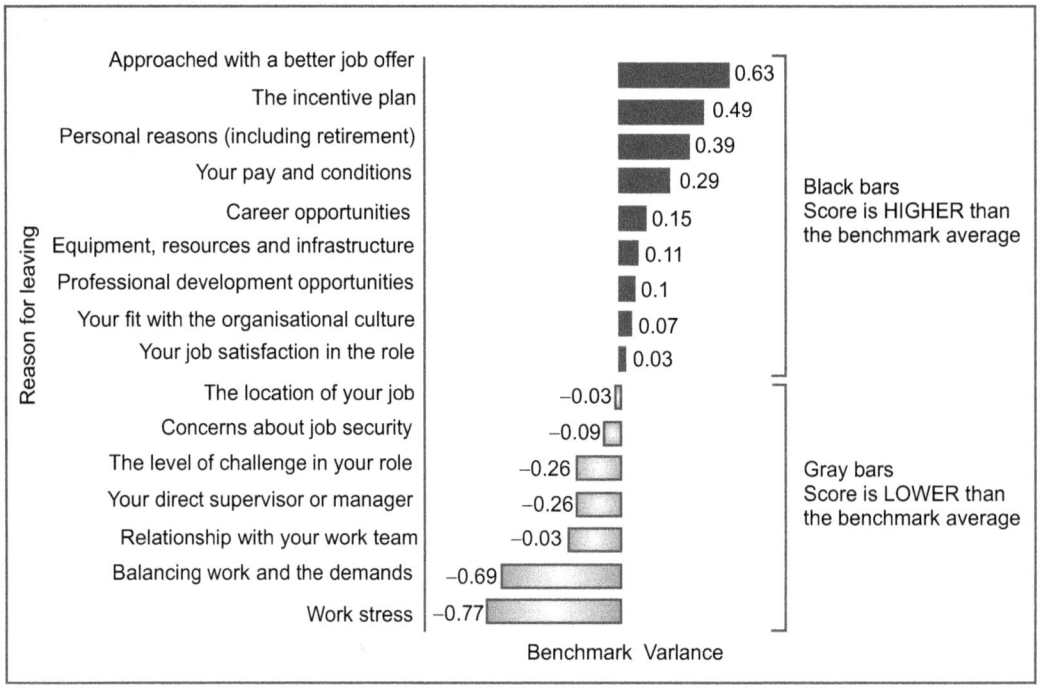

Chart 5.1: Reasons Employees Leave the Job

When an employee is to leave an organisation, certain procedures need to be followed by its HR department. These are termed as exit procedures and should always be followed without question. The exit procedures should aim at the following:

- Removing access to systems with confidential information (changing password, revoking certificates and keys, blocking accounts, and so on).
- Logging the actions of the employee leaving.
- Backing up all their work.
- Revoking their roles in incident management.

- Interviewing to hand over to the next person.
- Performing exit-interview to learn for the future.
- Announcing staff change to constituents, parent organisation, and other teams.

No matter how much the management trusts the person who is leaving, always log what he is doing and revoke access to the most sensitive systems.

5.9.1 Termination

During the course of an employee being with an organisation, it may come to light that the two parties are not in sync with each other. In such a case, employee termination is the only answer.

Termination occurs when an employer or employee ends an employee's employment with a particular employer. Termination can be voluntary or involuntary depending on the circumstances.

Voluntary Termination

In a voluntary termination, an employee resigns from his or her job. Resignations occur for a variety of reasons that include: a new job, a spouse's acceptance of a new job in a distant location, returning to school, and retirement. With valued employees, employers expend efforts on employee retention to limit preventable turnover.

Involuntary Termination

In an involuntary termination, an employer fires the employee or removes the employee from his or her job. An involuntary termination is usually the result of an employer's dissatisfaction with an employee or an economic downturn. Reasons for involuntary termination range from poor performance to attendance problems to violent behaviour.

Involuntary termination, such as a lay off, can also occur because an employer lacks the financial resources to continue an employment relationship. Other events that trigger termination can include mergers and acquisitions, a company relocation, and job redundancy.

With performance problems, the employer most often has tried less final solutions such as coaching from the employee's supervisor to help the employee improve. Escalating progressive discipline in the case of performance issues such as absenteeism is also the norm.

Employee termination must be carefully planned, with a heavy involvement of human resources, if this assistance is available. But the responsibility for how to terminate an employee is the job of the manager and not that of the HR representative.

If a person gets fired, more rigorous measures have to be taken. Besides the procedures mentioned for when an employee leaves the organisation, the following have to be done immediately:

- revoking access to the building
- escorting the person out of the building using a security officer or guard
- removing access to any system

The termination meeting should be brief i.e. ten to fifteen minutes is usually sufficient. The person affected may always want more but to no benefit. If possible, the meeting should be scheduled early in the week as the person affected does not have the weekend to brood about it. In the discussion, no attempt should be made to justify or defend the decision.

Employee termination is undoubtedly one of the most disliked requirements of being a manager. But the termination of a marginal employee, if handled compassionately and maturely, will only generate relief from those who have had to put up with them without being able to take action.

Occasionally, an employer and employee recognise that they are not a good fit for whatever reason. They mutually agree to part ways in a manner that makes neither party culpable for the termination. This approach to termination is called agreeing on an exit strategy. No pain. Unwanted employee, unwanted job: gone.

5.9.2 Resignation

A resignation is the formal act of giving up or quitting one's office or position before the end of the stipulated term. A resignation can happen when a person holding a position gained by election or appointment steps down. A resignation is a personal decision to exit a position, though outside pressure may exist in many cases.

Employees may resign at any time during their employment, provided they give reasonable notice. The employment agreement need to be checked to confirm notice periods and final pay should be calculated accordingly. If the employee gives the required notice, the employer must pay the employee to the end of the notice period, unless the employee is justifiably dismissed during that period.

The employee may be required to work for the full notice period or may be asked to stop coming to work before this date as is seen fit by the organisation. In either case, the employee should be paid to the end of the notice period. If pay is stopped before the end of the notice period, the employee may claim for wages owed.

If an employee leaves work without giving notice, the employer is not required to pay for time beyond the employee's last actual working day. The employer should not deduct pay in lieu of the notice from any amount that is owed to the employee. This can only be done if the employee agrees in writing to it or the employment agreement specifically allows it.

The employer must also pay all holiday pay that is owed to the employee in their final pay.

Forced resignation

Many a times an employer puts pressure (directly or indirectly) on an employee to resign, or makes the situation at work so intolerable for the employee that they may be forced to resignation. This type of resignation is often known as a "constructive dismissal".

A constructive dismissal may be where one or more of the following occurs:
- The employer has followed a course of conduct deliberately aimed at making the employee resign.
- The employee is told to choose between resigning or being dismissed.
- There has been a breach of duty by the employer such that the employee feels that he or she cannot remain in the job.

In the case of a forced resignation, an employee may have a personal grievance case that they would like addressed.

5.9.3 Downsizing or Lay-off

In a business enterprise, downsizing is reducing the number of employees on the operating payroll. Some users distinguish downsizing from a layoff, with downsizing intended to be a permanent downscaling and a layoff intended to be a temporary downscaling in which employees may later be rehired. When the market is tight, downsizing is extremely common, as companies fight to survive in a hostile climate while competing with other companies in the same sector. Businesses use several techniques in downsizing, including providing incentives to take early retirement and transfer to subsidiary companies, but the most common technique is to simply terminate the employment of a certain number of people.

Downsizing in an organisation is never a pleasant task to carry out. Everyone in the organisation is affected in some way when it decides to downsize the number of employees it has. Downsizing is usually done in cases where the company is making significant changes to either increase company value or reduce excess costs. Businesses use different techniques in downsizing. This includes providing incentives to take early retirement and transfer to subsidiary companies. The most common technique is to simply terminate the employment of a certain number of people.

Rightsizing is downsizing which is done when an organisation feels it really should operate with fewer people.

Dumbsizing is downsizing that, in retrospect, failed to achieve the effect it was meant to deliver.

Whatever the term used, downsizing is undertaken with a certain view in mind by the management of the organisation. A few of the considerations that are looked at as the desired result of downsizing are listed here:

- **Cost Reduction:** One of the primary reasons for employee downsizing is to reduce costs. Employee payroll counts as a liability on the organisation balance sheet and, therefore, reduces the owners' equity.
- **Productivity:** Organisation sometimes downsize their employee base to increase productivity.
- **Value:** Downsizing the number of employees an organisation has, generally signals that some restructuring and changes are underway. These changes generally take place for increasing profitability of the organisation.
- **Outsourcing:** The management may sharpen the focus of the organisation by eliminating some of the products or services that it offers. In doing so, a reduction in the number of employees may be necessary.

When a layoff is the only option, the employees who leave and the ones who are left will feel much better if the boss handles the situation respectfully and humanely. The situation is better handled if the bosses:

- ensure better communication
- allow for good-byes
- ease the transition
- reassure the remaining employees

Numerous terms accompany downsizing. Employees may be terminated, fired, laid off, made redundant, or released. A business may be optimised, rightsized, or experiencing a reduction in workforce. Some of these terms have different legal meanings depending on where one is in the world; a layoff, for example, may refer to a mass temporary release of employees who will brought back in once business picks up, while a redundant employee is one who is asked to leave permanently.

Numerous consulting firms offer assistance with downsizing, often with the use of specialists who visit a business to evaluate it. Since profit is an important bottom line for companies, downsizing measures should be expected by employees, especially when they observe a troubled market or they are working for a struggling company.

For employees, the process can be stressful, because they may feel uncertain about whether or not they will continue to employed. Sometimes, downsizing is very abrupt, with a huge batch of employees being released from employment on the same day, while in other cases it may be a more drawn out and nerve wracking process in which employees are slowly let go. Employers should remember that downsizing is very upsetting and stressful, and they should take steps to make it run smoothly while assuring valued employees that their jobs are secure.

5.9.4 Retirement

Retirement is the point where a person stops employment completely. A person may also semi-retire by reducing work hours. Many people choose to retire when they are eligible for private or public pension benefits, although some are forced to retire when physical conditions no longer allow the person to work anymore (by illness or accident) or as a result of legislation concerning their position. In most countries, the idea of retirement is of recent origin, being introduced during the late 19th and early 20th centuries. Previously, low life expectancy and the absence of pension arrangements meant that most workers continued to work until death. Germany was the first country to introduce retirement, in 1889.

Nowadays most developed countries have systems to provide pensions on retirement in old age, which may be sponsored by employers and/or the state. In many poorer countries, support for the old is still mainly provided through the family. Today, retirement with a pension is considered a right of the worker in many societies, and hard ideological, social, cultural and political battles have been fought over whether this is a right. In many western countries this right is mentioned in national constitutions. The "standard" retirement age varies from country to country but it is generally between 50 and 70 (according to latest statistics, 2011).

The mandatory retirement age in different countries is different. In some cases, the age of retirement is the age at which a person is expected or required to cease work and is usually the age at which they may be entitled to receive superannuation or other government benefits.

Unless it can be objectively and categorically justified, it is no longer permissible to dismiss someone on the grounds of retirement. Older workers can voluntarily retire at a time they choose and draw any occupational pension they are entitled to. Employers cannot force employees to retire or set a retirement age unless it can be clearly justified.

In the present globalised scenario and in order to meet the increased competition, right-sizing of the manpower employed in an organisation has become an important management strategy. The Voluntary Retirement Scheme or VRS as it is popularly known in India is the most humane technique to provide overall reduction in the existing strength of employees. The VRS is a technique used by the companies for trimming the workforce employed in the industrial unit. It is now a commonly used method to dispense off the excess manpower and thus improve the performance of the organisation. It is a generous, tax-free severance payment to persuade the employees to voluntarily retire from the company. It is also known as a 'Golden Handshake' as it is the golden route to retrenchment.

In India, the Industrial Disputes Act, 1947 puts restrictions on employers in the matter of reducing excess staff by retrenchment, by closures of establishment and the retrenchment process involved lot of legalities and complex procedures. Also, any plans of retrenchment and reduction of staff and workforce are subjected to strong opposition by trade unions. Hence, VRS was introduced as an alternative legal solution to solve this problem. It allowed employers including those in the government undertakings, to offer voluntary retirement schemes to off-load the surplus manpower and no pressure is put on any employee to exit. The voluntary retirement schemes were also not subjected to not vehement opposition by the Unions, because the very nature of its being voluntary and not using any compulsion. It was introduced in both the public and private sectors. Public sector undertakings, however, have to obtain prior approval of the government before offering and implementing the VRS.

A business firm may opt for a voluntary retirement scheme under the following circumstances:

- Due to recession in the business.
- Due to intense competition, the establishment becomes unviable unless downsizing is resorted to.
- Due to joint-ventures with foreign collaborations.
- Due to takeovers and mergers.
- Due to obsolescence of Product/Technology.

Though the eligibility criteria for VRS varies from company to company, but usually, employees who have attained 40 years of age or completed 10 years of service are eligible for voluntary retirement. The scheme applies to all employees including workers and executives, except the directors of a company. The employee who opts for voluntary retirement is entitled to get forty five days emoluments for each completed year of service or monthly emoluments at the time of retirement multiplied by the remaining months of service before the normal date of service, whichever is less. Along with these benefits, the employees also get their provident fund and gratuity dues.

The guidelines provide that the scheme of voluntary retirement framed by a company should be in accordance with the following requirements, namely :

- It applies to an employee of the company who has completed ten years of service or completed 40 years of age
- It applies to all employees (by whatever name called), including workers and executives of the company except Directors of the company
- The scheme of voluntary retirement has been drawn to result in overall reduction in the existing strength of the employees of the company
- The vacancy caused by voluntary retirement is not to be filled up, nor the retiring employee is to be employed in another company or concern belonging to the same management
- The amount receivable on account of voluntary retirement of the employees, does not exceed the amount equivalent to one and one-half months' salary for each completed year of service or monthly emoluments at the time of retirement multiplied by the balance months of service left before the date of his retirement on superannuation. In any case, the amount should not exceed rupees five lakhs in case of each employee, and
- The employee has not availed in the past the benefit of any other voluntary retirement scheme.

A company may make the following announcements while implementing a voluntary retirement scheme:-

- The reasons behind downsizing the organisation.
- The eligibility criteria for voluntary retirement scheme.
- The age limit and the minimum service period of employees who can apply for the scheme.
- The benefits that are offered to the employees who offer to retire voluntarily.
- The rights of the employer to accept or reject any application for voluntary retirement.
- The date up to which the scheme is open.
- The income tax benefits and income tax incidence related to the scheme.
- It should also indicate that the employees who opt for voluntary retirement and accept the benefits under such scheme shall not be eligible in future for employment in the organisation.

Points to Remember

- Managing employee relations in an organisation is the key towards achieving balance in the workplace.
- Managing employees and their requirements and needs may involve implementing a dedicated information system for the management of human resources.
- Some of the core issues that can be controlled with effective employee relationship management are communication, conflict management and employee growth.
- Induction is the formal introduction of a new employee to a new job with the information that employee needs to function comfortably, properly and effectively in the organisation.
- Induction helps to minimise what might be called the reality shock which some new employees undergo.
- New employees can adjust to their jobs or work quickly if properly inducted and this saves time.
- Induction develops a sense of belongingness and makes the new employees more responsible.
- The category that a worker falls into depends on what they actually do, the way they do it and the terms and conditions under which they are engaged.
- There are three types of employment status, a 'worker', an 'employee' or 'self-employed'.
- Flexible work arrangements are alternate arrangements or schedules from the traditional working day and week.
- Though flexible working arrangements are becoming popular, some issues if addressed appropriately ensure the success of this arrangement.
- Managing employee relationship effectively can be mobilised using employee surveys to engage employees in the issues that are most important to them.
- Conducting employee surveys is a useful tool towards reaching a beneficial level of employee relationship because they provide an opportunity for candid feedback and analysis that isn't possible in everyday business communication.
- Workplace diversity is an important subject that plays a significant role in how employees feel about their workplace and how customers and clients view the organisation.
- Employee productivity can be directly related to employee satisfaction.
- An employee handbook, sometimes also known as an employee manual or staff handbook, is a book given to employees and contains information about company policies and procedures.
- When a breach of policies and lapses in discipline comes to light the employee is warned or reprimanded depending on how severe the lapse is.
- Understanding why people leave is critical to managing staff turnover.
- When an employee is to leave an organisation, certain procedures called exit procedures need to be followed by its HR department.
- Employee termination must be carefully planned, with a heavy involvement of human resources, if this assistance is available.

- A resignation is the formal act of giving up or quitting one's office or position before the end of the stipulated term.
- Some organisations distinguish downsizing from a layoff by saying that downsizing is intended to be a permanent downscaling and a layoff is intended to be a temporary downscaling in which employees may later be rehired.

Questions for Discussion

1. Explain the concept of managing employee relations.
2. Why are managing employee relations important?
3. What is 'Induction'? Explain the objectives of 'Induction'.
4. Explain the meaning, objectives and advantages of Induction.
5. What do we mean by employee status?
6. Explain flexible working arrangements.
7. Why are employee surveys useful?
8. Explain what an employee handbook is and explain what all should it contain?
7. Write short notes on:
   - (a) Termination
   - (b) Downsizing
   - (c) Resignation
   - (d) Violation of policy/discipline
   - (e) Golden handshake
   - (f) VRS

Questions From Previous Pune University Examinations

1. Write Short Notes :

   (A) Lay Off.   **M.B.A. April 2005**

   Ans. Refer Article 5.9.3 of this chapter.

   (B) Suspension and Termination.   **M.B.A. April 2010**

   Ans. Refer Article 5.9.1 of this chapter.

2. Elaborate Various Methods of Employee Separation.   **M.B.A. December 2009**

   Ans. Refer Article 5.9 of this chapter.

3. Explain the different Methods of Separation of Employees from the Organisation.   **M.B.A. December 2009**

   Ans. Refer Article 5.9 of this chapter.

4. Describe various Kinds of Separation.   **M.B.A. December 2010**

   Ans. Refer Article 5.9 of this chapter.

***

Case Studies ...

Case Study 1: Training and Development

Is Satish in need of corrective Training?

Satish Sharma has been employed for six months in the accounts section of a large manufacturing company in Faridabad. You have been his supervisor for the past three months. Recently you have been asked by the management to find out the contributions of each employee in the Accounts Section and monitor carefully whether they are meeting the standards set by you.

A few days back you have completed your formal investigation and with the exception of Satish, all seem to be meeting the targets set by you. Along with numerous errors, Satish's work is characterised by low performance – often he does 20 per cent less than the other clerks in the department.

As you look into Satish's performance review sheets again, you begin to wonder whether some sort of remedial or corrective training is needed for people like him.

Questions:
1. As Satish's supervisor can you find out whether the poor performance is due to poor training or to some other cause?
2. If you find Satish has been inadequately trained, how do you go about introducing a remedial training programme?
3. If he has been with the company six months, what kind of remedial programme would be best?
4. Should you supervise him more closely? Can you do this without making it obvious to him and his co-workers?
5. Should you discuss the situation with Satish?

Source: http://www.citehr.com/143880-training-development-case studies.html#ixzz2mmZFZhnm

Case Study 2: Recruitment

Tesco is the biggest private sector employer in the UK. The company has more than 360,000 employees worldwide. In the UK, Tesco stores range from small local Tesco Express sites to large Tesco Extras and superstores. Around 86% of all sales are from the UK.

Tesco also operates in 12 countries outside the UK, including China, Japan and Turkey. The company has recently opened stores in the United States. This international expansion is part of Tesco"s strategy to diversify and grow the business.

In its non-UK operations Tesco builds on the strengths it has developed as market leader in the UK supermarket sector. However, it also caters for local needs. In Thailand, for example, customers are used to shopping in 'wet markets' where the produce is not packaged. Tesco uses this approach in its Bangkok store rather than offering pre-packaged goods as it would in UK stores.

- Tesco needs people across a wide range of both store-based and non-store jobs:
- In stores, it needs checkout staff, stock handlers, supervisors as well as many specialists, such as pharmacists and bakers.
- Its distribution depots require people skilled in stock management and logistics.
- Head office provides the infrastructure to run Tesco efficiently. Roles here include human resources, legal services, property management, marketing, accounting and information technology.

Tesco aims to ensure all roles work together to drive its business objectives. It needs to ensure it has the right number of people in the right jobs at the right time. To do this, it has a structured process for recruitment and selection to attract applicants for both managerial and operational roles.

Recruitment involves attracting the right standard of applicants to apply for vacancies. Tesco advertises jobs in different ways. The process varies depending on the job available.

Internal recruitment

Tesco first looks at its internal Talent Plan to fill a vacancy. This is a process that lists current employees looking for a move, either at the same level or on promotion. If there are no suitable people in this Talent Plan or developing on the internal management development programme, Options, Tesco advertises the post internally on its intranet for two weeks.

External recruitment

For external recruitment, Tesco advertises vacancies via the Tesco website www.tesco-careers.com or through vacancy boards in stores. Applications are made online for managerial positions. The chosen applicants have an interview followed by attendance at an assessment centre for the final stage of the selection process.

People interested in store-based jobs with Tesco can approach stores with their CV or register though Jobcentre Plus. The store prepares a waiting list of people applying in this way and calls them in as jobs become available.

For harder-to-fill or more specialist jobs, such as bakers and pharmacists, Tesco advertises externally:
- through its website and offline media.
- through television and radio.
- by placing advertisements on Google or in magazines such as The Appointment Journal.

Tesco will seek the most cost-effective way of attracting the right applicants. It is expensive to advertise on television and radio, and in some magazines, but sometimes this is necessary to ensure the right type of people get to learn about the vacancies.

Tesco makes it easy for applicants to find out about available jobs and has a simple application process. By accessing the Tesco website, an applicant can find out about local jobs, management posts and head office positions. The website has an online application form for people to submit directly.

Case Study 3: Employee Appraisal

Mr. Shah is a talented and well experienced human resources manager of Birdstar Company. He undertakes his role of HR manager by being an administrative expert and a change agent. He has always been an inspiration for his subordinates and the employees whose performance is measured and appraised by him. It is because of Mr. Shah's 15 years of experience of working in HR departments helped him to get acquainted with various Performance Appraisal methods for evaluating the performance of his employees in a better way every time.

He had always been implementing only those methods which he found result-oriented in terms of enabling the employees to know about their performance in the organization, to help them in providing adequate training, if required, to increase their potential, to provide concrete feedback and evaluate their current job performance to determine transfer, retention and termination of employees. He has been working in Birdstar since last 5 years and has gained good amount of respect and faith from his employees due to his appropriate and fair performance appraisal techniques that facilitated the uses of performance appraisal.

Because of Mr. Shah's good rapport and close relations in the recent months with his subordinates Ram Kumar and P.K. Gupta, he has developed a new tendency to appraise the performance of those employees known to Kumar and Gupta with leniency and because he finds them similar to him (personality and knowledge wise). As a result of this unfair and inappropriate appraisal of Mr.Shah, he also evaluates the performance of the employees taking into account their recent performances only. Hence, most of the employees' productivity has reduced and is inefficient, even some of the good employees have become irresponsible towards their tasks along with different behavior showing no interest to put in their best efforts to realize the goals and mission of the company. Some employees are planning to resign as no proper feedbacks are provided when required and no better prospects for Promotions are expected to see the light of the day.

Case Study 4: When personal issues affect employee performance: An Employee Relations case study

Mrs. Kale has been employed in your department for six years. During her tenure she has been a valuable employee, although during the past two years you've observed a drop in her work performance due to tardiness and absenteeism. The whole department is aware that Mrs. Kale is facing many problems at home, and her co-workers have covered for her and even completed work for her when necessary, but they are beginning to complain.

Although you had hoped that Mrs. Kale's issues would improve and she would return to being the dependable employee you once knew, you must confront her about the work piling up.

When you meet with her the next morning and begin the discussion of her work performance, she starts to cry and tells you her husband has been abusive, her son is failing in school, and she's been battling depression. You try to help her talk through these issues. You suggest that she visit the Employee Assistance Programme and see her physician, and by the end of the meeting, she seems better. She leaves your office and starts a one-week vacation that you've just granted so she can begin to deal with these issues.

You feel she is taking steps to improve her situation. You realize that you never really did discuss her work performance, but you're confident that she'll be fine once she takes your advice.

- What did this supervisor do right?
- What could this supervisor have done better?

Case Study 5: State Bank of India

State Bank of India is the biggest commercial bank in the country. It has approximately, 6000 branch offices across the country. It has been managing these branches with 20 regional offices located in important places in the country. One of those regional offices is located in Maharashtra.

Mr. Mishra is the Regional Manager of Western Region of Maharashtra and the Singh is the HR manager of western region of Maharashtra. Mr. Puri is working as the chief HR manager at the central office Mumbai. Earlier, the central office used to select candidates for different jobs and allot them to different regions. But the bank has recently decided to decentralise the hiring process and hence asked all the Regional Managers to select their own candidates. Mr. Mishra asked various departmental heads at regional office and branch managers to rewrite job description, job specification, estimate manpower needs to send them directly to him. Mr. Singh has received a letter to this effect in the capacity of head of personnel department in the regional office. Immediately he met Mr. Singh and told him that his job was to prepare job description, job specification, estimate manpower for the entire region and as such, he would be authorised to do all those functions instead of departmental heads at regional office and branch managers. But the regional manager did not accept his request and told Mr. Singh that things would go according to his own instructions. Mr. Singh told the regional manager not to discount his request and restore his positional authority.

Questions:
1. What are the main problems in this case?
2. What should be done to resolve the conflict between the Regional Manager and Regional HR Manager?

Case Study 6

Mr. Shrikant is in charge of a factory in Pune, which employs fifteen people, five of whom work in the factory, three of these employees run machines, one supervises and the fifth moves the finished goods by handcar. This fifth position which demands no skill other than driving a handcar, needs to be filled and three applicants have responded.

The first is Mr. Dutta who is forty-five, unmarried and a Navy veteran. Mr. Dutta has a poor work record. During his five years in Lonavala he has worked on seasonal labour and occasional odd jobs, he drove a forklift in the Navy while working at Lonavala. He has a strong build, which could help although the work is generally light.

Mr. Gaikwad age twenty-two came to Pune two years back from Orissa. He has done farm labour for many years and assembly-line for one year. His command over English is poor. He resides with his mother and seems certain to remain in the area for some time. After having run farm equipment, he should have no trouble steering a handcar.

Mr. Rao is a local boy who finished high school five years ago. Subsequently, he got a diploma from a local institute and is currently employed as an assistant is Gati Transport company, Nigdi. His character references are good. Mr. Rao is small, but he seems quick and was track star in high school.

Questions
1. How much consideration should be given to Mr. Dutta with poor work record? Should Mr. Shrikant check to verify it.
2. How important is a command of English to the job? How quickly could Mr. Gaikwad assimilate enough English to be effective?
3. Should Mr. Rao get the job? How heavily should his references be weighed against his inexperience?
4. Who should be hired? Why?

***

www.ingramcontent.com/pod-product-compliance
Lightning Source LLC
Chambersburg PA
CBHW081300170426
43198CB00017B/2865